School Days

A Life of Making a Difference at
Amherst College, Wesleyan University,
and Williston Northampton School

Nina,
Our friendship is very special and
your life in Fletcher House gave me
and my family much joy. Enjoy my book.

GEORGE B. DUNNINGTON

George

School Days:
A Life of Making a Difference at
Amherst College, Wesleyan University,
and Williston Northampton School
Copyright © 2022 George B. Dunnington

Produced and printed by Stillwater River Publications.
All rights reserved. Written and produced in the
United States of America. This book may not be reproduced
or sold in any form without the expressed, written
permission of the author(s) and publisher.

Visit our website at
www.StillwaterPress.com
for more information.

First Stillwater River Publications Edition

ISBN: 978-1-958217-01-6

Library of Congress Control Number: 2022906463

1 2 3 4 5 6 7 8 9 10

Written by George B. Dunnington
Published by Stillwater River Publications,
Pawtucket, RI, USA.

Publisher's Cataloging-In-Publication Data
(Prepared by The Donohue Group, Inc.)

Names: Dunnington, George B., author.
Title: School days : a life of making a difference at Amherst College,
Wesleyan University, and Williston Northampton School /
George B. Dunnington.
Description: First Stillwater River Publications edition. |
Pawtucket, RI, USA : Stillwater River Publications, [2022]
Identifiers: ISBN 9781958217016
Subjects: LCSH: Dunnington, George B. | College administrators--
New England--Biography. | School administrators--New England--Biography. |
Amherst College--Professional staff--Biography. | Wesleyan University
(Middletown, Conn.)--Professional staff--Biography. | Williston Northampton
School (Easthampton, Mass.)--Professional staff--Biography. |
LCGFT: Autobiographies.
Classification: LCC LA2317.D628 A3 2022 |
DDC 378.0092--dc23

*The views and opinions expressed
in this book are solely those of the author(s)
and do not necessarily reflect the views
and opinions of the publisher.*

Dedicated to my wife
Ann Elizabeth Dunnington
August 19, 1937 – September 2, 1999

If it was not for my wife's complete support—especially while working at these institutions—I could not have been so successful. The intensity of my jobs meant she had to do more than her fair share of taking care of our three wonderful children, Susan Elizabeth, Amy Byrne, and George Balfour III. Each time I changed institutions, the rigors of moving our household and finding the children new schools she did with great care and grace.

She was exceptional at entertaining, nurturing many students in our home, cooking delicious meals, and celebrating numerous special events with all of us.

To My Wife, Dorothy Lewis Dunnington

It would be nearly impossible to properly thank my precious wife Dorothy for her numerous contributions to this book. She has read every page many times, and carefully edited each of those many pages. She also traveled with me to research material at the various institutions that were discussed in my writings. Without her support, encouragement, and patience, this book would never have come to fruition.

Contents

Resume	ix
Disclaimer	xi
Acknowledgements	xiii
Amherst College, 1960–1969	1
Enter the Era of the Computer—the 1960s Variety	6
Some Interesting Stories	17
The President of the United States of America Comes to the Campus	19
Robert Frost, Teacher and Poet	24
Changes I Observed in the 1960s	30
Wesleyan University	39
My Introduction to Williston Seminary—Williston Academy— Williston Northampton School	51
First Introduction to Williston Academy—Unbelievable!	54
Williston Seminary— Williston Academy— Williston Northampton School	59
What I Did Not Know—Bank Debt	82
The Great Merger Questions	90
Wilmot Babcock—Coach and Business Manager	96
Robert A. Ward—Head of School and Great Friend	107
Christopher C. Corkery, Headmaster 1979–1984	137
Selling of the Northampton School for Girls Campus	145
Admissions—A Critical Story at a Critical Time	159
Early Alumni Issues	167
Williston Northampton School Health Services	172
Williston Welcomes Computers	175
Summer Programs—A Major New Happening	180
Legal Challenges and Campus Security Duties	185
A Few Faculty Stories that Made the Business Manager's Life More Interesting	198
Support Staff Stories	206
Pitcher House—A Dorm—Our Home—A Reason to Love My Job	216

Outstanding Williston People	227
Margaret Eastman French, Williston Trustee, Parent, and Grandparent	228
Roger P. Clapp, A Wonderful and Generous Human Being	238
An Unusual But Special Gift—Paul V. McCormick ('24), Greenwich, New York	248
Charles H. Peter Derby ('28) Estate	252
George E. Clapp ('20) Estate	257
Dr. Antonio J. Giacomini ('31)	260
Theodore (Ted) Adams, the School's Independent Plummer	263
Miscellaneous Attempts to Raise Funds For Survival	271
The School's Major Asset—The Physical Plant	278
Dennis H. Grubbs, Headmaster 1984–1999	299
Endnotes	*301*
About the Author	*306*

George B. Dunnington Background Information
Born: Brockton, Massachusetts July 24, 1937
College: Babson College BS BA 1960

In all of the following firms, colleges, and private schools, I was able to follow my own path to new adventures that led directly to the institutions' betterment. I am especially proud of what I was able to do at Williston at a most challenging time. This school is now flourishing, which brings me much happiness.

Employment:

>General Electric Company, Schenectady, New York
>>Finance and Service Operations

>Amherst College, Amherst, Massachusetts
>>Assistant To Treasurer and Director of Information Systems

>Wesleyan University, Middletown, Connecticut
>>Director of Information Systems

>Williston Northampton School, Easthampton, Massachusetts
>>Assistant Treasurer and Business Manager

>Milton Academy, Milton, Massachusetts
>>Business Manager

>Pine Point School, Stonington, Connecticut
>>Business Manager

>Providence Country Day School, East Providence, Rhode Island
>>Business Manager

>Mitchell College, New London, Connecticut
>>Assistant to the President and Business Manager

GEORGE B. DUNNINGTON

(Note: The last five institutions were all dealing with severe financial hardships—two were virtually in bankruptcy. I left all with a new lease on life, and all continue to be doing well.)

Retired: 2000

Residence:
    12 Jerome Ave. Mystic, Connecticut 06355
    6060 Perthshire Lane, Fort Myers, Florida 33908 *(November to May)*

Disclaimer

The written material in this book is from my own personal experiences as I lived them and observed them. It is possible, over such a long period of time, that I could have embellished or misremembered events, however, it is my memory and thus my memoir.

Acknowledgements

Rachel E. Jirka, Amherst College Library Archivist.

Deborah Richards, Mount Holyoke College Library Special Collections Archivist.

Amanda Nelson, University Archivist at the Wesleyan University Special Collections.

Richard Teller '70, Williston Archivist retired, who helped me on numerous occasions throughout all of my writing.

Roger Maroni '74, for many helpful ideas and his extensive knowledge about Williston.

Charles B. McCullaugh Jr., Chief Financial Officer, The Williston Northampton School, for his willingness to help locate financial materials for the book.

Gina Tirrell, Executive Assistant to the Chief Financial Officer, who spent many hours of searching for financial records and providing me with copies of the materials.

Susan Curry Barnett, whose 43 years of history at Northampton School for Girls and Williston were an enormous source of stories and ideas.

Glenn F. Swanson '64, Williston's long time beloved history teacher and coach, whose comments and assistance were greatly appreciated.

Thomas Evans, Williston's Director of Admission 1972 to 1976, whose comments were also greatly appreciated.

Robert A. Blanchette, Director of Admission 1976 to 1981, whose generous contributions were appreciated.

Anne Ritchie Duncan, Director of Admission for Girls 1977 to 1982, for her thoughtful comments.

DeWitt (Chip) Howell, a real special friend and colleague at both Amherst College and Wesleyan University. A great source of information for my book.

The Reverend Dr. Lynne C. Holden, who initially inspired me to write this story and gave words of encouragement along the way.

SCHOOL DAYS

Amherst College, 1960-1969

WHEN I GRADUATED FROM BABSON COLLEGE IN 1960, I WAS hired by General Electric Company, whose corporate financial headquarters were in Schenectady, New York. It was a time when GE and other similar companies were experiencing a recession and facing legal charges for price fixing in the large steam turbine business. Thus, it was difficult to advance in the normal manner within the company. However, I was fortunate that, as a trainee, I moved between the many departments within the Financial Services Division. I was working in a small department, Accounts Payable, which included a manger and two clerks. The manager became ill and had to leave, so I was asked to temporarily assume his position. I found several instances where the manger had failed to take significant exemptions for State Sales Taxes. I filed for refunds and received many thousands of dollars from these refunds. This brought attention to my work. I also strengthened some of the internal procedures, enabling the department to do a better job.

I was frustrated by the large amount of company "red tape," which seemed to prevent the obvious from happening without going through a long, arduous process. It was a good experience, but I did not like the very narrow focus of the position. I started a search for a position that would give me a better chance to use my varied skills.

My First Introduction to Amherst College

I contacted the Babson College Placement Office and told them I was interested in employment in a smaller company. They replied that Amherst College was looking for an Assistant Comptroller. It was

October when my wife, Ann, and I were invited to come to the College for an interview. We drove from our home in Schenectady to Amherst, Massachusetts through the beautiful Pioneer Valley. It was fall, and all the trees were in their beautiful reds, oranges, and yellows. The fun of the drive was enhanced as we were excited to be driving our new little sports car, an Austin Healy 3000. The beauty and the fun of driving that sports car around the winding hills made us both say, "We are ready to move to this beautiful little town in Western Massachusetts!"

I met with George May, the Comptroller. He was an Amherst College graduate, Class of 1946, and a very dedicated employee. Our conversations went well. There was an immediate, mutual good feeling. His wife, Ann, joined us for lunch. What a coincidence: George and Ann having lunch with George and Ann. It was a great start to a wonderful experience of almost ten years. I also recall Van Halsey, Dean of Admission saying to me that I was the first Non-Amherst College graduate to be hired in the administration. What an honor, and what a great team of people I had joined.

Here, I had the freedom and opportunity to venture into many new endeavors.

Early Business Office

First—and somewhat surprisingly—I noticed the Business Office had no automated systems. It was 1961, when computers had not fully made their entrance into the small business world, but unit record equipment (IBM punched cards) was in many medium to large companies. In the Amherst College Business Office, every accounting entry was made by hand, every column added by a mechanical adding machine. I also made sure I, by hand, made every entry that was required for several accounting cycles. Though tedious, it really helped me understand the Business Offices procedures. This was absolutely essential, as I had no experience with college accounting and was about to make major changes.

The College auditors, Coopers and Lybrand, had, as part of their annual audit, strongly suggested the College begin using some more sophisticated accounting equipment, the kind that left a printed trail, and automatically totaled numbers—not the hard-to-read handwriting.

When I arrived, in the corner of the office was a large, unopened box containing an NCR Accounting Machine. George May, the Comptroller, did not have the time to peek into the box, let alone figure out how to use it.

Fortunately, he had a very capable staff that were all willing to learn new things, and thus the NCR machine started to be an integral part of our office. This was extremely helpful to me as I ventured into these new tasks.

Working at Amherst was, you could say, kind of romantic. Our office was on the third floor of a very old, very stately beautiful building: Walker Hall, built in 1870. This building had some offices and several classrooms with a huge center staircase taking up what seemed like a third of the space. From my office I could hear some of the professors lecturing, especially one star professor, Benjamin M. Ziegler. He was very loud, rather intense, and very interesting. The students loved him. I should note that this building was later, in 1963, very carefully dismantled, stone by stone, so that those beautiful stones could form the base of the new Robert Frost Library.

Walker Hall being demolished to make space for the new Robert Frost Library. This was the location of my first Amherst College office.
(Buildings and Grounds of Amherst College: A History of Photographs of the Campus 1820–2007)

College Hall—The New Home for the Business Office
(The Buildings and Grounds of Amherst College:
A History in Photographs of the Campus, 1820–2007)

So, in 1962 we were informed that our office would be moving to new temporary headquarters in College Hall. This was a large, old, 1830s, all-wood structure consisting mainly of an auditorium with a surrounding balcony. It was sad to leave the glorious Walker Hall, but we managed.

The College Treasurer, Paul D. Weathers, was elderly and a member of the Amherst College Class of 1915. He was not a big fan of any kind of automation. He was a little scary; everyone seemed to jump when Mr. Weathers entered. He was "old school," very precise, and liked things his way. However, I moved on and I negotiated time on the unit record (punched card) equipment at the University of Massachusetts, just a short way down the street. In preparation for this change it was necessary for me to develop a chart of accounts, which basically means assigning numbers to every accounting account. That makes it sound simple, but because the "punched card" system sorted by the punched holes in the cards, the numbers were the key in breaking down the accounts by Fund—i.e., Endowment, Plant, Operating etc. It further broke down the accounts by assets, liabilities, income, and expenses. Then, it completed a further breakdown of the number by such things as departments. In essence, the chart of accounts is the foundation for the entire accounting system.

This was a new experience for me, but fortunately it was very successful. As a matter of fact, I was doing the same task—creating a chart of accounts—at Mitchell College in New London, Connecticut, in 1990. This was some 30-odd years later. At the time, I called Amherst College to see if they had developed a new, modern chart of accounts. The reply was, "No, George; we are still using the one you implemented in the 1960s!" That made me feel pretty good.

In 1964, I hired a young, very capable person, Paul Billings, to help operate the new unit record equipment located in a small room in the basement of College Hall. This operation was expanded, so we eventually had all the IBM unit record machines, key punch, sorter, and an IBM 407 Tabulating machine to produce the financial reports.

Enter the Era of the Computer— the 1960s Variety

THE COLLEGE REGISTRAR, ROBERT F. GROSE ('44), WAS MOST EAGER TO advance beyond the punch-card level of record keeping. He pushed hard for computers, along with a couple of faculty members—particularly Al Linnel, an astronomy professor, and Jim Chalmers, an economics professor.

The powers that be thought it would be wise to study the computing needs for the whole college, not just one or two narrow functional areas. So, they contracted with Systems Development Corporation—CDC, a firm with a national reputation for assisting the biggest and best companies. The cost of this study was approximately $100,000 and was to take several months. The lead consultant was an Amherst College graduate who was extremely capable. They interviewed faculty, administrators and flow-charted all of the many office's functions. Flow charting was the hottest new tool for doing systems design. Page upon page and book upon book was produced, and I worked closely with the consulting team. At about halfway through the study, I could clearly see what was going to be their conclusion, so I wrote what I thought would be the CDC's final recommendation and gave it to the College Treasurer, Dr. Stanley F. Teele ('28). He called me into his office and told me he really liked what I wrote and wanted me to present my conclusion to the Amherst College Board of Trustees at their upcoming Washington, DC meeting.

I had never had any previous direct dealings with the Board, and when I discovered the names of the Board Members who were serving, I became very impressed and somewhat concerned. These men were the very best in the field of Law and very high up in both government and business. On top of all that, I was not fond of public speaking.

The Vice President of IBM, George "Spike" Beitzel ('50), wanted to talk with me before the meeting and asked, "Could we 'jog' together from our hotels?"

What could I say but, "Yes."

At the time I smoked and was not a jogger; however, Spike was very fit and a jogger. Well, if you have never tried jogging while answering questions from the VP of IBM and a Board Member of the College, I can assure you it is not easy! Nevertheless, I went to the meeting and made my pitch to set up an all-college computer center. Having had no experience with computers or designing all-college computer systems, I set about the task as a one-person department. My first task was to hire the computer technical staff

Dr. Teele gave me a new title: Assistant to the Treasurer. Dr. Teele's faith in me was very uplifting and spoke to the kind of man he was. He was a fantastic person, very dedicated to the College, but unfortunately passed from an illness not too long after he gave me my new position. To fill my old position in the Business Office, I went back to the Babson College Placement Office and told them I needed an Assistant to the Comptroller as soon as possible. Fortunately, we found a candidate: a recent graduate, Clinton D. Howell. He came to campus, interviewed, and we hired him. He started to work in May 1966. He became a great member of the team and his family and mine became very close and longtime friends.

Amherst College's First Computer Department

In the mid 60s, computers were becoming more common. As directed, I set about the task of acquiring and setting up a computer department. It was again a challenge, but a project I really enjoyed. The College had, in 1965, just completely renovated the old, 1917, very classic, beautiful Converse Library into a Lecture hall and classrooms. I was given most of the basement area to use for the new computer center.

I always liked construction projects. I took the large, empty space and designed staff offices, a keypunch room, and a classroom. I constructed a raised floor in the area that would house the administrative computer

*Converse Memorial Library, built in 1917.
Remodeled to Administrative Offices Assembly Hall and Computer Center in 1965
(The Buildings and Grounds of Amherst College: A History in Photographs
of the Campus, 1820–2007)*

system and the academic computer system. The computers of those days generated a lot of heat, so computer room floors were often raised up to allow for the enormous number of interconnecting wires and for the air conditioning that would flow up and pass through the bottom of the equipment.

At the risk of being boring, I would remind the reader that the primary way you entered information into the computer and also stored information was by using IBM punch cards. This operation grew, but was limited by the IBM 1401 computer limitations; it had very little storage memory, very slow computing speeds, and magnetic tape was used as the primary means of storing data.

Again, I was fortunate to be able to find an excellent staff, including two keypunch operators, three computer systems analysts, programmers, and a computer operator. I was anxious to develop systems that were very sophisticated for the day, considering the limitations of the equipment.

Designing a comprehensive database was my objective. Fortunately, I hired Clela Reeves as a programmer and systems designer. She was previously a Dean of Students in an upstate New York university and had

A 1960s IBM 1401 Computer System
(IBM Archives Collection)

moved to South Hadley, Massachusetts. She shared my ideas and understood the college environment we were working in.

In those early days, after placing the order it took many months before your computer would be delivered. Hence, you were expected to have written a lot of the software and tested the programs on a similar computer system before yours arrived. IBM had test centers for their customers and ours was in Boston, Massachusetts. Because of the distance, we would try to schedule at least two one-hour time periods, a couple of hours apart on their computer. Getting hands-on time was very difficult and the computer was scheduled 24 hours a day, seven days a week. This would give us a chance to run four or five programs and then have time to try to de-bug any coding errors or logic errors. I did much of the systems design work and flow-charted the system for the programmers. They often were upset with me for I pushed the limit of the computer coding. The system/programmer team, however, was outstanding.

We chose the Admission Office to be our second application after the Business Office. Amherst had two very outstanding admission people, Eugene S. Wilson ('29) and C. Van Halsey, who were both extremely good at appreciating the applicants' struggle to get into a prestigious college like Amherst. They were also darn nice people. Well, while in Boston, as we were testing part of their system in the wee hours of the night, we were finding almost every student had near-perfect Board Scores. My background was not academic, and I think I got the most SAT points from spelling my name correctly; hence, perfect scores were not anything I had ever heard much about. Well, we went over and over the code to try and find the error.

I finally called Dean Wilson the next morning to tell him of my dilemma, and he nicely explained, "Almost everyone who applied to Amherst had near perfect Board Scores."

"Really!"

He said, "George, when we are selecting our students, we have to look beyond the Board Scores for someone who does something *else* that is exceptional."

In my new position I was also asked to establish the computer system for the academic side of the College. Initially we installed an IBM 1620 with the supporting punch card area for the students to enter their computer code. Fortran was the primary language. We held Fortran classes for the students, and they were an immediate success. I kept that facility open for nearly 24 hours. I also wanted to expand the user base to include the non-science faculty and students and show them how they might employ this new tool. Initially, the primary users were the astronomy department, an economics teacher, Jim Chalmers, and a couple physics teachers.

In my effort to get the non-science faculty to use the computer, Peter Marshall, a Greek teacher and a social friend who was attempting to do his doctoral thesis, mentioned he wanted to do a concordance of a very large Greek work.

I said, "We could do that by using the power of the computer."

To accomplish this, he would have to keypunch every word in the book, and then the computer could sort and count the words, etc. It is interesting to note now that almost all books are available on the computer, making this task very simple. It might have taken years to accomplish without the help of the "new" computer, but the concordance was completed in a relatively short time period. This fact, and the intellectual and human effort required, raised all kinds of questions by some Amherst faculty as to whether this project was worthy of a doctoral degree.

We installed Teletype machines so our users could transfer information from the other area colleges to our center. We also established a link with Dartmouth College in Hanover, New Hampshire. This was of particular interest to us because the Head of the Dartmouth Computer Center was a man by the name of John Kemeny. He and an associate, Tom Kurtz, had just developed a new computer language that was more user friendly than Fortran; it was called BASIC. For our students to have access to this new language was a great experience. When you have four elite colleges—Amherst College, an all-male school; Mount Holyoke College, an all-women's college; Smith College, an all-women's college; and Hampshire College, a coed college, sharing classes and using the Amherst College computer, anything can happen. And, it did happen. In those days, long-distance telephone calls were very expensive—until the students discovered they could call for free on our dedicated telephone line established for the Tele-type (TTY33). After dialing the computer station number, instead of placing the phone receiver on the Teletype cradle, they just talked with their friends. When I saw the usage bill from the New England Telephone Company, I was really puzzled by the amount of use this inter-college computer system was getting. Oh, how naïve I was!

IBM soon introduced a new, much more powerful computer, called the IBM 1130 with a line plotter. The students and faculty were delighted with what the power of this machine could do, and they "played" with it all day and night, doing some very sophisticated things. The computing speed enabled our users to develop projects that would previously have run well over 12 hours on the old first-generation IBM 1620, but now could be run in minutes.

A student, Tom R. Smith wrote in the newspaper, "Amherst College now has the biggest computer for student use among the Little Three...The IBM 1130 has been purchased by the college, complete with improvements for $121,000. The National Science Foundation, through its College Science Improvement Grants, is expected to share a large part of this cost."[1]

A rather interesting use of the computer was by one of the very accomplished faculty members, Professor Dudley Town, who designed crossword puzzles for the New York Times. He liked to come to the center after midnight to work.

*The Academic Computer Room's New 1967 IBM 1130,
with Director George Dunnington and Assistant Clela Reeves
(Amherst College 1967 Olio Page 39)*

The Amherst students did all the computer programming (very involved mathematical equations) that determined the shape of pieces of sculpture for a University of Massachusetts glass sculptor, Robert Mallory. These shapes were printed on the IBM 1130 Line Plotter. The artist published a book, for which he gained national notoriety for the techniques and the incredible shapes of his sculptures. In a biographical sketch in "comp**art**,": "Robert Mallory was a renowned artist early in his career already, and made a pioneering contribution to 'computer art.'"

It is almost impossible for computer users to realize how the students took to using this "new" device. I would have to ask them to leave the center at 10 or 11 in the evening. Many would have loved to stay all night.

In those early days of the computer there was an aura of having to be overly protective of this machine. There were lots of regulations; you had to sign in, you had to pass rudimentary tests, etc. I realized that our students were very responsible and were challenged by what they could do. Soon, I started giving out Computer Center keys to the students I knew well. I never had a problem.

There was a core of students who were absolutely brilliant and undertook fascinating projects. IBM had some software "bugs" in their new 1130—one of their newest computers—which they were diligently working to solve. Our students identified the bugs, fixed them, and sent the corrected machine language code by what IBM thought was a very secure phoneline to IBM's secure lab in Armonk, New York. The next morning, I got a call from an IBM executive asking if he could dispatch a team of his computer specialists to meet these students, and they were offered a summer job.

A group of our Amherst College football players had heard that the national football teams were scouting opponent games and entering the data in the computer to statistically analyze the plays. Hence, every Saturday a group of our students would sit at the keypunch machine and tediously enter the game's actual plays for both our team and the opponents. They had also entered several prior years of both our opponents and home team's handwritten football plays. There was so much data and so many complicated statistical analyses it would take this new "super" computer about five hours before printing out one, two, or three pages of facts.

It was really amusing to see our rather celebrated coach, James E. Ostendarp, look at the print-out and say, "I never would run the ball when we are on the 10-yard line on the third down."

The students would reply, "Oh yeah? You did it 85 percent of the time!"

I believe we were the first small college to employ the computer for the benefit of an already excellent football program.

The National Science Foundation and The National Institute of Health were offering grants to colleges for many different kinds of projects. Amherst College had a very prestigious name and the inter-collegiate sharing program, a "hot" new thing to do, with two well-known neighboring colleges helped to get our grants read. Grant writing was a new undertaking for me but fortunately the college had just hired a new Director of Development, John Callahan, and he knew the Washington, DC game. His plan was simple. I would take the 7:30 a.m. flight out of Bradley Field, arriving very early in DC. He had scheduled appointments with several of the division heads of these grant makers.

His plan was this: "George, ask all questions you can concerning what is going on within NSF and NIH—what is new, what grants they have made relating to computers."

I jotted down a few notes and when I went back to campus, I pounded out a proposal containing many of the very things I heard—and was successful at receiving a few sizeable grants. One of those grants paid for the IBM 1130 computer. I must say, John Callahan knew how to fluff up the proposal to be very impressive. I am pleased to say we used the funds very effectively for the reasons stated.

The Growth of Administrative Computing

It was easy for me to see that our computer hardware could handle much more work than we had at that time. I offered the other three private colleges in the area the opportunity to do their administrative computing at Amherst College. Mount Holyoke College signed up immediately and while Smith College did reluctantly join, they only stayed in the group for a short time. Hampshire College was just recently created and so I personally did much of their record keeping and ran the reports for their executives at the Amherst Computer Center.

There is a fascinating story about the founding of Hampshire College; the principal funds for this endeavor came from an Amherst College alumnus. A book was written about the involvement of the three colleges, Amherst, Smith and Mount Holyoke. In essence these schools were concerned about how many very well qualified students were refused admission. To try to help these many very capable students, they formed a new local college. Also, this new college planned to try to do things differently, more efficiently. For example, they were able to get IBM to help them study the feasibility of a "bookless" library. Dr. Steve Furth, an IBM researcher from their research lab, worked with us on this project. But, partly because of the primitive nature of computer terminals and partly because memory storage was so limited, at this time we were unable to digitally store the necessary data to make this goal possible. Also, we found that our library users wanted to touch the actual books and not try to search the library card catalogs using a computer terminal.

It is interesting to recall, in those early days of computers, the fear and trepidation that people had when you started to talk about collecting data and storing it in the computer. The "Big Brother is watching you" aura was prevalent. The College had no central database—a scary term—so we sent out questionnaires to begin collecting basic personal data. We held meetings to help assure employees that the information would be handled very carefully. We even found duplicate social security numbers—yes, true—and we randomized the social security number to be the main file identification number. The answers to my carefully designed data-collection sheet were just amazing: "Sex?" Answer: "Yes!" Overcoming the misconceptions people had about how computers would de-personalize the world, how they would put people out of work, and how information would be misused was constantly on my mind.

The computer was intimidating to some and threatening to others. A guest lecturer, an applied mathematician from Harvard College whom I had invited to talk with the math and economics faculty about computer usage, was particularly confused by it. We had the meeting in the newly renovated Converse Memorial Hall, where one of the theoretical math teachers actually stood up and said, "computers are for trade schools!" That's hard to believe today.

Computerization did require systematizing things so that they could be handled logically, and like things had to be identified as being alike. In this quest to have more universality to things, the library cataloging systems immediately were challenged. Amherst College employed the Dewey Decimal System for cataloging books, as did many other colleges. Melvin Dewey was the inventor of that system and was also the Amherst College Librarian, circa 1874.

By then, the Library of Congress had developed their system, commonly called LC system, so that every book published was cataloged by them and the number was printed in the front of all books. This had a couple of significant advantages over other systems. First, it saved a lot of time and money for the libraries across the country. The in-house cataloging effort was often backed-up so new books did not immediately get on the shelves in a timely manner. Secondly, the LC system provided for the cataloging of more than just books; it included items such as works of art. This feature in itself made hundreds of pieces of art available that were often stored deep in college and museum basements. Some very valuable art treasures were discovered during this cataloging challenge.

Some Interesting Stories

The Big Controlled Burn?

In the 1960s, this small-town Amherst was an idyllic college town. The University of Massachusetts was essentially, still, the Massachusetts Agriculture College, but it was about to burst into a full-blown State University. I become involved with the town in a small way and knew the Town Manager, Allan Torrey. The town had a huge problem with its volunteer fire department in that the firemen were not properly trained to successfully extinguish fires in this rapidly growing town. Mr. Torrey hired a new fire chief from a large New Jersey fire department. From my prior fire department experiences, I knew that a new chief would love to have a building that could be used to practice fire-fighting skills. His firemen could set the building on fire and then have it extinguished by these trainees. Amherst College was about to demolish an enormous old wooden structure that had many, many apartments. I offered this to the new chief, and he was delighted to have this building where his men could practice setting and putting out fires. Sitting in my second-floor office, in College Hall, at the corner of Route 9 and South Pleasant Street, I began hearing the town fire whistle blowing over and over. Soon thereafter, I looked out my window and saw several fire trucks coming into town with their sirens screaming. Engines from Northampton, Holyoke, and even Springfield were roaring into town. Yes, you guessed it: our new chief lost control of his "controlled burn," and the building burned completely to the ground! It did save us a lot of demolition expenses. Also, my face was a little red.

The Big Dig

I belonged to a small, very old church on the edge of the Amherst College campus whose membership was growing. To accommodate this growth, the church acquired a new piece of property on the edge of the University of Massachusetts's campus, upon which they built a new church structure. The only problem with this location was that going down a very steep hill, behind the church, was a swamp. It was planned to be the parking lot for our parishioners, but it was a swamp-wetlands. They had exhausted their building funds. Thus, making a parking lot out of a swamp land had to be postponed. In 1963, Amherst College was about to start constructing the Robert Frost Library, a structure that was going to be at least two floors below ground.

Lots and lots of dirt needed to be excavated. It was just what was needed to make a swamp go away and a parking lot to emerge. Problem: the enormous trucks—18- wheeler, trailer dumps—when loaded, needed a special permit to go through town. My friend, Town Manager Mr. Torrey, gave us permission and so the trucks started to roll. A huge, special, conveyor belt machine located on the soon-to-be library basement could load a truck at a rate of one about every five minutes or so—many, many tons of dirt. The State of Massachusetts had just paved the main road to the UMass campus, right by the front of our new church. The first truck upon arriving turned sharply and went down the very steep hill and mired down in the swamp. I thought that was the end of my dream of free fill. Not to worry, George—these enormous trucks faced the challenge and conquered it. The excavating company brought down a front-end loader with wheels taller than I stood to pull the truck out of the muck. I drove down from the College at noon to see what progress was being made in filling our swamp. Upon arriving, my heart went into my throat. Huge chunks of the new State of Massachusetts road were all pushed up from where the trucks had turned to enter the church property. They looked like icebergs, all pushed up on top of each other. I immediately thought about the potential cost to repair the new street. Somehow, it got fixed without my further involvement! And the swamp was gone.

The President of the United States of America Comes to the Campus

Hail to the Chief

Having the opportunity to be close by and listen to the President of the United States speak was an amazing experience for me, back on October 26, 1963. The process, even back then, to prepare for a presidential visit was extensive and very involved. The Secret Service said a college campus was a difficult location for them to provide security. There are all the dormitories, with their many windows and rooftops along the President's campus route. I supposed a campus rebel was a worrisome possibility, and the college had its share of rebels.

They did background checks on taxi drivers, bus drivers, and anyone else who had business on the campus and around town. In addition to Secret Service protection, what seemed to me like all of the Massachusetts State Police cruisers were parked on the athletic fields adjacent to the College's Field House. There were only 250 police officers! I had no idea that the State owned that many vehicles. The State Police presence was everywhere—dormitory windows, building rooftops, etc. Very impressive.

The event was for the dedication of the new Robert Frost Library. President Kennedy was an enthusiastic Robert Frost fan, and Frost had read at his Presidential inauguration. Amherst College felt very fortunate that the President would honor this dedication with his presence.

I was personally involved with some of the setup in the College Field House. It was a large building with a dirt floor and was used primarily for baseball practice and Track and Field events. A large stage was constructed with elaborate sound devices, flags, and chairs for the dignitaries. They included, President of the College, Dr. Calvin Plimpton , John J. McCloy ('16), former President of the World Bank, poet Archibald MacLeish, and many other dignitaries.

The New Robert Frost Library Amherst College
Dedicated on October 24, 1963
(Amherst College Archives Kennedy Convocation)

The person doing the sound system was a man I had known for several years, as he did all the intercom work in the newly constructed Computer Center. All the many wires and cables were carefully and neatly laid to the various amplification speakers around the hall, under the stage, and to the microphones on the stage.

The Secret Service told us they would provide the podium, the President's water, and guards around the stage so no bad things could happen.

I was there very early to make sure all the setup was happening and talked with Secret Service personnel. The weather was rather unusual in that there were extremely heavy and low clouds and dense fog. The plan was for the President to fly into the Westover Air Force Base, not too many miles from the College.

People were taking their seats, the dignitaries were settling in the assigned seats on stage, and the President of the College, Dr. Calvin Plimpton, started his opening remarks. Disaster struck on his very first words! The elaborate speaker system screeched ear-piercingly. Only a few of President Plimpton's words came out sounding normal; the others were ear-piercing screeches.

My sound person furiously checked the amplifier and the wire connections to it. We followed the wires and checked each connector. He

*The Convocation Stage, crushing the speaker wires
(Amherst College Archives Photographs of John F. Kennedy Visit
to Amherst College 1963 October 26 Page 39)*

could not find anything wrong. I immediately ran up to the stage and was about to go under it, when out of nowhere the Secret Service grabbed me.

"But sir—"

"No buts, period. No one goes under the stage!"

The next speaker on the program took to the microphone and still, this horrible screeching continued. Fortunately, we got word that there would be a delay in the President's arrival. In this interim time, we discovered the problem: we had put all the speaker wires and cables under the metal stage frame, and the weight of the fully loaded stage was pinching the wires. Because the stage was constructed on the dirt floor of the Athletic Fieldhouse, we could easily dig out the dirt and relieve the pressure on the wires.

No President yet, thank goodness! An hour went by—still no President, and no word when to expect him. I walked out behind the Field House and saw that they had cleared a huge area for helicopters to land. The extreme fog was causing some delays, as the helicopters were coming from nearby Westover Air Base. I think there were three or more, and they all looked alike.

While I cannot remember exactly how long the wait was, it finally happened, and we were told that the President would go immediately to

Presidential helicopters landing behind Fieldhouse
(Amherst College Collection John F. Kennedy Convocation Page 37)

Amherst College Convocation, October 26, 1963
President Kennedy receiving an Honorary Doctor of Laws Degree
(Amherst College Library Archives President Kennedy Convocation October 26, 1963)

a smelly locker room for his makeup to be applied. That process was close to an hour, and then the thrill of a lifetime came over me. A live band played *Hail to The Chief,* and down the center aisle came the President.

I was a Republican at that time, but in spite of that I was very proud to be an American and to see in person, up very close, a couple of feet from where I stood, our President, John F. Kennedy. He gave a fantastic speech, as he was known to do, and was bestowed an Honorary Doctor of Laws Degree.

And the microphone and sound system worked as it should for his speech. Sadly, this was one of the President's last public appearances before he was assassinated on November 22, 1963. Such a horrible tragedy after his special appearance at the College.

Robert Frost, Teacher and Poet

I FEEL I WAS VERY FORTUNATE TO HAVE HAD THE OPPORTUNITY TO restart my career in a new direction: the field of education—and especially fortunate to begin at the truly renowned Amherst College. Working at a prominent College means you meet some of the most interesting people in the world. Amherst was certainly a very large, but closely knit family, all very proud that they worked there. Many had actually graduated from there.

In earlier years Robert Frost was a teacher and lecturer at Amherst College. A good friend of mine, Robert A. Ward, when he was a student at Amherst in the late 50s was Frost's campus personal assistant, guiding Frost back and forth from the College to the nearby, very quaint Lord Jeffery Inn, where he stayed. Mr. Ward enjoyed talking with Frost, discussing his many poems. Later, Mr. Ward became a Robert Frost scholar. Years later, when he became Headmaster at Williston Northampton School, we worked together and he often shared a Frost poem with me. The poem almost always was a metaphor for me to contemplate. Robert Frost, at Amherst, was the Simpson Lecturer in Literature and would often do a reading of his poems in the auditorium in College Hall. I attended one of these events. The auditorium was filled to capacity with students. This was my first time to hear a poet read his own poetry, and I thoroughly enjoyed his readings. It was very special. Shortly thereafter, College Hall, built circa 1830, was gutted and converted to temporary offices—mine being one of them.

Emily Dickinson Home

In 1965 the College purchased the poet Emily Dickinson's home. It had not been significantly improved since her life there. Having recently read a book about Emily Dickinson written by Polly Longsworth, I had

The Emily Dickinson House
Purchased by Amherst College in 1965
(Buildings and Ground of Amherst College, A History in
Photographs of the Campus, 1820-2007)

learned that Emily Dickinson led a rather traumatic, stressful life and had endured the hardships of going over the mountain by horse-drawn carriage to classes at Mount Holyoke College. She was also somewhat of a recluse. In 1965, I went to her now empty home and inquisitively started looking all through the house, from the attic to the basement, in hopes I might find something that actually belonged to her. No such luck, but I was impressed by a very large copper kettle in the attic that evidently held water for the family.

Branching Out—New Experiences

While my tenure at Amherst College was going along very comfortably, I believed it would be beneficial to gain experience at another institution. Along this line of thinking I saw an advertisement in an educational newspaper for a three-year financial position at the American University of Beirut. This sounded perfect for me as it would give me experience away from the prestigious Amherst College. It would also allow my whole family to go with me, which would give us a chance to see another part of the world. I followed up on this and got some very encouraging replies from the University. Now it was time for me to tell my "boss," the College Treasurer, Kurt Hertzfield, what I was thinking. This made me a little concerned, as I believed he was not the most open-minded person and could be easily upset by this plan. While pondering this dilemma, I got a call from the President of Amherst College, Dr. Calvin H. Plimpton ('39), asking me to come to his office. What could this be about? Did he hear from the University of Beirut before I had a chance to tell him? Yes, he certainly did hear from the University of Beirut, and they expressed a genuine interest in having me come and be their chief financial officer.

President Plimpton sat down with me and said; "I hear you're interested in going to the University of Beirut for three years."

I innocently replied, "Yes, I was thinking this might be a very enriching experience for me. May I ask how you heard about this?"

"Yes, of course, I am the Chairman of the Board of the University."

"Oh," said I, a little dumbfounded. And thinking to myself why did I not know this? Well, after a gulp or two by me, President Plimpton enthusiastically supported me.

He said, "I think three years would be too long for us to operate without you, so would you consider one or two years? You still will need to get the Treasurer, Kurt Hertzfield's, approval."

We both had some skepticism as to what he might be agreeable to do. The decision became irrelevant. The next day on the national news it showed planes bombing Beirut. Bombs and I are not a good match, and so ended this potentially great escapade.

Community Involvement

The Town of Amherst in the 1960s was an picture-perfect college town where the center of Town had all the stores and banks we needed to enjoy our lives. Shopping was fun and we knew many of the shopkeepers. We had parades wherein my children would march as Brownies or Girl Scouts, and we had carnivals on the town green. Part of this very pleasant ambience was created because many of the townspeople participated in the institutions that served the town. My wife, Ann, and I bought our first home from Elder – Jones, a local developer. I remember we paid $18,000, a huge sum for us, and it was financed by Amherst College. Walter Elder was a great gentleman who owned the local lumber company and from whom I purchased many things, as I was essentially building out the interior of our new home myself. His son Doug, with whom I also worked, was a Williston graduate, class of 1954. The builder, Tony Conklin, was a fantastic guy and went out of his way to make the construction experience wonderful for both Ann and me. He also served on the Building Committee at the Church with me. I tried to do my share to make our town a little nicer, and as I write of the few activities I supported I wonder how I ever found time to take part. I never was content to just be a member, I had to take a significant role in whatever organization I joined.

The Little Church on the Green

As previously mentioned, the quaintness and the small size of the town made it so you could easily get to know many residents and town leaders, and they knew you. The town was growing rapidly, especially with the major expansion of the University of Massachusetts.

One of my first extracurricular activities involved the church, which my family and I attended. The pastor, Ewald Mann, had moved from Estonia and was an extremely hard worker, a great preacher, and a wonderful person. He introduced himself to me on one of our family's first visits to his church, and the next thing I know, he was telling me a terrible tale of woe about his need for someone who could help the church with their finances. Yes, I became the Church Treasurer. The membership was getting older and declining. Fortunately, the growth of the town brought more new, younger folks, including college students. It was evident that the church building was too small and its physical, downtown location prevented it from expanding. The thinking was that by moving closer to

UMass we would attract younger members. No surprise—soon I was deeply involved with the church leadership in buying property and constructing a new structure on the edge of the UMass campus. This was very successful—even the construction of the church's parking lot, as referenced earlier.

The Little Music Camp in the Hills

One day while busily working in my office in College Hall, there appeared a woman, very shy, asking if she might have a minute to talk with me. She was Elsa Brown, the wife of the Amherst College's doctor, Steve Brown ('28). We had met at a social function and chatted, and I remembered she was a rather well-known musician and played in the Springfield Symphony Orchestra.

She started our conversation by saying, "George, I have a serious problem. The Cummington School for the Arts has asked me to be their Treasurer. I have no idea what to do." She went on to say the previous treasurer was a well-known poet who had died, leaving her with all the records.

I said, "I am not sure I can help you, but bring in the school's books."

The next day she showed up at my office with three large, brown, paper bags and handed them to me. Upon looking into the bags, all I found was many years of unopened bank statements and scribbled financial notes. So, late that evening, I began examining the contents of the bags and decided it was mostly useless trash and I would have to start from the beginning. The summer camp was extremely well known and had graduated many very successful musicians, poets, and artists. The new President of the Board, Ned Ryerson, was a very wealthy person and very supportive of the school. He also asked me to help and join the Broad of Trustees. For several years I managed their finances and attended meetings. It was the 60s, and touch-feely things were all the vogue. This I was not fond of, but I joined in with the students and "bonded!" The head of the school, Chris Horton, was a very successful artist. In 1969, he gave me one his engravings, "Apple," which I continue to enjoy and still hangs on a wall in my home.

The New School

My oldest daughter, Susan attended kindergarten at the University of Massachusetts School of Education and my wife, Ann, of course became involved in her program.

One night after dinner Ann said to me, "Mrs. Johnson is starting a new school based on the Montessori teaching method, and, she wants me to help."

At first it was easy; I was building giant plywood boxes on wheels in which the children could store things and hang their clothes and boots. I think I built ten and painted them. I became further involved being on the Board and helped with their finances. The school was very successful and grew and so, I was very busy with another wonderful task.

Changes I Observed in the 1960s

WORKING AT AMHERST COLLEGE WAS AN EXTREMELY ENJOYABLE experience. While my various positions there were very challenging and rewarding, the people were what made this time period for my family and me very special. The 1960s were a time when I saw many changes happening at the college and across the country. The changes I noticed might mean very little in the big picture, but nonetheless, from my personal viewpoint, I felt they represented a real change in the character of the college. The following are but a few of these changes:

1. In my early years at the college, perhaps 15 to 20 faculty and staff would all go to the Dining Hall for the morning coffee social time at about 10:00 in the morning. The discussions were often very interesting, ranging from what was happening in the world to proposed changes to the curriculum. A few of the names that I recall include Frederick King Turgeon (a professor of French), Gordon Bridges (Head of Dining Services), Charlie W. Cole (retired President of the College), George B. May ('46, the Comptroller), Charles Morgan (Head of the Fine Arts Department), Benjamin M. Ziegler (Political Science professor), Robert F. Grose ('44, Registrar), and Ralph C. McGoun, (Director of Theater Arts). This group began to shrink in numbers as everyone became too busy to socialize and, while I hate to say it, this group was getting old. Nonetheless, the group was very eclectic and thus the conversations were most interesting.

2. In those days, the older faculty prided themselves in the fact that Amherst was a teaching college, not a research college, not a

"publish or perish" college. While there was some research always happening, it often actively involved the students. This generation of faculty always cherished the number of "contact hours" they had with the students. They were there for the students! In the mid 60s, some of the newer faculty started talking about how few contacts hours they had. They looked at this as a good thing; it meant their research or book writing was being recognized. Was this good? I cannot answer that, but I felt student contact hours was a core value for the college.

3. There were no computers, either in the academic programs or in the administration when I arrived in 1961. In the 60s, I was the center of a change that brought computers to campus and the computers began to become more and more a part of the students' academic lives. The faculty was starting to integrate the computer into their courses. Economics and Astronomy were early users. A prominent Professor of Physics, Arnold B. Arons, once told me that one of the projects his students did each year involved calculating something to do with the stars, which would take the students many days of hard, tedious work to prove. With the computer, the same calculations took only minutes. At a lecture I sponsored, I invited Dr. Kenneth E. Iverson, a Harvard applied mathematics professor, to talk to the math and science faculty about a new computer language he developed called APL. He was truly an amazing guy. He would ask the math faculty to give him the equation for a mathematical algorithm and he would write it on the "chalk board" with his left hand and at the same time ask another faculty member for the same formula and write it with the other hand! They were both different, but supposedly for the same purposes. He said mathematics often did not have a commonly accepted language and his new language, APL, would help address that problem. This was when one of the Amherst theoretical mathematicians stood up and said he thought computers were for trade schools—an opinion I referenced earlier. This might have been a clue that indeed, things were changing. Computers were here to stay. That does not mean I did not have

many issues as I launched Amherst College's first computers—not only in the academic programs, but also as the use of computers began to be an integral part of the administration as well. When I came to Amherst College in 1960, the Business Offices' accounting functions were all done by hand! When I left, virtually every function was aided by the computer.

4. Amherst College's Kirby Theater was known throughout the area for its outstanding student productions. It often had sold-out performances. Again, the town was a closely-knit community of Amherst College faculty and widows of faculty that loved attending college functions, with the theater being a special treat. Then came a new "shock" play that not only made me feel uncomfortable but also embarrassed me, and that is not easy to do. The "F" word was in almost every sentence, the actors ran down the aisle half naked, screaming and shocking the audience. These risqué performances became more commonplace, and the theater audience changed.

5. The three, single-gender colleges, Smith, Mt. Holyoke, and Amherst, began talking about the issue of continuing as single gender colleges or becoming coed. These colleges were very strong in their belief of remaining single gender, but other colleges across the country were making the change. Dartmouth College and Williams College became coed, among others. Fortunately, a long-standing tradition of allowing students to take courses at any of the five colleges continued and was enhanced by a regular bus route connecting the colleges. While this was not coed education, it meant that the classes and activities were often coed. Prior to having regular bus schedules, hitchhiking was the norm, but the rapid expansion of the University of Massachusetts meant that large numbers of construction workers from all over the country were now around town. I remember being very surprised when the construction companies building the new high-rise residence halls contracted with American Indians from upstate New York who specialized at working on projects that were very high. I first experienced these workers at the

local drugstore when, on payday, they were lined up at the Western Union money wiring window to send money home. These people were not accustomed to seeing young college girls hitch hiking and misread what they were doing. Because this practice had the potential for trouble, a five-college bus service was initiated. This not only enhanced the five-college exchange programs, but it also enabled the libraries to easily loan books between the libraries—by just sending the books on the bus. The Computer Center seemed to always have a lot of women from the other colleges using the Amherst facilities. It was truly coed.

6. In the 1960s, students began to become deeply involved in the way our country was being run. The integration of the South was very emotional. Students by the thousands went South to take part in marches and to boycott places that remained segregated. The Vietnam War was also a very highly charged topic, as most students believed we should not be involved in the war. Peaceful protests often became violent, with people getting hurt and killed

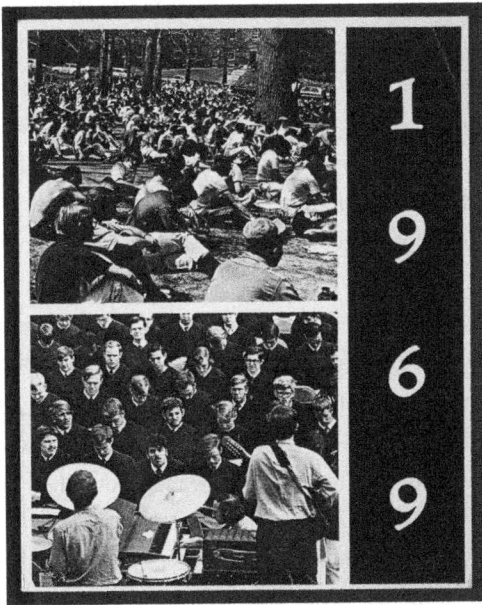

(Amherst College Yearbook Olio 1969)

and property being damaged. Fortunately, the college's leadership did an amazing job at keeping the fringe advocates from being too destructive and unhelpful to the cause.

7. Amherst College was always very fortunate to have many graduates who cared deeply about their college and gave generously, and therefore they had a sizeable endowment and an extremely functional and beautiful physical plant. However, until the 60s, they had never had a formal Development Office. In 1960, they hired Charles Longworth ('51) as the Assistant to the President and Director of Development to start to plan the college's first major fundraising campaign. This was extremely successful.

8. Marijuana and drinking always were big problems for colleges, especially for the Dean of Students. Massachusetts drinking age was 21, and the Associate Dean, William L. Swartzbaugh, and others theorized that if the age was reduced to 18, students could drink more safely on campus, which eventually did happen. Amherst had a long, "sacred" tradition of campus fraternities, and there were some very large and beautiful fraternity houses that housed and fed their members. These structures were owned by the various fraternity chapters. The college had a person, Arthur Davenport ('32), Business Manager of the fraternities, who was responsible for overseeing the many fraternity programs. It was not long before the frat parties were big drunken affairs and became wilder than usual. The damage to the properties was prevalent, a new and worrisome concern for the college. Soon, smoking pot became very popular; it too was illegal, but it had an advantage in that the damage to the physical plant seemed to go way down as everyone enjoyed smoking a "joint" and sitting down and listening to music. A peaceful event.

9. As the Amherst town budgets got tighter and the town fathers started looking for other sources of tax income, they began looking at the enormous, beautiful fraternity houses, which had been

real estate tax exempt. The town won the battle of the taxability of the fraternity houses. The taxes that were levied on these buildings were so burdensome on the fraternity members that they simply could not afford to operate the houses and pay all the expenses,. The college eventually took over ownership and classified the houses as dormitories, which had the effect of making them again tax exempt. The college did make payments to the town in lieu of taxes, but assumed all the care and expense of operating these dormitories/fraternity houses.

10. The drugs, the Vietnam War, and the equality demands of people of color began to challenge many of the old ways of our country. There were marches to the South, there were boycotts of places that had restrictions on blacks, and there was a general outcry for more minorities in our mostly white educational institutions. Colleges, like Amherst, customarily heavily recruited students from prestigious, independent schools. With these changes, the prestigious colleges, in order to increase the number of minority students, began to focus their recruiting in public high schools. This movement had some significant impacts on our colleges. Amherst College was a relatively peaceful place to learn and work. Yes, there were issues that students were concerned about, and even passionate about, and they would often respond by writing articles in the student paper and would invite speakers representing both viewpoints to come to campus to speak on the subject. Soon, this peaceful form of protests was not enough. Changes were not happening fast enough to satisfy the protesting groups, and then we had sit-ins, marches, and some destruction and violence, a new and difficult issue to deal with. Dr. Calvin H. Plimpton, President of the College, immediately spoke strongly about the fact that the College was an open and accepting institution, so certain forms of protest were simply not going to be tolerated. My recollection is that he did not make exceptions even with military recruiters, who continued to come to campus as students went to their various activities. On other campuses, there were complete

take-overs and shutdowns. Buses went to Selma and other similar destinations for student sit-ins and marches. We set aside times and places where the college body could gather in smaller groups and discuss issues, with the expectation that some issue might be mollified in a mutually accepted manner.

11. It was also a time when the college lost one of its great and respected teacher/poets, Robert Frost, who passed on January 29, 1963, at age 88. His passing was just nine months before the dedication of the Robert Frost Library on campus. The college was shocked by the tragic death of President John F. Kennedy on November 22, 1963. This tragedy was just a few days short of a month from when President Kennedy spoke at the dedication of the Robert Frost Library.

12. Amherst College decided to increase the size of its student body.

1959–1960	**1969–1970**
Seniors: 242	Seniors: 304
Juniors: 234	Juniors: 287
Sophomores: 251	Sophomores: 304
Freshmen: 260	Freshmen: 313
Total: 990	Total: 1208

This meant new buildings would be needed to accommodate all the new students and associated programs. To mention a few new structures:

- Walker hall, an 1870 stone structure, was demolished in 1963.
- Crossett Hall, a residence hall, was constructed in 1963.
- Davis Hall, a residence hall, was constructed in 1964.
- Pond Hall, a residence hall, was constructed in 1964.
- Stone Hall, a residence hall, was constructed in 1964.
- Robert Frost Library was constructed in 1965.

- Converse Memorial Hall was remodeled in 1965 from a library to a lecture, classroom, and computer center facility.
- The Emily Dickinson Home was purchased in 1965.
- The Walter S. Orr Skating Rink was built in 1965.
- Coolidge Hall, a residence hall, was constructed in 1966.
- Arms Music Building and Buckley Recital Hall was built in 1968.
- Merrill Science Center was constructed in 1968.

My time at Amherst College was truly memorable for my family and me, but I continued to believe that to advance my career, I should experience working at another college, along with its unique issues and challenges. The Town of Amherst was also a wonderful place to live and raise a family. Fortunately, my family was always willing to support me in my new endeavors.

Wesleyan University in Middletown, Connecticut sent a representative to Amherst, and soon thereafter recruited me to come there to start a new computer facility and develop programs for modeling assumptions for their future growth, a project I had tried to do and failed to accomplish at Amherst College. Little did I know what I was getting myself into!

Wesleyan University

Old Challenges, New Adventures

WHILE AT AMHERST COLLEGE I WAS APPROACHED BY PROFESSOR Singleton, an applied mathematician from Wesleyan who was attempting to do some computer modeling of how the University might function under various financial assumptions. He was working for the Treasurer, Colin Campbell. He had learned of some of my work as Director of Information Systems at Amherst College, and we discussed his desire to implement some of these techniques at the University.

Soon thereafter, I received a call with an invitation to come to Wesleyan and establish their computer center and information systems office. I was anxious to explore some new ideas, and Wesleyan supposedly had ample money to support this endeavor, as well as the money to start up a new computer center. Much of Wesleyan's endowment came from a deal where Wesleyan sold their very famous and profitable "*Weekly Reader*" to the Xerox Corporation for 400,000 shares of their stock, worth approximately $54,000,000.[2] Wesleyan was being required by the IRS to operate this publication as a for-profit enterprise, a strong incentive to sell this successful operation.

I accepted their offer of employment and, in mid-December 1969, our family settled into a lovely historic, old, Wesleyan home, complete with its very old, severely slanting floors. Initially it felt great to be on campus in a historic campus house. This style of living was what I had become accustomed to. Little did I know of the challenges that would soon be coming my way. I was not told of the serious unrest happening on campus and in the black community. This friction had started several years prior but was escalating to another level. The New York Times, on January 18, 1970, wrote an extensive story, "The Two Nations At Wesleyan University." This went into the background of many of the black student concerns, going back several years. I cannot help but wonder: had I known about these issues, would I have accepted the position?

Prior to my actual move to Middletown, I made a few trips to the Wesleyan campus. I hired my secretary, Marilyn Stepanski, and set up my office in South Hall on the second floor over the President's Office. It was a very comfortable office with lots of old school charm, a fireplace, and dark, rich woodwork.

At the same time, the college hired a new Treasurer, Robert Siff ('48). He hired an assistant, Kenneth W. Cunningham. These men were very capable, a real pleasure to work with. It was good and important to be part of this team.

Shortly after moving to campus and settling into my office, I heard a gunshot from the first floor, right below my office. This concerned me, as I never had experienced anything like this. This scared my new secretary, Marilyn, half to death. Being this close to gunshots was not something I had ever anticipated. It was very concerning to me. Quickly, I guided her down the exterior metal fire escape to the ground outside. What had happened was some students had taken over and occupied the President's Office. This kind of event had happened in other major Universities, so it was not unique to us. I had no idea this was just the beginning of a black-student-issue related crisis.

It was my understanding that Wesleyan had made a commitment to have a rather high percentage of its student body be black students. During this same time, many other colleges had also made similar plans for the make-up of their student bodies. This resulted in many highly competitive colleges looking, all at the same time, for a few well-qualified black students. The movement encompassed many things, but it was primarily to offer equal opportunities to a population that rarely considered a college or university with a high academic reputation.

At this same time, these colleges and universities were also having serious student unrest over the Federal Government's handling of the Vietnam War. The students did not want the Government to continue this terrible war and they wanted immediate action, while at Amherst we had sit-ins, related discussions, and lots of disruptions. Fortunately, Amherst's President Calvin H. Plimpton took a firm stand and insisted the college be open to all persuasions. I felt this was not the case at Wesleyan, and from there, matters got worse. What was about to happen on the campus was very shocking and completely unexpected.

Given these unusual and serious concerns surrounding the workplace, I nevertheless felt it was time for me to begin hiring my computer support staff and adding office equipment to the Information Systems Department. Also, it was time to move our entire department to a small house located at 36 Wyllis Avenue. Conveniently, the location was located just across the soccer fields from my campus house.

I was very fortunate to hire an extremely capable computer support staff. Through some very difficult and unusual happenings on campus, they all remained dedicated and stayed with me until I left Wesleyan.

The first person I hired was Steve J. Friedman, a public-school teacher who was from a NYC classroom. He was also a very devout and practicing Jew. I learned much from him about his faith, including attending his son's Bris at his home. Being an Orthodox Jew made this ceremony very special to both Steve and his family. I was impressed and want to share a little of this very interesting story. All the women in attendance went into the kitchen while the Rabbi, Steve, and his eight-day-old son were at the front of the living room. I stood with the men as witnesses to the ceremony. Never having ever experienced this ceremony, I stood near the front so as not to miss anything. Oh, my goodness, I was shocked and quite uneasy to see that the circumcision was really going to happen then and there! I felt uneasy and rather quickly went to the back of the room while they cut-off the little guy's foreskin.

Next, I hired our second systems analyst, Frederick Stefanowicz, who was then employed by a large Hartford insurance company. He had no college working experience but fortunately adjusted well to campus life, even at this very radical institution.

An old Amherst College colleague and a Babson College graduate, D.C. (Chip) Howell, joined us as a Programmer Analyst. I originally hired Chip through the Babson College Placement Office to replace me as the Assistant Comptroller at Amherst. We had remained good friends and we continued our friendship until he passed in 2019. Interestingly he remained in the Wesleyan Information Systems Office doing special projects until just before he passed. He was an exceptionally skilled and competent person.

Jerry Pandisher was working at the University as the Data Processing Supervisor and directed the key-punch staff. He continued on with us as our computer hardware manager.

After we had installed our computer and were deeply into developing systems and software, we hired Nancy A. Taylor, again from a Hartford insurance company to be a Programmer Analyst.

We all began to work very aggressively to design systems beginning with the Business Office and the Admission Office. Also, we started our search for the actual computer. This was a very difficult task, as the computer technology we wanted—specifically, randomly accessible data—was not fully developed nor generally available. Most hardware relied on sequentially accessible data, such as with magnetic tape drives. We choose a Burroughs 2500, as their computer did use randomly accessible disks. This choice was a little risky, as the big and most well-known company was IBM.

We soon began planning for our complete department to move to the newly constructed Science Building. We occupied all of the 5th floor. It was a perfect space for us to function with adequate office spaces and room for our data processing and computer equipment.

I hired a helicopter to lift the computer center's new, six-ton air conditioner onto the roof. It was up on the roof and attached to the supporting bolts in all of 30 minutes. So much easier than hiring a large crane to do the same thing. It is interesting to note, several years later, when I was a Vice President at Mitchell College in New London, I hired the same helicopter pilot to fly Jesse Jackson from Bradley Field to campus where he was to be our graduation speaker. The pilot remembered me and was pleased to help out again.

Meanwhile, reflecting back at our quaint little office building on 36 Wyllis Avenue, all was going well. The staff was very productive and getting to know the members of the Wesleyan community.

Then, on one very peaceful night in May 1970, I was home sleeping only to be awakened by a phone call and heard, "Hello this is the fire department. Your office is on fire."

SCHOOL DAYS

Information Systems Office On 36 Wyllis Avenue
(Wesleyan Argus October 13, 1970 Photo by Jeff Baskin)

"Information Systems Office Firebombed A Second Time"
(The Argus October 13, 1970)

At first, I thought it was my father, as he was always up early and he assumed the whole world was up at that hour. He was also a fire department volunteer and prone to using related comments. Once I realized this was the real thing, I immediately dressed and ran out the back of my yard across the soccer field to see the flashing lights of the fire engines as they were working to put out the fire. I ran inside to see what I might rescue from my office, only to see a firebomb sitting right on top of my secretary's desk. Yes, it was Marilyn's desk, the same person who I had ushered out of the building when the gunshots happened. Thankfully the firebomb had not ignited. There was another bomb just outside on the ground made from gasoline and fuel oil in a whiskey bottle wrapped in cloth. The third bomb that exploded was in the back of the house, causing some serious fire damage to the building. Interestingly, the file cabinets in my office were tightly packed with files, which actually protected their contents from the fire. But what later became a major challenge was removing the many paper clips holding the paperwork together. They had quickly rusted solidly onto the paper. Most paper clips could not be removed. Secured firmly by rust, they had to be individually torn off the paper, a long, tedious job.

In the October 27, 1970 Wesleyan Argus (the student newspaper), it was written, "Last May, the house was one of three buildings damaged by fire (the others were the College Store and the Music Building on Williams Street)." This article said, "Few understand why the vandals chose the house. Since last January, the house has been occupied by The Information Systems Office. The name, at least sounds like a symbol or institution of American injustice, this leading many to think that the vandals were actual revolutionaries. But when one realizes what goes on inside that innocent-looking house one begins to think that the revolutionaries must know more than we do. 'There is absolutely nothing here at the present time,' said George Dunnington who, as Director of Information Systems, is trying to program all of Wesleyan's scattered and complicated records into a computer." [3]

For sure this thought crossed my mind and made me wonder if we were going to be ongoing targets for the so-called revolutionaries.

In another story, the Argus said, "On this same occasion Downey House which housed the bookstore was bombed at 3 AM. Also, the Music Annex building was fire bombed at 4:35 in that morning."

This building housed a very expensive, large Indian Gamelan musical instrument. Fortunately, it was saved. Yes, we had more than our share of fires and disturbances. Just a couple houses from where I lived on Washington Avenue the newly, beautifully renovated Alumni and Development building, on February 2, 1971,was firebombed and totally destroyed. One has to ask why "revolutionaries" would target these buildings. This action seemed, to me, to be just plain vandalism. Through all these distractions our team kept on plugging away. I gave frequent interviews as to what we were actually planning and doing, hoping to keep the community informed.

About this same time, a student was shot in a dormitory. This happening frightened the President's wife, Mrs. Etherington, and she and her family quickly moved off campus to their home in Old Lyme, Connecticut. Edwin D. Etherington '48 had been president from 1967 to 1970 until the time of this shooting, when he resigned. I was shocked when he called me to tell me of his decision. This also added greatly to my concerns, for he was supportive and involved in my hiring and my work.

My wife and I decided to build a new house before moving off campus. It was a beautiful saltbox style home located on the edge of the marsh in Old Saybrook. The decision to move to this quaint shore town was primarily because their public schools had a very positive reputation. Our children's education was a major concern of my wife, Ann. Our best friends, Chip Howell and his wife Susie, also moved nearby in Old Saybrook. This enabled us to continue our close friendship and also to commute together to Wesleyan daily.

Very late one night, I received a call at our house in Old Saybrook from the Acting Wesleyan President, Robert Rosenbaum, telling me, "The Registrar, Harold Boling, has suddenly quit and left campus." That in itself was a big problem. Surprisingly, he then said to me, "I would like you to be the University Registrar!"

Wow, very shocking! Without a great deal of thought I told him, "Bob, I do not want to be the University Registrar. I have no experience at that position."

He pleaded with me, "We must have someone to do the job immediately."

I said to him, "I will think about this and meet with you in the morning."

Why did he choose me to do this job? Was it because he was impressed by the tasks I had been doing?

Crisis after crisis—would it ever end? Obviously, the position of

Registrar was critical because this office records all student courses and grades, and helps students plan their future courses. It is the Registrar who certifies that a student is eligible to take a course and has met all prerequisites. And, very importantly, the Registrar determines if the students have met all the academic requirements needed to graduate and receive his/her Wesleyan Diploma. There were other very difficult issues that came to the attention of the President's Council that required prompt attention, in which I had tertiary involvement. One of them was a large housing development called Wesleyan Hills. This was a community where the University owned the land, but the people owned their homes located on this property. The homeowners were also faced with many rules and regulations. This living concept was not really a comfortable New England lifestyle. Eventually, it went back to being a community where people owned their homes and land. We terminated the architect and, I believe, a psychologist who together played a major role in designing this community. This experimental project cost the University a great deal of money.

It is not difficult to imagine, as Director of Information Systems, our team was extremely busy trying to meet systems design deadlines for the new computer, which was to arrive at the University campus soon. Our two big projects at this time were designing the systems and programing software for the comptroller's office and the admission's office. Since these systems were our first, it meant we had to also design and program many supporting systems that would be shared by these offices and others that would be coming online soon.

My nature is to very seldomly say NO to a challenge. So, feeling lots of pressure, I shared the missing Registrar problem with my staff. My thinking at the time was that our office would run the Registrar's Office as a team.

However, I said, "Only one of us would be the University Registrar."

In thinking about this proposition, I am very proud of our team and how they were all willing to pull together to help the University through this crisis. After much discussion with my staff, I selected Fred Stefanowicz, one of our Systems Analysts to be the Registrar. I was always thinking this would be a temporary fix which would allow the University to continue to function while a search for a well-qualified and experienced registrar went on. That turned out not to be the case, as Fred stayed in that position for many years.

Running the Registrar's Office was not without some very serious issues. Perhaps the previous Registrar knew of these issues, and that may be why he disappeared in the night without any notice. Wesleyan was such a hotbed of emotional causes—for example, black issues and women's issues were very important and somewhat radical, at least at that time. In response to these pressures many new courses were quickly introduced to educate the students in these disciplines. It was not long before Fred discovered that many students at the end of four years at Wesleyan did not meet the academic criteria necessary to receive a diploma and graduate. I met with Fred and reviewed what he had discovered to be sure his conclusion was correct. I took this information to the provost and of course he was shocked to hear of this seemingly unsolvable problem. We went to the President's Council Meeting and I explained, for example, some students had taken Art History 102, but had never taken the prerequisite Art History 101. This would mean no credit could be given for Art History 102. Some students had never taken some of their required core courses. Again, I ask, did the previous Registrar know of these serious issues? And that they could not be easily solved? After much discussion with the faculty, exceptions were granted.

While the fires were burning, both figuratively and literally, Treasure Robert Siff ('48) and his Assistant, Kenneth W. Cunningham, decided to leave the university on July 1, 1971. The craziness of the continuing campus crises may have seemed to them unsolvable—or, at least, made their jobs much more difficult. They both started work at the university when I did, and as I have previously said, were wonderful people with which to discuss issues and were supportive of my work. Their loss had a very negative impact on my plans as Director of Information Systems.

Eventually, Colin Campbell became the university's president and began to try to settle the campus down to a more traditionally functioning institution.

I was now comfortable knowing I had completed the major tasks I had been hired to do. But I remained very uncomfortable with the chaos at the university. Previous attempts by the university to install a computer system had completely failed. I did set up the Information Systems Office, hired a very competent staff, laid out the computer center on the fifth floor of the new Science Center, purchased and installed a new computer, and successfully developed major software that was up and running.

The university hired a very competent treasurer to replace Mr. Siff, but after a brief stay, he left for a more significant position in another company. Unfortunately, a new treasurer was hired but did not have the necessary understanding of what an information system office meant. Immediately I felt he did not really appreciate the concept of a central computer system with central databases. He was an accountant with unit-record (punched card) experience. Rather surprisingly he, the university treasurer, would show up in the unit record room and start sorting the IBM punch cards. My staff thought this was strange. His viewpoint was so distant from mine and my staff that we quickly had issues.

As it seemed like one crisis after another, this conflict had me searching for another opportunity. I was interviewed and hired by the University of Pennsylvania in Philadelphia. The position was as Assistant Controller and it, too, had many interesting challenges, but the Controller was very competent and he was a great person to work with. The big city life was something I had never really experienced. In searching for a home, I was shocked at the "big city" prices. While I was searching, I lived on the 20th floor of a campus residence hall. It was fun meeting the students and walking to work. This work style was something I was used to doing. However, this was not the work style of most of the other employees in the Controller's Office. They were primarily commuters, with their work schedules controlled by the big city train system schedules to their suburban homes. During this time, while searching for housing, I was also commuting home to Old Saybrook on Friday nights and commuting back to Philly on Sunday nights; not a fun trip.

I was approached and begged to take my next position as Assistant Treasurer and Business Manager of a private independent school. Given the "Big City" issues I was facing and the radical change of lifestyle, I decided to accept this offer. Somewhat sadly, I notified my boss of my decision.

At the time, had I carefully studied the school's issues—mostly financial in nature—I probably would not have taken the position. This time it was the whole school that was endangered and threatened with failure. My skills dealing with a wide variety of issues and my like for challenges turned out to be what was needed at that school at that time. I believe the new Head of School and myself played a significant role in its survival.

My Introduction to Williston Seminary—Williston Academy—Williston Northampton School

THE CHAPTERS THAT FOLLOW ARE A MOST REVEALING STORY OF Williston Seminary, Williston Academy, and Williston Northampton School's efforts to survive through some very difficult times. I reflect back to the beginning of the school in 1841, and then delve more deeply into the years beginning in 1960 through 1972, looking for possible reasons for the near collapse of the school in the 70s. Most readers will be very surprised at what the administration and the Board of Trustees had to deal with, just to keep the school functioning in the time period 1972 to 1986, when I left the school as its Assistant Treasurer and Business Manager.

It was also very notable to see how Sam Williston had been a significant financial benefactor to Amherst College. It made me very jealous, and you will see why as you read of his generosity. Also, you will be surprised at how many Williston faculty and Trustees were connected to Amherst College

The research I did from 1959 through 1972 was most revealing and, I must say, surprising. In Philips Stevens' days as the Headmaster of Williston Academy, many Trustees seemed to focus heavily on whether the school was making a profit. Indeed, that was the sense I got from attending my first several Board meetings. Unfortunately, making the financial reports show a "profit" is not that difficult to do, and of course was very misleading in the case of Williston. Quality, or the lack of it, can be completely covered up—quality in teachers' salaries, quality in the physical

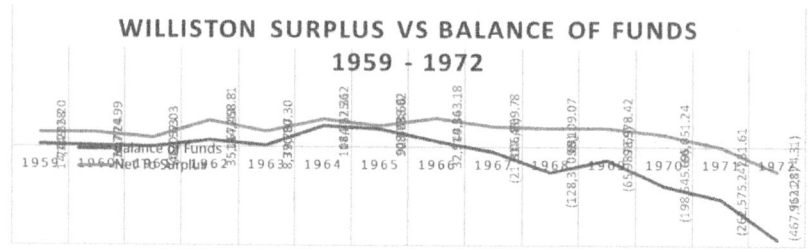

plant, and quality in other important parts of the school's programs. I can only surmise that the Trustees were duped by just reading the audited financial statements. Or, if by reading them very carefully, they could see an enormous infusion of money would be required to right this ship. This fact could have left many of the Trustees not willing to attempt to address the many issues.

As you can see from the chart above, Williston Surplus vs. Balance of Funds, the administration was reporting a surplus "profit" in the years from 1959 to 1970. This I find very hard to believe was possibly true, for several reasons which will be discussed throughout the book.

In many schools, tuition income is the primary source of revenue. As such, having full enrollment is critical to being able to have a strong academic program along with the other supporting functions.

Enrollment had always been a struggle for Williston in the past, even from its beginning in 1841. The school's enrollment, as shown in the chart on page 53, beginning in 1959, began leveling out in 1964 and then dropped drastically in 1970, just before the merger with Northampton School for Girls. This book will reveal what was going wrong, and perhaps why the merger of the two schools happened so quickly.

Take a couple of looks back on tuition income as a percent of total income. In 1959, Tuition Income was 90.2 percent of Total Income and in 1960 it was 89.7 percent, an extremely high percent, indicting the other two major sources of income, Gifts and Endowment Income, were very low. Over the ensuing years, working very hard at improving Gift Income as well as Endowment Income, the percent of Tuition Income to Total Income in 1986 was lower, at 70.7 percent, a healthier rate.

Robert A. Ward, Headmaster 1972 through 1979, exerted tremendous energy just addressing one challenging crisis after another. He was

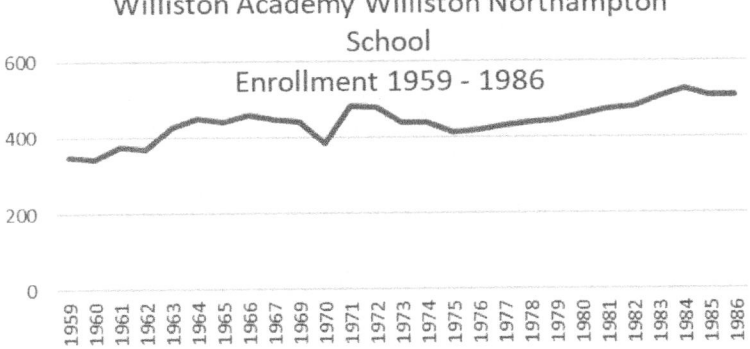

followed by Christopher Corkery from 1979 to 1985, who was tasked with looking ahead to the school's 150th Anniversary. It was Headmaster Denny Grubbs whose fundraising efforts were finally able to begin a very successful period of raising money—Gifts. He was the first Head of School since its founding to do this! Today, Williston Northampton School is an example of a very successful private independent school and an envy to many such schools.

It is my opinion that reading this book will be of interest to any graduate of the school and also very enlightening to anyone who worked at the school, be it as a teacher, administrator, or other employee. It will, I believe, make a Trustee wonder how this all could have happened.

Going to a school such as Williston is not just a learning experience. For many students, teachers, and administrators, it is an experience where you invest your heart and soul in the whole experience.

I invite you to read this revealing story and be thankful that Williston turned out to be a very successful school with great leadership and a place where you can thankfully, continue to invest your heart and soul.

First Introduction to Williston Academy—Unbelievable!

MY INTRODUCTION TO WILLISTON ACADEMY CAME WITH A CALL from an old Amherst College friend, Charlotte Turgeon. At that time, I was the Assistant Comptroller at the University of Pennsylvania. I had only been at the University for a short time, and she wanted to know if I would consider the Business Manager's position at Williston Academy. I was not at all familiar with Williston Academy or private school life. She told me the story about all the changes that were happening at Williston, including the fact that the Business Manager of 33 years was retiring.

I explained, "I have just taken a job at the University of Pennsylvania, and so I do not think I could make a change at this time."

Soon thereafter I got a call from a Northampton School for Girls Trustee, Emmy Snyder ('56), also an Amherst College friend, asking me to consider the position.

I again explained, "I do not want to take time away from work, as I have only been on this job for less than a year."

To my surprise, they agreed to charter a private plane and to fly me to Northampton. They also agreed to charter this plane after my workday, so I could be back in Philadelphia that same night.

I do not like to fly, but I reluctantly agreed to flying to Northampton, Massachusetts to meet some Williston people. Park Rouse, a resident of Philadelphia, also a Trustee of the NSFG, picked me up at the university and we drove to a small airport north of Philadelphia. We met the pilot in the lobby of a now closed airport.

Immediately he informed us, "I can't fly the plane until I find a regulation, required co-pilot."

As we were talking, in walked a little, very old custodian, carrying a broom, who immediately became the copilot! Amazing to me, and somewhat worrisome, we took off to fly to White Plains, NY airport to pick up Emmy Snyder. After she boarded the plane, we then took off on our journey to Northampton, Massachusetts where there was a reginal, Williston alumni meeting happening.

It was February, and the Western Massachusetts area had lots of snow and ice on the ground. I sat in the back of the six-passenger plane, where I could easily hear the pilot say, "Where are the damn runway lights?" as he headed down ready to land the plane.

He said this a couple of times and he said he thought the lights were not working. Having lived in this part of the country for many years, I quickly recognized that we were not over the runway at all, as the area must have looked to the pilot, but we were about to land on the frozen Connecticut River. I yelled out my observation. On hearing me, we headed up, rather steeply just clearing the top of the Coolidge Bridge over Route 9 in Hadley. Now, I was really wondering why I ever agreed to this jaunt. I then told our pilot where I thought the airport was and as he turned the plane in that direction, and like magic, and as programed, the blue runway lights came on when we made our landing approach.

After landing I was still shaking, and the pilot asked, "Where is the location of the nearest bar!"

That infuriated me to say the least. I told him my thoughts on drinking and flying in no uncertain terms. We drove to the nearby Hilton Inn to attend the big alumni meeting. We were entertained by two fantastic choral groups: the women's ensemble group, the Widdigers, under the direction of Jon Arterton, a school faculty member; and, then by the men's group, the Caterwaulers under the direction Richard Gregory, also a school faculty member. We also listened to a few speakers talking about how well the school was doing. I was introduced to the Head of School, Philips Stevens, and many others, including some school Trustees.

It was getting late and time to leave, and board our plane. I reluctantly settled into my seat knowing that it was now snowing and icy. The pilot started up the plane and it began snowing much harder. Immediately, he got on the plane's radio to get clearance to land at White Plains, New York, not very far away as the crow flies.

The airport radio tower came back and we heard, "Sorry captain, White Plains is closed for plowing—could be several hours."

When we took off, the pilot headed directly toward the nearby Mount Tom, which he seemed not to see. Soon it was very evident the mountain was directly in front of us and he made a steep climb up and over the mountain. We were now headed to White Plains in spite of the warning from the flight controller. When we arrived, we were told to circle the airport along with other planes.

Now a little frightened by this pilot, I asked, "What about flying me to Providence RI?" The pilot called there to find the airport was open and clear. Because of my wish to get on terra firma, I said, "Take me there, and I will rent a car to drive back to Philadelphia."

The pilot and my friends discouraged me from that venture, but in spite of my plea, the pilot said, to the tower, "I am going to land now!"

He was again told in no uncertain terms, "You cannot land, and if you do, you could lose your license."

He said, "Emmy, be ready to jump out the door as soon as we touchdown so I can immediately takeoff."

Down we went, in poor visibility with snowplows all around. When we touched down on the not well plowed runway, the snow flew everywhere. The pilot opened the cabin door, Emmy jumped out into the deep snow, and off we went. Lots of radio talk came from the tower—none very good. Seemingly, not fazing our pilot. As we neared Philly our pilot complained about how sluggish the plane seemed to be flying. About then, I was looking for my chute! We made it down and upon deplaning, we indeed found our wings were heavily iced over.

The pilot nonchalantly says, "The deicer must not be working."

Was I ever glad to be back in my office the next day?

A Campus Visit

Shortly thereafter, I visited the Williston campus for a final interview with some Trustees from each of the schools, Williston Academy and Northampton School for Girls. The two schools had agreed to be merged as one school on the Williston Academy campus. Frank Conant

('35), a long time Board member, was the treasurer-type person at the meeting and asked me several business-related questions. This group of men were members of the Prudential Committee (Executive Committee) of the Board. We were meeting in the Homestead, in a very eloquent Board Room. This was the home that Samuel and Emily Williston built for themselves to live in.

Not completely understanding what was really going on as far the merger of the two schools was concerned, and also a little puzzled about the way they explained the retirement of the Head of School and Business Manager. I, with some trepidation, decided to take the position of Business Manager.

When I arrived home to Old Saybrook, Connecticut, adding to my concern, I tried to call Mr. Babcock the Business Manager several times and each time I was told, "He is at the pool."

What I did not know at the time was Mr. Babcock was an outstanding swim coach and that coaching was his first love and concern. Again, my lack of familiarity with private schools made this seem very strange. I was thinking, a school facing so many challenges would certainly demand 100 percent of the Business Manger's time. In fact, I later learned that many administrators do coach or take part in student activities. To me, it seemed more like Nero playing the fiddle while Rome was burning.

As part of my contract, I was promised housing on the campus, in a beautiful, very large house dating back many years to when the original owner was Mr. Pitcher, Class 1891, the wealthy treasurer of a large local mill. He spared no dollars on the house construction.

The problem for my housing was that the former Head of the Northampton School, Nate Fuller and his family, were now living in Pitcher House, and by agreement could stay until the end of June.

Hence, there was no place for me to live on campus in March, my scheduled start date, as there were two acting heads, Stevens and Fuller, still living on campus. Fortunately, the Northampton School for Girls campus, located in nearby Northampton, was now empty, so I was able to move my family into the former Head's house. My good friend from Amherst College and Wesleyan University, Chip Howell, helped us move our household belongings. When Chip and I did things together we were always very successful and enjoyed many hearty laughs in the process. This move came close to disproving our claims of being successful. While Chip and I were carrying in the refrigerator from the back of the school's dump truck, we left our sons, Tim and Geordie, two seven-year-old boys, in the cab playing "truck." Yes, you are right, probably not a good decision. They found the lever which would dump our half-unloaded truck. When we looked out, we saw the dump all the way up, with Ann's precious piano up in the air sitting very precariously tied by a small rope. We both made a dash for the truck and lowered the dump.

Ann and I had custom built our beautiful house in Old Saybrook and thus it had many fond memories. Fortunately, she supported this move, as difficult as it must have been. Our children, Susan, Amy, and Geordie, were wonderful considering they were moving away from friends. The other member of the family, Penny, our English Setter, joined right in at our temporary house—the Logan House. We were all happy on the otherwise vacant, NSFG campus, and we enjoyed having our own gymnasium where we could play and shoot hoops. There were also several other large houses, formally dormitories, administrative, and dining facilities where we could also play.

At that time, the middle of the children's school year, their smooth transition into a new school was of prime concern. That huge worry was solved by the fact we could enroll them at the nearby Smith College Campus School, a school with an exceptional reputation for their programs that worked well for their student body.

As I look back on this journey it is a wonder that I actually settled into this job. But as it turns out, it was the beginning of a wonderful experience for me and my family.

The time passed very quickly, but I longed to get settled on the Williston campus where I could walk to work and visit more with the faculty and students. Finally, we were able to move into Pitcher House. After serving as both a home for Henry Teller, a long-time faculty member, and his family and a dormitory for eight boys, Pitcher House was in very bad disrepair. Very little or no maintenance had been done over its many years. We decided not to do any repairs. This decision was made mostly because we knew the faculty were living in homes that were also in disrepair.

Williston Seminary—
Williston Academy—
Williston Northampton School

IN MY FIRST FEW WEEKS AT WILLISTON, I HAD AN OPPORTUNITY TO look through some of the prior year's financial reports and could clearly see the school was often operating with a deficit, or close to one. I also was able to have several talks with Mr. Babcock, the Business Manager of the school since 1943. He was quite forthright and told me he attributed the financial problems to the low enrollment. He did not offer any reasons for the enrollment being low, except he thought the cost of tuition was high. As the person in charge of the school's finances, it appeared he just continued reacting to declining income by cutting the expenses, hence enormously deferred maintenance costs kept increasing and the physical plant was visibly falling apart. He was also depleting the human assets, which are the most valuable to a service organization like a school. It was alarming to me to see how old and in disrepair the school vehicles and equipment were, a real handicap to the workers trying to do their jobs.

It appeared to me that the Head of School, Phillips Stevens, likely "pressured" Mr. Babcock to make the finances look better than they were. I have no real facts to back up this statement, except a few comments Mr. Babcock made to me.

While spending time with Phillips Stevens, who was the retiring Head of School, he also said, "enrollment was a problem and the alumni participation in the annual fund was low." This I surmised from looking at the financials. What I did not understand was why the Annual Fund did not continue to grow as he so enthusiastically had described in writing about his first ten years (1950–1960), "The Plus-Decade" as Head of School. A possible reason was the solicitation of funds was focused on a select few capital projects and at the expense of the Annual Fund gifts.

The new Assistant Head, Nathaniel Fuller, the prior Head of Northampton School for Girls, felt the school needed to update its curriculum and needed to encourage its faculty to enroll in more enrichment programs. He also was distressed about the condition of the physical plant and how it negatively impacted enrollment. Interestingly, neither Stevens or Babcock ever mentioned the run-down condition of the plant. Perhaps they were too embarrassed to raise this issue.

Most of this was obvious to me, but the most surprising thing was, for the past several years neither Stevens nor Babcock offered any plans for increasing enrollment, increasing alumni participation, or increasing giving. There was a study in 1962 by Marts and Lundy with recommendations about strengthening alumni involvement.

These were very serious issues. It was strange to have no obvious concrete planning underway to deal with such basic but critical problems.

I talked with several of the Trustees and they shared their concerns very honestly with me. The younger alumni Trustees in the 1970s were extremely capable and caring people, although few were really in a position to give meaningful gifts. Some of the older Trustees made only token gifts, and likely were never pressured to help the school. I was told Headmaster Phillips Stevens nominated these people primarily because of personal friendship, and he likely never told them he expected significant gifts for the school. It was hard for me to believe that some of the trustees did not give at all, and others only made very small, token gifts.

Original Ford Hall

The seriousness of the school's fiscal health made me wonder about the school's financial history. Was it always as bad as this? There were few signs of significant alumni giving, going way back to the start of Williston Seminary. Ford Hall, the first dormitory on the new campus, did have the name of a donor, John Howard Ford, Class of 1873, who made a very generous gift of $100,000. With this gift and contributions from about 60 more donors, Ford Hall was built.[4]

The gym did not have a donor name, but fortunately it was constructed with good architectural features and with quality materials, similar to those used in the construction of Ford Hall. There also were some alumni who donated gifts to help with the construction of this building. Most of the other campus buildings did not seem to have donor names attached and were built with, cheaper "construction grade" materials, not of institutional quality. It also meant that much of the construction costs came from operating funds. An exception was the Homestead; constructed by Samuel and Emily of the best material, sparing no expense, it was a gift of the Williston's.

Another beautiful home, the Pitcher House, was purchased from Mr. Pitcher, a Board Member and a member of the class of 1891. He also built his home with the finest materials and craftsmanship. When I was living there, I discovered that all the room ceilings on the first floor were made of a silk like material, not traditional sheetrock. That was rather surprising to me as I had never seen anything like that. This is the house where my family and I lived.

*Pitcher House—Home of Mr. Pitcher 1891,
The Teller Family, Dormitory and The Dunnington Family
(Williston Archives)*

As I was doing my writing, many questions piqued my interest and I felt it necessary to look at the school's history beyond my brief time at the school. I searched for books that might reflect on the history of Williston Seminary, Williston Academy and Williston Northampton School. My research was not extensive, but did answer some of my questions.

One book was extremely enlightening to me: *A History of Williston Seminary* written in 1917 by Joseph Henry Sawyer (Amherst Class 1830 and Williston Seminary Trustee, 1841 – 1897).

I was immediately surprised by how many people involved in the early days of the Seminary were "men of the cloth." Much religion was brought into the daily life of the school. This practice, seemingly, was not unusual in the early days of educational institutions.

Henry Mather Tyler wrote the introduction to the book, which started with The Williston Constitution:

> "Goodness without knowledge is powerless to do good, and knowledge without goodness is power only to do evil; while both combined form the character that most resembles GOD, and is best fitted to bless mankind."[5]

Another interesting quote from Mr. Tyler was, "And the history adds to this large illustration of the truth that it is personalities rather than funds which make a school as Williston a success." [6]

This statement, I certainly believe, is so true and so significant. I remember in the early 1970s, in the former Language Building, when Lorraine Teller, a respected, long time Latin teacher literally fell through the patched, rotted wooden, old factory floor, of her classroom, to the sand beneath (only up to her ankles).

In spite of this physically horrible classroom, the students continued to learn and learn well. This embarrassing incident upset Mrs. Teller so much she immediately came to my office, next door in the Schoolhouse, with tears in her eyes saying, "I can no longer teach in that room." We made a few more patches to the floor and she returned to her classroom. People like Lorraine Teller, the exceptional teacher, helped make Williston a success, just as Mr. Tyler said, in the very early years of the seminary. I might add this building was in such disrepair that I had no choice but to eventually tear it completely down.

The picture below of the "ivy covered," once factory building may look attractive, but I will tell you the ivy covered up lots of decaying wood and lack of paint. Naturally, the ivy saved—or I should say, hid the need for—maintenance money.

The Ivy-Covered Language Building and One Time Chapel
(Williston Archives)

The Language Building Demolition in Progress
(*Williston Archives*)

This is but one example of many, showing how the students respected the personalities that made the school successful. The drab, unkempt buildings did not interfere significantly with the students' learning experience or affect the quality of their education. Nonetheless, I do believe new, clean, well-equipped classrooms lift the spirits of the teacher as well as the learner and help foster the love of learning.

To further illustrate the influence religion had on the times, I quote the following: "It was in 1837, during the sickness of his last child, that Mr. Williston, feeling that he had not done his whole duty as a steward of the Lord's property, consecrated himself anew to His service, set apart the principal and interest of a considerable investment for benevolent purposes, and thus entered on a new Christian life."[7]

After this very upsetting experience it was interesting to note that Sam Williston said, "He consulted his friend, Professor William S. Tyler, (Amherst College 1830), and came slowly to his decision to found a preparatory school of high grade. He chooses to call it an English College. He was not a wealthy man in 1840."[8] He was however a true entrepreneur of his day.

Another troubling thing for me to understand was why Mr. and Mrs. Williston gave so generously to several other churches, town buildings, and colleges. "Amherst College was then in its second decade, and in need of friends and money. Mount Holyoke Seminary was in its first decade, and, if possible, in greater need of friends and money. Mr. Williston helped both."[9]

Samuel and Emily Williston–Benefactors to Many

"He was an early benefactor to Amherst College, and for thirty-three years a member of the Board of Trustees, giving as freely of his time as of his money."[10] He built a significant building on the Amherst College campus. While at the same time he was trying to keep the school he founded, Williston Seminary funded and functioning.

Finally, after much discussion and many letters published that winter in the *Hampshire Gazette* about whether a school was needed, it was decided to formally establish Williston. "On February 22, 1841, an act of incorporation was granted..."[11]

On the Campus of Amherst College
(Amherst College Archives The Buildings and Grounds of Amherst College,
A history in Photographs of the Campus, 1820–2007)

It was not easy for me to fully comprehend how long ago that was, nor what the times were like then. To help understand that time period, President Martin Van Buren was completing his term in the White House. President William Henry Harrison was assassinated while in office. And John Tyler served our country as President, 1841 – 1845.

Both Sam and his wife Emily were very kind and thoughtful people, always willing to help when there were difficulties, usually of the kind that could be helped with monetary gifts. Frank P. Conant's ('35) book, *God's Stewards*, speaks to Sam and Emily's generosity when disasters happened. "The new Payson Church was destined to have its trial by fire." This church was started because Sam felt his school had overwhelmed the only Town church and he and Emily paid for its construction, some $14,500. "Early Sunday morning, January 29, 1854, the new building burned...Another building was begun that spring and, when nearly three quarters finished, it, too, burned...The cost of $14,000 was once again borne by the Willistons. This church remains today as the Easthampton Congregational Church."[12]

His deep and generous involvement at Amherst College began in 1841, when he was a member of the lower house of the Massachusetts Legislature, and then in 1842-43 as a member of the Senate. "While a member of the legislature in 1841 he was chosen by that body as a trustee of Amherst College."[13] He was also one of the early trustees of Mount Holyoke Seminary.[14]

Again from Mount Holyoke archives come several remarks that help one to better understand this caring and generous man: "This reference to Mr. Williston in the history of our first half-century, is significant not only because his gift, increased to $10,000, the largest received, made possible Williston Hall, the first science building, but also because it was characteristic of the giver, to come to the rescue of Mount Holyoke when he was needed, to stand by it at all times, when things were going well and when they were not, and to do it all so unobtrusively that often no one realized what he was doing."[15]

Ms. Edwards, a Mt. Holyoke teacher, wrote, "Mr. Williston was a man of strong religious character and conviction. From the many little visits, which I made to the Williston home (the Homestead on the Williston campus) during the last 15 years, there is one picture-memory which I

Williston Hall with Shattuck Hall—front

shall especially treasure, and that is the morning prayers at the breakfast table. Mrs. Williston reading a few verses from the Bible, Mr. Williston following with a simple, earnest prayer. A busy, practical man, he was not too busy to give religion a place in his daily living."[16]

From the Mount Holyoke Archives, a former teacher, Ms. Anna Edwards, in her written remarks, states that Samuel, "was one of our first trustees in 1836, succeeded Hon. William Bowdoin, as treasurer, [18]39 – [18]62. This was a man of imposing presence, and I will remember his appearance on Anniversary (Commencement) occasions in the early (18)50s, and hearing it said we were indebted to him for many contributions never made public." She goes on to write, "I never pause too, over our precious copy of Raphael's Transfiguration in Dwight Hall, without affectionate remembrance of Mrs. Williston's part in securing it for us, and still more for the fact that she shared full-heartedly in all her husband's efforts in our behalf."[17]

Mr. Williston, throughout his career, made many contributions, not only to his school, but also to other churches and colleges that were never made public. Hence, we will never know the full extent of his gifts. That seemed to be the way he wanted it to be.

Annette Esty wrote in *Amherst Graduates' Quarterly*, May 1941, "For fifty-two years Samuel and Emily remained united by a durable affection, until he died. During much of that time they shared a meager life of the parsonage. Of their five children one died in infancy. In 1827 Ellen was born. Two years later came Delia Lord. But, like 'sweet flowerets born to fade,' these two children died of scarlet fever within a few days of each other. Another Ellen came. She lived to be five and a half. Another Delia Lord. And then ('So huge, so hopeless to conceive' as this which 'twice fell!') the two little girls, like their sisters and namesakes before them, were swept away by scarlet fever within a short time of each other."[18]

As previously mentioned, these tragic happenings, his daughters' sicknesses and deaths, caused Mr. Williston to pledge to his maker that he would endeavor to do whatever he could to please his Lord.

There were signs that Mr. Williston had financial challenges early on: "He could and did pay annual deficits, but he could not, with business safety, take from his capital what would have been an adequate endowment of the school." [19] One could say, if he only directed a greater portion of his benevolence toward the endowment of Williston Seminary instead of supporting so many other worthy causes, Williston Seminary might have had a financial experience that was less erratic and less disruptive to the program.

"On April 14, 1845, Mr. Williston gave to Amherst College a gift of $20,000 to fund an endowed professorship. Shortly thereafter, he gave $10,000 to fund part of another endowed professorship."[20] Again, Mr. Williston, the founder of Williston Seminary, said, "…he could not, with business safety, take from his capital what would have been an adequate endowment of the school."[21] I ask, "Why did he make a distinction between his endowment giving to Amherst College and his own school, Williston Seminary?"

Beginning as early as 1847, the school faced the start of an enrollment crisis. Over the years there were often many causes for declining enrollment beyond which the school had little or no control, i.e. the Civil War (1861-1865), competition from new public schools, World War I (1914–1918), and World War II (1939–1945). I also read about many other not-so-dramatic reasons for not reaching the enrollment goal. Perhaps this is, at least for a second-tier school, a built-in risk of being in the school business.

Enrollment 1847–1862[22]

Year	Enrollment
1847	286
1851	235
1855	163
1859	155
1860	136
1861	124
1862	86

This chart clearly indicates how enrollment had significantly declined, going from 286 in 1847 to just 86 in 1862, a short 15 years. Enrollment would constantly threaten Williston over the years, and it was the primary cause of deficits even in 1972, when I became Business Manager. The endowment was not of a size to help the school through troubled times in 1847, nor was it in 1972.

In the 1870s Mr. Williston, "…had most embarrassing business troubles…"[23]

"In 1874 the total amount of funds given by the Founder amounted to $270,000."[24] In those days, the school was having issues of accounting; this total included the cost of a building that was totally burned, it included cost of wear and loss in buildings and apparatus. It is interesting back then they appeared to recognize "depreciation," which wisely helped to protect the value of assets. This accounting practice (depreciation) sometime in the future was no longer continued in school accounting standards. However, in the 1970s, depreciation was again adopted as a standard for not-for-profit institutions. I was involved with the National Accounting Standards Committee that later led to this controversial change.

"Thirty-three years had passed since the opening of Williston Seminary when the founder died in July, 1874, aged 79 years and one month."[25]

His obituary in the 1874 Boston Globe stated, "Mr. Williston had long occupied a leading position among the citizens of Western Massachusetts, and his extensive charities have made him widely known throughout the country…To his enterprise and the extent of his varied industries his native town has grown largely within the past few years, its population amounting at present to about 4,000 inhabitants. In 1845 (sic.

should be 1841) he founded Williston Seminary an institution which has no superior in the country for the completeness of its equipment and the thoroughness of its discipline...He has already given it $275,000, and it is anticipated that the provisions of his will may raise the total expenditures and endowment to at least $500,000."[26]

"It is difficult to really understand his total giving to the Seminary, as some went to deficits, some money to plant and equipment and some to endowment. This kind of giving was very generous and totaled, $1,000,000, and by his will he had distributed $500,000, more."[27] It went on to say, "As soon as the estate was settled, the Seminary should receive $200,000. A fund of $50,000 was to be held in trust, and when with its accumulations it amounted to $100,000 it was to be paid to the school. A fund of $150,000 was to be held in trust for Mrs. Williston. Upon her death it was to remain in the trust until with its accumulations amounted to $300,000, when the whole was to be paid to the Seminary." [28]

Mr. Williston's businesses had their ups and downs, and naturally it was the downs that seemed to have had a greater effect on his ultimate planned generosity.

In the *History of the Endowment of Amherst College*, there was an interesting statement that illustrated Mr. Williston's difficulties. "One of the difficult problems handled by Whitcomb for the Finance Committee in his early days as a trustee resulted from the will of Samuel Williston. Mr. Williston died in 1874. His will, executed the previous year, left specific bequests of over $700,000, with the residue to Amherst College. While Mr. Williston had been extraordinary as a businessman and had accumulated perhaps the largest fortune of his day in Western Massachusetts, his final business venture, the erection of a large thread mill in Easthampton, to compete with one of the old thread manufacturers of England, had been unsuccessful. And, as a result, his fortune was much reduced in the final years of his life. The (Amherst) College received title to this mill. After prolonged negotiation the College was able to sell the mill for some $103,000 to one Albert Abbott, taking $3,000. in cash and five serial notes of $20,000 each...The first note was paid at maturity; then Abbott failed...Finally, in 1888 Whitcomb was able to sell the remaining $80,000 notes and mortgage for $5,000…The $28,000 realized from the Williston

Estate was added to the Williston Contingent Fund, which Mr. Williston had established in 1872, by the gift of $50,000, bringing the fund up to $78,000."[29]

While he was alive, Mr. Williston gave Amherst College gifts which grew over time, so that in 2018 they amounted to approximately $3,256,590 in endowed funds. He made several other endowed gifts along with other Amherst donors, but the funds do not carry his name. He was on their Board for 33 years and it would, in my opinion, be reasonable for him to also have given a respectable annual donation, as is the custom for most Board members. As previously noted, he also built Williston Hall on the Amherst campus. This does not include any of his gifts to Mount Holyoke Seminary. It is not surprising that Amherst College offered to change its name to Williston, which he refused to do. "...The Trustees of Amherst College voted "that in the opinion of this Board it is expedient to change the name of Amherst College and to affix to it the name of its most liberal benefactor: Samuel Williston."[30]

Somewhat disappointing and surprising on the records of Williston Northampton School in 2018, Mr. Williston's endowed gifts have a market value as noted below:[31]

Samuel Williston Memorial Scholarship 1874	$86,339
Samuel Williston Fund 1939	$51,952
Samuel and Emily Williston Bequest 1962	$234,024

These endowed funds from Samuel Williston only total $372,315, about 11 percent of the amount he gave to Amherst. This makes me wonder why he chose to be so generous to Amherst College. Did he feel his practice of covering the Williston Seminary's annual deficit from his income was significant enough so that he did not have to provide more endowment monies? He also built buildings and provided the campus for the Seminary—significant as this was, did he believe this was enough? It could also be possible that there were other monies of his that went to school emergencies over time and were not properly recognized, such as possibly funding the building that burned and had to be replaced. We may never know, but it is clear that his gifts to the Williston Seminary did not come anywhere close to his gifts to Amherst's endowment. Mr. Williston was characterized as a modest gentleman and enjoyed helping various causes without recognition. But I wonder if the Amherst Trustees, most of which were likely wealthy, very prominent, and respected in their occupations, subtlety made Mr. Williston feel like he wanted to be a "player" in this group? After all, we do know one of the best ways to obtain a significant gift is to have the "asker" be a giver of the same amount or more, i.e., "won't you, John Doe join me in giving our school $1,000,000?"

It was not my intention when starting this writing project to write a complete story about the Willistons; as a matter of fact, I had no idea of the extent of his overall generosity. Edward Hitchcock, Junior ("Old Doc") Williston 1844, who was educated at Williston Academy and afterward taught there, has left this piquant portrait: "Mr. Williston, 'the father and founder of us all,' as we used to call him, was never an approachable man. He was of the stern old Puritan type, dignified, austere, and grand in all his ways. Everybody stood at a distance from him. But he was susceptible to flattery in everything except getting some of his money. In this he felt that he was a steward of the Lord, and felt he must give it all back to Him, but he said he never enjoyed giving away any of his money. And this penuriousness always hurt him and his work."[32]

As I have said so many times, he gave to such a number of causes, it would be very difficult even to discover who had benefited and to list them all. Many of these gifts were relatively small and often were anonymous.

On With the "Williston Seminary" Story

A familiar note: "in the summer of 1863 Williston Seminary approached a crisis in its history of which few were aware."[33] This was an enrollment-driven financial crisis, another precursor of many similar threats to the school's existence.

Also, it is puzzling to ponder why the school, over all these years, did not try to raise more endowment funds from its many very successful alumni. When the founder was alive, one answer to that question might be, Williston Seminary was Sam Williston's idea and a project he controlled and financed, so he likely would not have encouraged other donations.

I am a graduate of Babson College, the Class of 1960. Roger Babson founded the College in 1919, and purchased all the many acres of extremely valuable, Wellesley, MA land (as Samuel Williston did for the Seminary) for the college to build its beautiful new campus. On one of his visits, I met Mr. Babson, and ushered him into Knight Auditorium, on campus, for the Founder's Day celebration—and yes, he, like Mr. Williston, had his peculiar ways. Many alumni of both institutions thought their founders were rich and therefore did not need help from its alumni and friends. Hence, these institutions had little or no endowment funds, and most detrimental was that in the early days, they failed to groom their alumni and instill the ethic of annual giving. For both of these institutions, this stigma has been thankfully lost. They are now both prospering from the generosity of their many dedicated alumni and friends.

In the early years of Williston's existence, around 1870, Rev. Henry Clay Trumbull, Williston Class 1844, started an alumni association. He was a part of every anniversary (reunion) until he moved away.[34] In my reading up until 1919, I do not recall any further mention of the alumni association helping to raise funds. Again, I ask, "Why?"

The annual deficit raised its ugly head again when, after the first year of Dr. Whiton's administration (1876-1878), "…the treasury showed a deficit five times greater than any annual deficit the school had known."[35] As was previously mentioned, in the past, while Mr. Williston was alive, he covered these deficits from his (personal) income. And, as was previously stated, he believed that by taking it out of his businesses' capital he would deplete the school's (eventual) endowment.[36]

Times were very stressful, and June, 1877 was significant. There were drastic cuts in salaries and consideration was given to eliminating Mr. Williston's "English College."[37]

> *"Williston Seminary continued to struggle and accumulate deficits. The school desperately needed the $200,000 endowment that was to happen on his death. There were two significant issues the school had to deal with; first, the $200,000 that was left in stocks of Easthampton firms were not producing any dividends; secondly, as I previously stated, because the founder was thought to be rich, others did not give.*

The Trustees were able to change the management in the firm and it paid $5,000, a year so that at the end of the decade, in 1886, the deficits accumulated since 1878 had been very nearly paid."[38]

I keep wondering why, over the many years, the Trustees and the several heads of school did not realize that the school needed to seriously consider the need to raise endowment funds, or for that matter, annual funds. An endowment fund would help temper the ever-recurring, erratic, and disruptive operations budgets. It is my opinion that serious planning for raising capital gifts did not begin until the mid-1970s. It was then when the newly appointed Head of School, Robert A. Ward, Amherst College '51, saw the need to start a modern development office. Headmaster Robert Ward and I knew how a successful fundraising operation needed to be structured, as we both had experience at Amherst College where, in the early 1960s, they launched their first, major, and very successful capital campaign. I will reveal more of what happened at WNS in the 1970s and 1980s later.

Another interesting story shared by the old Williston and the modern Williston occurred in 1884, when the Seminary went without a head for two years. The Principal, Dr. Fairbanks, resigned, and eventually ended up at Amherst College as its Treasurer. The Williston Seminary trustees choose not to appoint a new Head. They did appoint a teacher to act as Head.

WNS, in 1973-74, also went without a Head, but for just one academic year while the school anxiously waited for Robert A. Ward to complete his final year as Dean of Students at Amherst College.

WNS appointed Dean Robert St. George to be the spokesperson for the committee of four, who were responsible for the daily functioning of the school.

In the spring of 1885, Mrs. Williston died. She lived very frugally after Sam's death, but continued to support many of the charities that she and Sam did when he was prosperous. She gave significant gifts to the town, its public library, helped with the building of new churches, and to the endowment of the Easthampton Village Improvement Society. It was clear she understood the importance of building an endowment, but did not include any endowment funds for Williston Seminary. However, on her death, she gave her home, the Homestead, and 23 acres of contiguous land to Williston. This property, located at the corner of Payson Avenue and Park Street, is now home to the Admission Office and Development Offices. In her will, she restricted the residence to be the home of the school principal.

Perhaps she concluded the money previously designated by her husband for endowment was adequate?

"The enrollment of the school had declined through the preceding decade. The enrollment in 1876 had been 217; in 1886 it was 133. For the year 1886-1887 it was 89."[39]

This serious decline in enrollment obviously resulted in large deficits and, since the mill property had been sold, there was no income from that source. It was a real financial crisis.

"Williston Seminary was not in financial condition to satisfy expectations of friends."[40] Thus, they did not dare to try to borrow funds from a bank. Again, the school's very existence was challenged, and they, apparently, were unable or too embarrassed to ask friends and alumni to make gifts. This was a very serious problem, which I believe has existed for almost all of the years of the school's history through the 1970s.

It is with great difficulty that I look back on Mr. Williston's generosity, helping numerous organizations without making "his" school the primary focus. And yes, as I struggle to accept all this, perhaps I am just selfish! He was a very caring person and reached out to help many causes in the Williston Seminary, Amherst College, Mount Holyoke Seminary geographic areas.

Hopefully the following is not just a boring review. Perhaps just bewildering to the writer?

In reviewing Mr. Williston's gifts, you may better understand my feelings: "Early 1845 he founded the Williston Professorship of Rhetoric and Oratory in Amherst College. (According to the current records of Amherst College, this fund had a book value of $25,600. And, in 2018 it has a market value of $683,776.) In the winter of 1846-7 he founded the Graves Professorship, now the Williston Professorship of Greek, (this fund had a book value of $20,300. And in 2018 a market value of $542,213) and one half of the Hitchcock Professorship of Natural Theology and Geology in Amherst College, thus making in all the sum of $50,000.00 which he had

Samuel and Emily Williston Home, Constructed by Sam
(Williston Archives)

already given for permanent foundations (endowment) in that institution."[41] He also gave to Amherst's permanent endowment; this has a book value of $76,024 and in 2018 a market value of $2,030,601. [42]

His factories were expanding and he felt financially comfortable supporting organizations like Amherst College. Again, I have to ask, "Why did he not add real cash, not promises of funds, to the Williston Seminary endowment?" You can just imagine what that would have done to help the Seminary grow stronger with fewer, or possibly not as severe, financial crises. As an example of the power of these generous gifts to Amherst College, the Samuel Williston Fund is estimated to payout, toward Amherst's operating funds, $89,423 in 2019!

As an aside, when I was at Amherst College in the 1960s as their Assistant Comptroller, I undertook the task of setting up all the endowed funds that composed their endowed holdings, to function much like a mutual fund, with each having shares in the total fund. This allowed each fund to receive their share of capital gains and capital losses and income. I also, tediously, read the documents delineating the donor's restrictions and their intended use of the fund's income. While this was extremely interesting, it pointed out some legal challenges, i.e., some funds could only be invested in railroad bonds. In those days, the railroad was "king." As I recall, it was Mr. Williston's Professorship of Greek that had grown to such a size that it really would be difficult to spend the income for the purposes designated. This situation was created as the teaching of Greek had become less popular over the years. It also illustrates why most not-for-profits want a donor to provide a way for the trustees to modify any restriction that may, over time, become no longer appropriate. I went through this very same process upon arriving at Williston as their endowment records were in a similar state.

Other Early Challenges and More Stories

When a school or college occupies a major part of the town in which it functions, there can be stress, as this quote suggests: "school is a little world apart. An endowed academy exists in a community, but not as part of that community. The proverbial lack of harmony between town and gown has been a result. The thoughtless escapades of some students, now and then, and the raids on school property by the mischievous and lawless of the town, has not destroyed that friendly relation."[43] This was all happening around 1885.

When I arrived on campus in 1972, Williston Northampton School was also experiencing some very bad relations with the town kids. The school did not have any security personnel, hence I was it.

There was fighting and stone throwing, and broken windows. How interesting to note that some 80 years ago, the school was dealing with this same difficult problem. Fortunately, I had an intimidating deterrent with which to confront the "townies." Our night watchman from the NSFG campus patrolled that vacant property every night and, during that time, I never had so much as a single pane of glass broken. This night watchman, Frank, was one of the biggest men I have ever met. His hard-working farmer hands were absolutely huge. With one squeeze of a person's hand, he would put that person in excruciating pain. So, I made a visit to Frank's farm in Hadley and asked him if he would help again. He was anxious to help me.

After his hiring, I had only one final rather significant incident. On that dark quiet evening, Frank, my giant, Polish, Hadley farmer, and I stealthily waited near the back of the Schoolhouse. Soon, the kids slowly appeared from behind the adjacent railroad station, only to meet us. Frank greeted them, and immediately picked up two townies—one in each hand—by grabbing the necks of their jackets, shook them really good, and hung them by their jackets on the chain link fence. Then he grabbed another and squeezed his hand so tight that he kicked and cried in agony. (I cannot imagine this happening today.) A scary sight for me, but most likely scarier for those hanging on the fence. Fortunately, this ended the episodes of bad relations with the "mischievous and lawless of the town." I will revisit this problem later in my story, as it is very important for a private non-tax paying school to have very good town/gown relations.

Enrollment continued to challenge the Seminary. Finally, it began to increase, until in 1906 the total was 221.[44]

In the years following 1893, the school added some prominent men to its Board. "All these gave the school highly prized aid, especially in service on committees."[45] Not the badly needed monetary gifts!

An incident of great significance to our newly merged schools occurred way back in 1913, when Robert P. Clapp, Williston Seminary Class of 1875 from Lexington, Massachusetts, was elected to the Seminary Board.[46] He was the father of Roger P. Clapp, our primary donor to the Williston Northampton School, the Robert P. Clapp 1875 Library, and other funds. Roger was one of our first real generous supporters. In addition to funding most of the Library, he also made several other significant gifts during his lifetime—some gifts even before the gift of the library.

Roger became a close and very special friend of mine. We shared many interesting stories, some of which I will talk about later in the book. One story he shared was how his dad really cared deeply for Williston Seminary and how it was his practice, after he had attended a Board meeting, to bring home, to Lexington Massachusetts, the blueprints for the yet-to-be-constructed Ford Hall. He enthusiastically shared these blueprints with his son, Roger. This active involvement by his father, Roger told me, was what excited him to become more involved with, and help, Williston.

Beginning in 1896, there began some movement to reach out for gifts. However, many of the gifts received were not for major capital projects.

There were many gifts of portraits, a teacher's desk, prizes, and art. These gifts were very nice to receive, but not what was really needed.

Of significance was, "Beginning with 1915 the graduating classes are promising that each member shall for a term of years send each year a small gift to the school. An alumni fund will be the results..."[47] As important as this was, Williston struggled all the way through to the 1970s trying to get alumni involved in the school and to make regular contributions toward the current operations of the school.

"Before the sale of the mill property in 1899, and when no other relief was in sight, the principal (Head of School) began soliciting contributions from alumni. The effort was to get $25,000 to be used by the trustees, as they should decide. The effort failed through the inexperience of the solicitor, and his distaste for the part beggar."[48] Yet again, the principal attempted to raise funds. The amount sought was $100,000. Less than $6,500 was obtained. The financial crisis was so severe that the principal felt compelled to attempt a third effort to pay off accumulated debt of $150,000. This time they had a pledge for $25,000. This effort also failed.

A fourth attempt was undertaken, but with more professional help and more involvement of the alumni. The amount sought was $250,000 which was to be used for the erection and furnishing of new buildings. The school was able to get a couple of major gifts. Cleveland H. Dodge, Class of 1875, made a generous gift to build a room at the back corner of what was the gymnasium. It is believed that Cleveland Dodge's son may have given the money for this memorial room.

The Dodge Room, with its warm, knotty pine paneled walls, was a great place to entertain visiting athletic teams and hold other small functions. To this day we continue to enjoy the pine-paneled Dodge Room, still located in the same place but now surrounded by the beautiful Reed Campus Center. This was accomplished in 1996 by the generosity of John Reed ('33).

In the 1970s, Head of School Robert A. Ward developed his dream of a new library. Schematic plans soon were drawn and we started to solicit gifts. This initial attempt to fund the library failed. These failures to raise funds for the school plagued the school up through the 1970s. There might be one or two exceptions, but they all failed because the leadership of the school was not able to direct the development of a strong alumni association until the mid 70s. They also failed to get new members on the Board of Trustees who had both the financial means to make significant capital gifts, and had the inclination to do so.

Back in the mid 1970s I did some research on Cleveland Dodge and found that he was living in New York City. Bob Ward and I were able to arrange an appointment to visit him. From the beginning of the visit, things were a little different. His house was a beautiful old brownstone building of perhaps seven floors. We entered, and it was as though we were back in the 1920s. The house had gorgeous dark mahogany woodwork, high ceilings, and lots of intricate detail to the wood trim. We rang the bell, or I should say, turned the handle on the polished brass ringer, making a loud ringing sound. The door opened, and we were cordially welcomed into the house by an elegantly attired butler, whom we later determined was also Mr. Dodge's secretary.

He said, "I will inform Mr. Dodge that you are here."

We waited somewhat nervously, not knowing what to expect. Soon, a very elderly, hunched over man appeared and came slowly over to shake our hands. We introduced ourselves and then, practically knocking us off our feet, Mr. Dodge, threw up his arm and stuck a big trumpet-like device in his ear. Well, for a few seconds, which seemed like hours, Bob and I did not know what to say. It was difficult having a discussion with him, as his hearing was extremely poor, even with his accoutrements, so we thanked him and left. This was probably a big mistake. In hindsight we should have struggled a little longer to see if he could really hear us, and whether he might have been interested in helping the school.

Reviewing the early days of Williston, from its founding to the early 1900s, was enlightening and yet not so different from what I experienced beginning in 1972.

First, the faculty were extremely dedicated, a common characteristic of many private school teachers, be it 1841 or 1972. They were paid low wages. And, unfortunately, the school often took advantage of their dedication; including having them provide, from their own funds, some of their teaching books and equipment. Worst of all, their jobs were often in real jeopardy, thus leaving them anxiously not knowing if the school would even open in the coming fall. Our very dedicated faculty had similar fears in the 1970s, which were partially precipitated by the merger, which caused a need to reduce the number of faculty. These trying times were exacerbated by the already existing financial issues.

Second, for many years the school never had leadership that recognized the need for and importance of raising both annual gifts and capital gifts. They did not focus on growing and strengthen the alumni association.

Another rather surprising finding from reading this history was how Williston Seminary and Amherst College employed so many of their respective alumni. Williston graduates went on to graduate from Amherst and then returned to teach at Williston. The Williston Board had many Amherst graduates as members. And, of course, Mr. Williston helped build buildings, fund professorships, and was an Amherst College Board member for 33 years himself. Our new Head, Robert A. Ward, was an Amherst graduate. I remind readers that I was a member of the Amherst College administration for several very wonderful years.

Headmaster Ward was a Robert Frost scholar and spent time with him when Frost was on the Amherst Faculty. Robert Frost came to Williston several times at the request of Headmaster Archibald Galbraith (circa 1938) to lecture the students. Upon reading this story in a Williston Archives story I was very surprised. I never heard Headmaster Ward mention this story. I believe, if he knew this, he would certainly have talked about it.

Was all this information necessary? The reader will have to decide. But for me, it was rather astonishing that the school made it through all these troubling years and today has become a very successful institution, one we can all be very proud of.

What I Did Not Know—Bank Debt

I ARRIVED AT WILLISTON AT A TIME OF CONFUSION DUE PRIMARILY TO the pending changes in the top management and the school's merger issues. I am not sure how I missed seeing it, or if I was even fully informed about the amount of debt the school was obligated to pay. Nor did I realize how the administration had virtually stripped all of its functional departments of the necessary funds that would be required for them to do their jobs. It was just amazing how the faculty and administrators caried out their work under these constraints.

So, the day I became Business Manager in March of 1972, the bank debt was a whopping $1,100,000. That was a staggering amount, considering the school's very limited finances, meaning they had no real way to satisfy their loan. I also had no idea that the bank borrowing extended all the way back to 1959, when it was $425,000, (that was as far back as I searched). Just where the Trustees concerns were on this matter was unknown to me.

Very soon after I settled into my job, I received a call from the President of Valley Bank, Steve King in Springfield, asking for a meeting. I was nervous and very concerned as to the reason for this request. It turned out to be a cordial meeting, but he made clear to me that the type of loan the school had was a working capital loan and not a mortgage. Therefore, the loan conditions stated, it should be paid up for a period of time each year. As can be seen by looking at the chart "Notes Payable Valley Bank" on page 84, this never happened. This chart showed the loan reaching its peak in 1973, at $1,250,000!

Why did the school keep borrowing over the extended time period of 1965 to 1973, without having a plan to retire this debt? My answer to this is, although unlikely, perhaps Philips Stevens believed the proceeds from the "Progress Fund" capital campaign would be used to retire this debt, or some portion of it. Through his rose-colored glasses, he went ahead and started construction on various projects included in the Progress Fund campaign even before the actual gift money was received. My observation of the campaign was that from its very beginning it was not successful. By the end of the 1965 schoolyear he had already spent $1,145,472 on the designated projects.

At this time the school was in dire straits, but did the Trustees know this? More importantly, who was making plans to deal with this problem? On March 14, 1972 (soon after I began work), Philips Stevens wrote a few interesting comments to me just before leaving for his vacation home in Grenada.

"I want to introduce you to the staff, go around the school with you and have the whole school community see us together."

Interesting statement, considering he was about to be retired. How did he not realize this?

He then went on to say, "George, we must settle on a budget and see to it that nobody exceeds any part of it. This has been one of the hardest problems that I have had this year with steadily rising debt in the annual operation and principal debt, too."

In my opinion, as previously mentioned, budgets prepared by most departments in the school were already at barely functional minimums, so that statement was meaningless. He, after all, controlled the already out of control budgets, including the debt costs.

The following comment is also a little bit strange coming from Head of School: "It is staggering to me that that we should owe over a million dollars. It has taken me better than twenty years to build our endowment from less than half a million to two-million-six. And now to have half of that hypothecated is a tragedy which I am going to have to live with and do my best to reduce, if not eliminate."

It is evident from the following information that he had been building debt for over 13 years. In my initial meeting with the Board of Trustees I do not recall the bank debt or the looming deficit ever being a big concern. I certainly never saw any financial plan for the school.

The annual interest cost of these notes was very significant as can be seen in the chart on page 85, "Interest Expense On Bank Notes." It

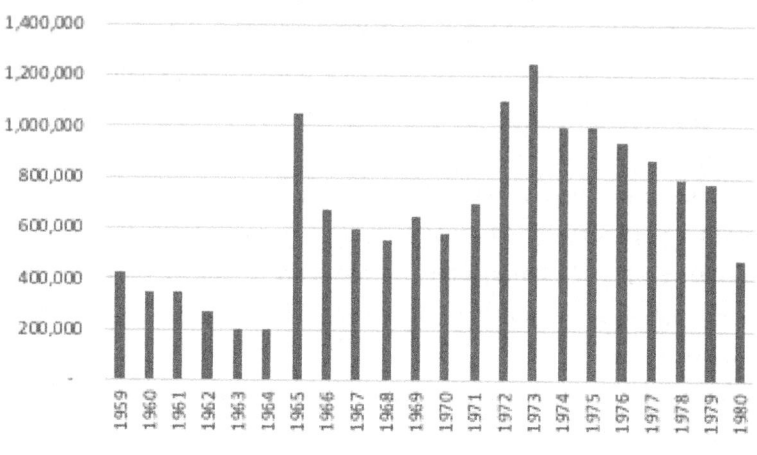

(Williston Annual Financial Statement)

makes me wonder whether they ever considered taking out a mortgage on one of the larger projects, such as The Hockey Rink? Had they done so, this would likely have meant a fixed interest rate and therefore would likely have been less expensive. Fortunately, the bank was willing to turn a blind-eye to the fact that the school was not retiring the notes, at least for a period of time each year. The bank wanted a plan to retire the debt. This finally happened in 1980. The interest rate on the note floated with prime and this became an enormous financial burden. In March 1981, the interest rate was 17.25 percent.

With this costly incentive, and working closely with the Board of Trustees, in fiscal year 1980-81, when rates were sky-rocketing, we decided to retire the last bank note of $475,000. Interestingly this was about the same amount it was in 1959. To accomplish this, we used money from the school's Unrestricted Endowment Funds. Included in that decision was also a motion to pay this now internal debt back to the endowment at the annual rate of $50,000 with no interest.

The chart on Page 88, Net Operating Gains/Losses, reveals a very interesting accounting fact. From fiscal year 1959 to fiscal year 1971, the school reported "profits." Again, this was a curious problem for me to comprehend. Did they really have excess income over expenses? What was the

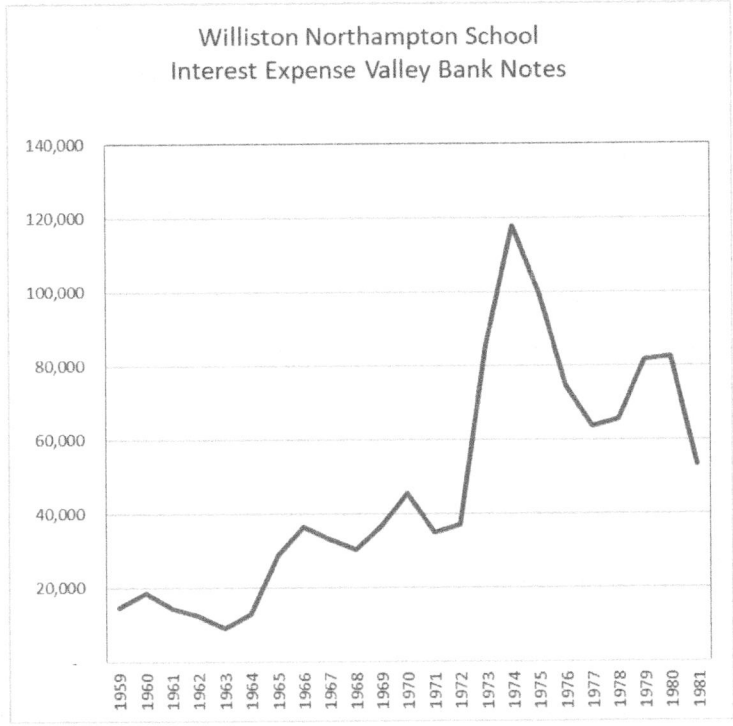

communication between the Board of Trustees and the management? In my brief time working with Mr. Babcock, I believe he felt pressure to "make things look good," or perhaps I should say, "look better than they actually were." Also, again looking at the chart on Page 88, Operating Gains/Losses, it is clear that the surpluses began to disappear in 1970 and were virtually gone in 1971, the year of the merger. When I started at Williston as its Business Manager, there was a real and significant deficit. In my opinion, the school should never have shown surpluses over most of the 60s decade. I say this because they were underfunding so many accounts and programs, they were in fact actually doing harm to the school's overall program.

In 1972, the first year of the merger of NSFG and Williston Academy, there were many extraordinary expenses related to converting a shabby looking, all-boys school into a coed school, fitting for girls. This should have been expected, and realistically planned for, something I did not see.

While functioning in a crisis mode with no plan for me to follow, many improvements were made to the physical plant just because they were deemed necessary but not planned, i.e., leaking roofs. These significant expenditures resulted in our borrowing internal funds from primarily the Quasi-Endowment Fund.

As Business Manager, I was particularly fortunate to be working with Headmaster Ward and a Board of Trustees that had confidence in us. They fully relied on me to respond to the many plant issues, especially those that negatively affected the prospective student campus tours. Also, the Chair of the Buildings and Grounds Committee, Margaret E. French, was extremely involved and understanding of the importance of physical plant improvements to the survival of the school. She was very supportive with both her time and treasure.

Another very puzzling practice of the Babcock era was how they employed an account they termed "Surplus Account," which I believe, in standard college and private school accounting, to be the same as the "Balance of Funds Account."

In his transmittal letter to the Board of Trustees, dated August 29, 1969, Mr. Babcock writes, "The Surplus Account, (which is the net operating account over the years after sundry cash transfers have been made) showed a deficit of $128,310.69 as of June 30, 1968. This deficit was reduced during the year by an additional loan from Valley Bank in the amount of $150,000.00…and an excess of income over expenses for the year ended June 30, 1969 of $98,978.42."

I believe this practice in which the financials were presented to the Board was very deceptive. It was not correct to have shown the cash/loan going directly into the Balance of Funds account. The accounting entry that would have been proper would be to put the loan/borrowed amount directly to the Cash Account and to an off-set account, Loans Payable. A bank loan does not improve (increase your surplus); it increases your liabilities and cash. It is possible this practice misled the Board of Trustees as to the real significance of the bank debt and how seriously troubled the school's operations were.

Another issue that troubled me was, how could the Academy possible operate at a "profit" for all the years from 1959 to 1971? I cannot help but think the accounting was not truthful and the management of the Academy were not acting properly. I ask, where were the auditors?

I soon discovered that the faculty salaries were amongst the lowest in the group of ABOPS schools, a group of schools with which we compared ourselves. This fact had many negative effects on the quality of the academic programs and the recruitment of new teachers.

Another serious issue was the support-staff salaries which were also very low. Fortunately, the staff members were very loyal to the school, but it also meant it was very difficult to hire new, *qualified* personnel. One of the most obvious reasons for not legitimately being able to show an operating profit was they ignored the huge amount of deferred maintenance. This fact resulted in the deplorable state of the physical plant.

Who was at fault? I can only offer a few suggestions, derived from my observations:

1. Headmaster Philips Stevens would be the person who was most responsible, as he was constantly pushing for plant projects without having the necessary cash. So, I believe he likely wanted to show that the operations were "profitable" so the Trustees would not be alerted to a pending crisis and, likewise, the bank would not get overly concerned about their outstanding school banknotes.

2. Business Manager Wilmot Babcock, in my opinion, was somewhat intimidated by Mr. Stevens. So, he tried to make Stevens happy with the financial reports so not to upset the Trustees and, thereby, upset Stevens. Should he have said something?

3. The auditors, Doubleday, Allen, and Grimaldi, had been auditing the school for many, many years with Mr. Doubleday as the partner in charge. I sensed immediately that Williston Academy was an important account for their firm.
    a. Did they avoid any critical analysis of the school finances for fear of stirring up trouble and losing the account?
    b. Did they have the skills required to understand private school and college accounting regulations?
    c. Did they ever meet with the Trustees and share any fiscal operating concerns?

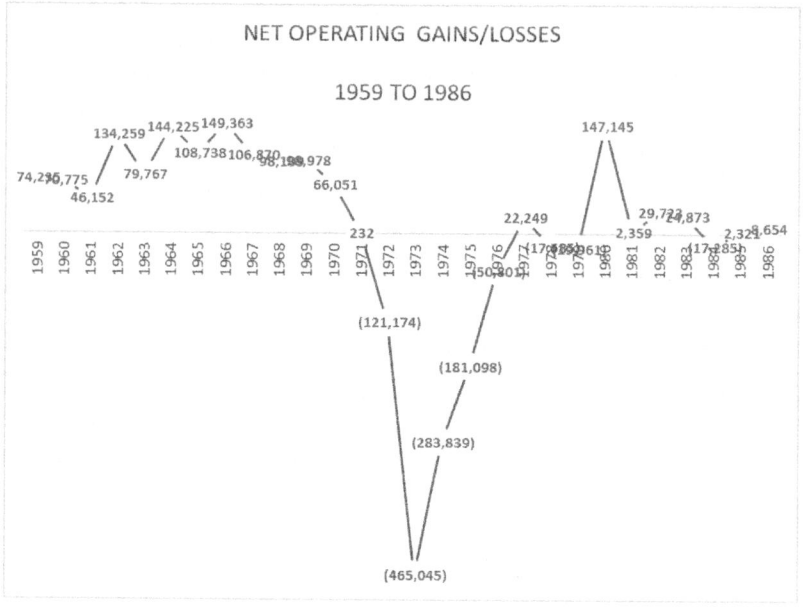

d. In a very short time after assuming my position as Business Manager, I met with the auditors and found them unable to be beneficial to the school's financial success. I terminated them at the end of the 1972 fiscal year.

4. Did the Trustees who were on the Board, at least from 1959 to 1971, really have an understanding of the school's finances?

   a. There was evidence that many of the Trustees did not even financially support the Academy with annual fund gifts.

   b. Did the Trustees, when on campus, observe the serious depletion of the physical plant?

   c. I would also offer a comment about the merger of the Academy and NSFG. There were the obvious reasons for the merger, such as increasing the enrollment, thereby making the school fiscally more viable. However, I believe one of the most import results of the merger was that it gave both Boards a chance to refresh the quality of the Board membership. This was likely the most important benefit of the merger.

As you can see from the chart on page 88, "Net Operating Gains/Loss" the gains presented were very significant. The reader has to wonder about how that could have happened. With the full support of the Trustees and Head of School Robert Ward, we vigorously began to address the issues that, once solved, would eventually contribute to saving the school.

The Great Merger Questions

THE QUESTION OF WHETHER TO BECOME COED HAD BEEN DIScussed by Williston Academy for many years. I believe at this most gloomy time in the school's history, what was really being said was, "Would going coed help to increase our dwindling enrollment?" Likewise, the question of increasing the number of day students had been considered on more than one occasion.

Head of Williston, Mr. Philips Stevens said, in the 1971 Yearbook, "The future of the one sex boarding schools is not so great...Until the latest revolution in education, there have been hardly any coeducational schools existing in New England, where there are hundreds of independent schools." He also said, "There are also going to be a greater number of day students and a decreasing number of boarders."

When asked by the LOG (the student yearbook), "Was coeducation instituted because of the economic problems existing at both schools?" Stevens replied, "No! By no means. There was never any suggestion that the merger was being done for economic reasons. Quite the contrary. I remain convinced that if, for some reason, this merger had not gone through, which of course, it has, Williston Academy would still have survived. I did not ever believe that we were going out of business."

This response to the student newspaper was completely fabricated by Head of School Mr. Stevens. He had to know how terrible the school's finances truly were.

Mr. Fuller said, "But even if Williston had not approached Northampton School on May 16, 1970, we would have stilled continued."[49] This also was more of a dream than fact.

Unfortunately, I have not found many poeple of authority from the 1970 time period who have been able to discuss the merger issues with me. When I arrived in March 1972, there were still many deeply concerning issues that were discussed with me by Trustees, the Head of School Philips Stevens, and Associate Head of School Nathan Fuller. Shortly after the merger, the combined Board had decided that having two former heads of school was not going to be conducive to strengthening and to growing the new school. The friction between the Heads and within the faculty was very disruptive. The Board in 1972 essentially terminated both Heads, effective June 30, 1973.

A student of both schools, Diane Eskensy ('70), in a recent email said to me, "Over the decades I think a lot of the animosity came because we (NSFG) felt we were not important as an entity, that Williston was in fact the big benefactor and NSFG was just being consumed." This was a feeling held by many NSFG women and drove a lot of the decisions in the next several years.

One big item, that caused many ill feelings was what was to be the official public name of the merged schools. Marketing the schools as The Williston Northampton School, located in Easthampton, seemed to be less than a catchy or even an easily recognizable name. In fact, Williston Academy was the more recognizable name, being founded in 1841 and with the larger alumni body. That is not to say the Northampton School for Girls, founded in 1924, was not a recognizable name. The name combination was just a marketing nightmare for a school that needed lots of first-class promotional material. This issue was of great concern to many other private independent schools, i.e. Choate – Rosemary Hall, Andover and Exeter Academy.

Also, there was definitely a group of Williston Academy faculty members that opposed the merger. They kept the fire of dissention burning for a few years. And, the combining of the two faculties drove the discourse, for there was an issue of how many faculty members were really needed in the new merged school. The reduction of faculty, even if not by attrition, was understandably worrisome to the whole faculty. There was not always a clear, credible way of deciding which faculty member was better than another.

The decision was driven from the top as well as from small groups friendly with the former Head and his family. One day, while working in my office, Sarah Stevens, the wife of Headmaster Stevens, called and said,

"George would you mind coming up to my house and talk with me about a few things?"

Out of courtesy I went, though somewhat reluctantly. When I arrived, she invited me in and then we went into the office just inside the front door of the Head's House. We did not sit down, but she immediately said, "I want you to help me to get Phil to stay on. With your help and with the help of Phil's supporters we can change the decision."

I had to say very clearly, "That decision is a Board decision, and I cannot get involved."

She was a little teary eyed, and we rather uncomfortably said, "Good-bye." The fight to keep her husband Philips Stevens continued, and it was sad and upsetting.

The Board of Overseers was constituted in 1954, "to survey and study the needs of the school and then pass on or recommend ideas to the Board of Trustees." Frank Conant ('35) was a member of that Board and eventually he became a WNS Trustee. Moving from one board to the other rarely happened, as he said: "WNS Board was self-perpetuating and largely unwilling to look much beyond their own country clubs for new talent." He also said, "his impression was that it was a way for Phil (P. Stevens) and Bab (W. Babcock) to schmooze with a lot of local persons of influence and keep them friendly." This Board became very vocal, supporting Phil Stevens to stay as Head of the School. But, by then, it was too late, as the WNS Board had made their decision and its membership had expanded to include NSFG Trustees. On more than one occasion, a Board of Overseers member approached me trying to get me to support them. Peter Knight ('58) was friendly with me and wanted very much for Phil to stay on—and he wanted the continuation of the Board of Overseers. It was finally dissolved in 1974.

I can say, with some certainty, that both schools were in very poor financial shape.

In the LOG article, Mr. Fuller stated, "You cannot deny that there are economic factors involved in any of these school mergers." He further comments, "Don't forget that Williston has over a two-million-dollar endowment, while Northampton School for Girls has had virtually a zero endowment."

From my experience, it is unquestionably clear that economics were the driving force. When tuition is providing almost 100 percent of the revenue and you admittedly say enrollment is declining, for the boarding students, that is the nail in the proverbial coffin. Fuller implied that two million dollars in endowment was a lot, but I assure you that it was not so. Even if they spent 5 percent of the endowment market value it would only amount to approximately $100,000. per year. Yes, that is more than Northampton School, but still not enough to save a school with all of Williston's financial issues from ruin.

From my observation, both schools had a very poor giving record, both from Board members and alumni. For many independent schools, gifts are a very important part of their income. Emily Snyder, a 1956 graduate of NSFG and later a Board member of NSFG in 1968, who then continued on the new merged Board, said, "the Board's giving was extremely poor, with some members not giving anything!" As a relatively young women, at a regular Board meeting she once challenged the Board members by going around the table to each member and essentially asking for a pledge. She, being very emotionally involved and choking up, said, she would pledge $5,000.00.

Another Trustee, Charles Johnson, said, "I cannot give anything as I have a mortgage and four children."

The other tell-tale indication of very troubling finances was the horrible, deferred maintenance issues that were blatantly obvious anywhere you looked around the campus. Emmy Snyder said, "When Nate Fuller arrived at NSFG to be the new Head of School, he was appalled at the fact that all the front doors showed peeling paint." Williston had similar problems. At that time, many of the independent schools were just beginning to build new, very impressive structures and refurbishing their campuses. Eye appeal was often very important in the extremely competitive student recruiting process. Both of these schools were having significant difficulty recruiting new students.

Even as late as 1977, Joe Lucier ('50), the newly appointed Director of Development, said, "No one was asking for money." This was very evident to me. I could see no real significant sign of any gifts being generated by the Development Office prior to the merger or major gifts generated by the Head of School, Phillips Stevens. Head Stevens did work with the Parents Association to raise some capital gifts. I believe none of the Williston buildings, up to the merger, were fully paid for by capital gifts. In the private independent school arena, as well as with private colleges many of the campus buildings were paid for by the generosity of donors. Williston seriously lacked in both capital giving and annual giving.

For these reasons and others, the merger was clearly for the financial survival of both of these schools. Contrary to what Philips Stevens said or implied on many occasions. I can personally attest that for the next several years Williston Northampton School was on the edge of financial doom.

When I finally sat at my desk and took inventory of the situation, I was faced with many imminent and critical problems that needed immediate attention.

First, there were a few good things I inherited:

1. The Business Office staff was very competent and hardworking. They were a real pleasure for me to work with.
2. The faculty were also very dedicated to the students and worked extremely hard.
3. The facilities, or Buildings and Grounds staff, were very dedicated.
4. The school had a new, very competent Dining Hall Director, largely because of the arrival of the girls who expected better quality food than had been fed to the boys.

However, there were some very important questions making life very difficult for the new management:

1. Enrollment was decreasing, especially the all-important boarding students.
2. Annual giving was very low and there was no real knowledgeable support staff in place to help in the turn around.
3. Deferred maintenance was absolutely terrible, resulting in the buildings looking old and unkempt.

4. The school did not own the necessary equipment nor did it have the skilled manpower to make meaningful improvements to the physical facilities.
5. The Business Office records were all recorded in long-hand.
6. There was no chart of accounts, which is necessary to produce meaningful information.
7. The endowment records were very primitive and each fund was not allocated its share of gains and losses over the years.

Enrollment was clearly the most important issue to tackle in order to ensure the school's future success. Just to emphasize this, in the *Williston Northampton Bulletin,* autumn 1971, Headmaster Stevens wrote in his letter, "In the last five years, our inquiries from prospective students, interviews, and applications have fallen off from approximately twelve hundred to six hundred. Last year we had the most precipitous drop and ended up with seventy fewer boarding students this fall than we opened with last year."

Five years is a long time to be in a period of declining prospective students, and obviously this was causing some of the unhappiness that was brewing concerning Philips Stevens leadership abilities and his future.

This, of course, was painting a very bleak picture of the school's future, but it clearly indicates that a merger of NSFG and Williston Academy could not do anything but improve both of the school's well-being. And, I might add, it did just that.

Wilmot Babcock—
Coach and Business Manager

CHARACTERS, SUCH AS WILMOT S. BABCOCK, CAN ONLY REALLY BE fully appreciated and understood by those who have attended a private, independent school where students are directly involved with the faculty and staff not only in the classroom, but on the playing field, in the dormitory, in the administrative offices, and in all other areas of campus life. I never attended a private school, so this "person" was not part of my life growing up. I quickly learned to appreciate what such a person meant to the students and the life of the school.

"Bab," as he was affectionately known, was Williston's Business Manager. He was in the process of retiring in 1972, when I was hired to be his replacement. As I wrapped up my job at the University of Pennsylvania, I knew that I needed to get to know more about my new school and my new job. I wanted to gather information from Bab and also wanted to arrange a trip to the Williston campus. However, when I initially called, I was told that Bab was "out of the office." That was okay, but I called again and again and received the same message. Finally, I talked with his Office Manager, Ann Tourville, and she said, "He was at the pool."

Exercising?

"No, coaching a very successful swim team."

As a matter of fact, the team was somewhat legendary. For the years 1953 to 1972, he had a record of 341 wins, 47 ties, and only two losses. His first love was coaching. He devoted an enormous amount of energy and love to his swimmers. Bab's teams were so good that they often beat such competitors as the West Point freshman swim team and other first-year college competitors. Of course, nothing breeds success like success.

The more Bab teams won, the more he attracted top swimmers to the school. Also, keep in mind, as the Business Manager, Bab controlled the school's money—so, looking back, I could see that may have helped attract swimmers, too. I'll have more to say about Bab's swimming teams in the section where I discuss admission to the school.

Bab graduated from Springfield College in 1930. He immediately started his career in the private school business. He taught and coached at Country Day School in Newton, Massachusetts and was Assistant Headmaster at Kimball Union Academy, 1935 - 1943. He came to Williston Academy as a physics teacher in 1943. Headmaster Archibald Galbraith appointed him Business Manager in 1945. His career path to being a school business manager was not uncommon during this and prior time periods. I have known several teachers, secretaries, and clerks who also became business managers; the job requirements were not as highly technical or professional as the position became during the mid 1970s.

Bab came to Williston primarily to teach physics, but, suddenly upon the resignation of Mr. Hodgkinson, the previous acting Business Manager, he took over the work of Business Manager.

When Bab first came to Williston, he coached soccer, and the ski team. He even built a rope tow on the west side of Mt. Tom. The picture below was what was left of the car and engine that pulled the rope up the hill.

Mr. Babcock's Ski Tow
(Williston Northampton School Year Book 1972, Page 182)

Grooming the hill was always difficult, and poor snow conditions were common. Fortunately, a better ski venue began to develop, still nearby, but on the other side of the mountain—the large Mount Tom Ski Area. The school began using this commercial facility for both competitive skiing and recreational skiing. So, eventually, Williston's rather primitive facility was abandoned and our grounds crew removed the tow motor and other remains.

While Bab had the title of Business Manager, you can see it was not his first love, but he did work hard at the job. His business office was very competently staffed with Ann Tourville, who acted both as his Bookkeeper and Office Manager. He also had two other staff members. Ann Tourville was most helpful to me in the years to come. She continued for several years at Williston as my Office Manager.

Bab's business methods and procedures were very basic. Everything in the office was handwritten; no mechanical aids were present except what was done on a typewriter and adding machines.

Immensely important to the success of all private schools and colleges are gifts, especially gifts with a donor designation/restriction. The courts have protected and enforced donor's restrictions. He kept track of some of the smaller designated or restricted gifts using cigar boxes stored in the walk-in safe. He carefully labeled the boxes. They often contained gift receipts, expense vouchers, and sometimes there was actual cash inside. For the more significant, designated funds, he would open a savings account at the local Easthampton Savings Bank. These funds were not all included as part of the school's formal record books, but the savings passbooks were in the safe. These gifts were safe in their own special way!

Just prior to my coming to Williston, Mr. Babcock announced he would retire after 33 very dedicated years. He stayed on to help me through a few months of transition. When I met him in his office, he seemed rather small in stature, a bit red in the face, and soft-spoken. He was very helpful, and thoughtful, he went out of his way to be sure he was not interfering with what I was trying to do.

From some of our conversations, it was clear to me that the Headmaster, Philips Stevens, put a lot of pressure on Bab and often wanted him to perform financial "miracles." This concerned Mr. Babcock and upset him, especially when Mr. Stevens would go ahead and do what Bab indicated the school did not have the necessary funds to accomplish. The fact was, you simply couldn't make silk gloves out of a sow's ear, no matter how hard you tried. Yet, Philips Stevens wanted to spend money that didn't prudently exist. That was a problem, especially in later years.

The school's financial base had been declining in many ways for the past several years, especially as a result of decreasing enrollment and low alumni participation in the annual fund. Tuition was the primary source of income, not only for Williston but also for many similar private schools. In 1971, Williston Academy's gross tuition income accounted for 90 percent of all income[50]. Williston did not have a large endowment; the reported investment income in 1971 was a mere 6 percent of total income. And, the annual fund was very small, with low levels of participation, resulting in the gift income being only 3 percent of total income.

The other big albatross at Williston was deferred maintenance. When a school cannot balance its budget because it does not have the necessary money, it then attempts to reduce spending wherever it can. Often that reduction is taken from the critical physical plant maintenance, i.e. repairs to equipment and to buildings. Why? Reducing building repair funds does not directly impact any specific individual, group, or program directly. So, there was less grumbling that Bab had to deal with from the cutbacks in maintenance or replacing failed equipment. However, this decision sadly, bit by bit, led directly to significant depletion of the investment in the physical plant. The decay of Williston's buildings was readily visible wherever you looked. This short-sighted cash saving tactic went on for many years.

One of Bab's cost-saving tricks was to paint only the front of buildings, the side that showed; and few or no repairs were actually made, just more paint on top of paint. This strategy, or lack of strategy, was not unique to Williston. Many schools and colleges were not allocating sufficient monies to maintain and protect their significant investment in the physical plant. Seeing the terrible conditions of the buildings and equipment was shocking to me when I first toured the campus. I especially remembered walking behind the Gym, a large, very attractive 1930s brick structure, now the Reed Campus Center, with the very large Georgian style windows with many small panes of glass. The ivy had never been maintained and now covered the whole back side of the gym, including the windows. When a building was constructed at Williston, more often than not, there was very little gift money to help with the construction. Hence, the buildings were built using the least expensive materials and employing very modest architectural design.

The idea of schools and colleges addressing deferred maintenance was, in the early 70s, just starting to be recognized and moved higher up on the agendas of many independent school boards of trustees. The well-known national accounting/audit firms could see that the plant assets were depleting and that there were no funds being allocated to protect these valuable assets. Also, at that time, most schools did not recognize depreciation on their balance sheets. I served on a committee for the national accounting firm of Coopers and Lybrand that eventually put forward a requirement for recognizing depreciation in the "Not for Profit Manual of Accounting Practices." The school's rationale for not depreciating their assets on their financial statements was simply that they could not possibly afford to fund the depreciation. So, why bother to show it in their financial statements? A sentiment of many older business managers.

Enrollment was very often a challenge for many independent schools at that time. Keep in mind that the post-World War II baby boom peeked in 1957.

That meant that by the early 1970s the pool of new students was getting smaller. A major blow to schools such as Williston, where tuition was often over 90 percent of their income. There was both a demographic problem and a stock market problem too.

While those things were happening, many schools and colleges were still in a building mode. The new and wiser thinking was this: we will not only raise, through gifts, all the necessary construction money, but, before breaking ground, we will also raise enough gift money to endow the upkeep of the building. This plan was new, important, and realistic thinking, but it still mainly only worked in the wealthy institutions, at least for the next several years. Not in Babcock's school.

Another of Bab's money saving methods was to paint almost everything "Babcock green," his favorite color of paint. It really was everywhere. I guess it made purchasing paint, patching, and decorating easier! So, the interior color of many Williston buildings was very dated, a rather drab green.

Yet another shocking experience I had with Mr. Babcock was when he introduced me to the school's very elderly auditor, who had worked for Williston for many, many years. In my previous positions I had had many years of experience working with Coopers & Lybrand. The firm had a whole division dedicated just to not-for-profit institutions and I had been involved directly with them in trying to upgrade the quality of non-profit accounting standards and procedures. Soon after I started working, I observed Williston's CPA/accountant start the annual audit by looking at every paid invoice voucher and, one by one, rubber-stamping each one "audited." I never could figure out what this tedious process proved. He did a similar thing with bank deposits. I asked for a meeting with the partner doing our audit, and I very gently told the very elderly Mr. Doubleday that I felt we needed a major accounting firm to do our audit so we could make sure we were in compliance with the latest accounting standards for schools and colleges.

He actually teared-up, making me feel terrible, and then proceeded to tell me, "I have public accountant certificate number 1, from the Commonwealth of Massachusetts!" That was an amazing statement for me to hear. It may have been an honor to him, but it said to me he was very old.

Now back to Bab's swimming program. About this same time, the competitive school and college swimming rules changed, making it much more difficult for small schools with just a few star swimmers to win events. The old rules allowed points to accumulate enough to win a match if your team had only two or three first and second place winners. Williston often did have the necessary number of swimmers to win the first, second, and third places. Some alleged the swimming association was waiting for Mr. Babcock to retire before implementing the new rules, which allowed points to accumulate for five or six places in each event. This gave an advantage to teams with larger swim teams.

It was also a time when the management of schools and colleges were becoming more professional and our independent school's national leadership was developing more professional standards. The National Association of Independent Schools had guidelines for granting financial aid.

And, at the time, Williston may not have been wholly in compliance with those guidelines. Soon after Mr. Babcock left, our Financial Aid Committee reviewed the previously awarded financial aid awards and discovered a few awards did not seem to pass the "smell test." A basic rule of independent schools at the time was that schools did not grant any athletic scholarships. The Financial Aid Committee was confronted with a few of these instances with Bab's swimmers and recognized it was not the student's fault—it was the school's fault. A compromise was the only way out. It was common knowledge that the swimmers were given lots of special care by Mr. Babcock. For example, he and his wife Wilma often had the boys over to their home, which was, by the way, located tightly between Memorial Hall and Payson Avenue. The little house is now gone, but that was the sight of occasional swim team dinners, a special treat, especially given that the quality of the food in the Williston dining hall was not known to be the best. I was told the swimmers lived on campus, but they did not live in regular dormitories with the other students. Rather, they lived above the gym like a fraternity. Bab built quite a swimming franchise that put Williston on the prep school map. But in the early 1970s, times were changing, and Bab's hugely successful swimming program was about to face tougher competition. While the swimmers had an especially sweet deal, I should note that many other faculty members generously had students over to their houses just as the Babcocks did. My wife, Ann, and I had many student dinner parties and gatherings at our home. It was fun to have the students visit in an informal atmosphere. I will speak more on this special opportunity our family and some students had at our home, Pitcher House.

During this transitional period, Williston became less formal than it had been. Mandatory chapel attendance was abandoned. The dress code for students no longer required coat and tie. But, the "Infirmary" was still of the old style, mostly serving those who were really sick. Not a lot of concern was focused on promoting good health via preventative maintenance. As Mr. Babcock controlled the Infirmary, on many mornings he had the swimmers go to the Infirmary where they were given a regiment of vitamins to help them be "stronger" swimmers. I do not know of other Williston teams being granted this privilege.

Bab fortunately had some very dedicated and capable office personnel, which helped me immensely as I was settling into the job, especially since many procedures were being changed and we began the conversion of all the accounting systems and records.

The school's endowment records were often incomplete and there was not a system for establishing the gains and losses, income, and expenditures for each of the individual funds. At the time, Mr. Babcock had been at the school for so long and likely had personal knowledge about the funds, and so he never bothered to properly document the gifts. I went through all the files in the big walk-in safe located in the basement of the Schoolhouse. It was necessary for me to carefully read as much as was available about each gift, trying to ascertain the intended purpose of the gift and any related restrictions. This was a very informative process and an interesting experience that helped me to better understand the school's past. Keep in mind that Williston was founded in 1841.

The next big, time-consuming project was to set up each donor fund, much like a mutual fund, with its own shares in the endowment pool, gains and losses, and income and expenditures. A ledger was established into which could be recorded the activity of each of the funds. I started by assigning one share for every dollar of principal in the individual, named funds. This ledger was important enough to me that I personally maintained it with hand entries for all the years I was at Williston. These endowed gifts often had an important story to tell about the donor's experience at the school, and it was important to me to know the donor's history with the school.

We also began the conversion of the accounting records using the chart of accounts that I had developed. I had to develop this at the time so that computerization of the records could happen. The chart of accounts was essentially the same one I had developed at Amherst College in the early 1960s, and had also implemented at Wesleyan University. The way in which financial numbers are accounted provides useful information, especially in budgeting. I added many new accounts to Williston's system. This would help me know where we were spending our scarce resources. Likewise, it helped me carefully track our income from the smallest sources to the major activities.

Mr. Babcock was very active in an organization of business managers consisting of 32 residential private schools, the Association of Business Managers of Private Schools. ABOPS, as it was known, was a data gathering and data sharing group that met three times a year. The work of this organization was extremely beneficial to me as it allowed me to establish goals, such as faculty salaries, etc. Each school took its turn at hosting the three-day annual meeting, and the members slept in the host school's student dormitory rooms. This was often a test of one's constitution. I especially remember going to St. Andrews School in Delaware for our annual meeting. It was held at Christmas break so the student rooms in the dormitories were available. When I was leaving the Williston campus it was snowing hard, so I decided not to drive but to take the train from Springfield. It snowed so hard they had to actually stop our train to remove trees from the tracks, and when we finally arrived at the New York City terminal, all the train schedules were late or cancelled. Hence, I arrived at Saint Andrews around midnight. It was the height of the 1970s energy crisis, and even though St. Andrews was a rather wealthy school, the frugal, hearty business manager had all the heating thermostats set to go off rather early in the evening. This practice was not so uncommon in our schools. My room was very cold and the blankets so threadbare I could not get to sleep. I was freezing cold. This room was directly above the Headmaster's office where, in my search for warmth, I found a large oriental rug that I borrowed for my blanket.

These meetings were considered an honor to host, an opportunity to show off our schools. It was hard, however, to compete with the big, old, well-endowed schools. Philips Exeter, for example, housed the attendees in the famous Exeter Inn. It seemed to me that Exeter had two of everything—two hockey rinks, two swimming pools, etc.

Although it was a special honor to host these meetings, it involved a huge amount of work. At one point, when I was President of ABOPS, Williston was the host school. I recall that as the students hastily moved out of their dormitory rooms to begin their Christmas vacation, we pleaded with them to help us by leaving their rooms clean. High school kids, really? You can just imagine what that was like. Our housekeeping staff had to very quickly clean the rooms and make the beds for every guest.

It was also a time where we showed off our dining service. Fortunately, Williston had a relatively new Director of Dining Services, Armand Davy, and he could tastefully prepare whatever meals I wanted. The culmination of this annual meeting was the exchange of financial data, consisting of many confidential and detailed facts and statistics. This allowed each school to rank itself with similar institutions, the wealthy and not so wealthy, the large and small,

This was an invaluable resource for me. Sadly, the many years of financial struggles had put Williston in the lower quarter of almost every collected category of information. For example, faculty salaries were of real concern for Headmaster Robert Ward. He was concerned because our salaries were so low, he believed it was difficult for our faculty to live a comfortable life, even though their families enjoyed free meals at the dining hall and free housing on campus. It was also a time when there was above average faculty attrition. We had to compete with all the other day and boarding schools for new talented faculty. Hence, with this comparative information provided by ABOPS, we could set a goal for our salaries and better plead our case for more money at budget meetings with our Board of Trustees.

Another cost center that ABOPS compared was the cost per meal to serve our students. Again, Williston was in the lower quadrant. As mentioned, we had a new director of dining services, Armand Davy, who had been severally restricted in what he was able to do to improve the quality of the food because his budget for food products and the necessary equipment to prepare the food was severely limited. Mr. Babcock liked using the government-provided free food products. That in itself is good, but some products were not of good quality. However, being in the program made it a requirement that you take what was offered. For example, Armand had to wash the provided pasta several times and it still was mostly starch and really of poor quality. The so-called provided "mystery meat" we did not even try to serve. We gave that to the local high school. Armand and I worked out a budget that would substantially increase the quality of what was fed to the students.

ABOPS continued to be of immense benefit to me. I served as its president and was always an active member. I also was President of the

National Association of Independent School Business Mangers, again another very helpful resource in my transition.

Mr. Babcock's retiring ended an era. His was a time when an individual could be primarily a coach, and on the side, be the school's business manager. A skill Bab learned by doing it, not as an apprentice in another similar position or even by attending a business college. He had no formal training in not-for-profit accounting procedures.

At the time I started work at Williston in 1972, schools were starting to learn that the business executive had to be a well-trained professional.

In my fourteen years at Williston, I focused completely on the school's business operations—its physical plant, dining operations, summer programs. However, I definitely believed helping with activities with the students was a beneficial thing to do for some administrative people. During my time at Williston, I had four assistant business managers who also coached and lived in a dormitory. They also felt it was a valuable experience.

Mr. Babcock was well-respected by the school community and was totally dedicated to his coaching and to being the school's business manager. He served from 1945 to his retirement in 1972. Bab passed on May 29, 1978. The Trustees recorded in their minutes on June 10, 1978, "Bab left his mark upon this school and all who knew him and worked with him are richer for that experience. His memory will forever be a part of the rich heritage of the school."

Robert A. Ward—
Head of School and Great Friend

THE MEETING OF THE BOARD OF TRUSTEES ON SATURDAY AUGUST 19, 1972 was a particularly momentous one for the future of Williston Northampton School. In accepting his election as Headmaster, Dean Ward stated: "I am deeply honored by this appointment and look forward to serving the school. The future of independent secondary education is not, as some would have it, bleak, and I have every confidence that Williston Northampton School will continue to command a leading position in the ranks of vigorous and forward-looking schools."[51]

In one of his regular messages "From the Headmaster," he said, "Two schools with distinguished reputations, are now one. We can take justifiable pride in the separate histories of both schools, but we can express even greater confidence in the present vigor and future strength of one school." He concludes his article with, "The future holds both great challenges and great opportunities. Many independent schools fear for their very existence, and only the hardiest in spirit will survive. I am convinced we have that hardiest—in our academic programs, in our faculty and students, and in our parents and graduates." And, quoting from his friend and favorite poet, he said, "Robert Frost was once asked if he believed in the future, and he replied: 'No, I believe the future in!' We can believe the future of our school "in" if we have the imagination to meet the challenges before us, the faith to hold fast to our fundamental purposes, and the will to make reality of our dreams for the school."[52]

Head of School Bob Ward grew up as a son of a maintenance person at the Kent School in Kent, Connecticut, where he also completed his secondary school education. Attending the school where his dad worked gave Bob a real deep understanding and genuine compassion for the support staff at Williston. Williston needed this caring compassion at this time. Bob's dad, Alex, was a kind and sharing person. He was a man who cared very deeply for the school where he was employed—his employment was not just a job, but a way of life.

After graduating from Kent School, Bob went on to Amherst College. It was at Amherst College, when Bob was a student, that he developed a love for the poet, Robert Frost. He was Frost's personal "caretaker" while Frost was teaching and lecturing at Amherst College and living at the nearby Lord Jeffery Inn. Bob walked Frost back and forth from the College to the Inn. And, up in his room at the Inn, they read poetry together, discussed the meaning of Frost's poems, and talked about their lifestyles. This very special experience, to be intimate with Frost, lasted Bob a lifetime, shaping his efforts to be a Robert Frost scholar. He frequently called on Frost's teachings and poems in his speeches and in his counseling of students.

After graduating from Amherst College, Bob went to Loomis Chaffee School where he taught English for several years. He was a favorite teacher there and many of his students continued stay in contact with Bob for his lifetime.

Bob then went on to Harvard University to get his master's degree in education, where he worked in the Harvard Admission Office.

He was invited to return to his alma mater, Amherst College, where he eventually became Dean of Students. In this position he enjoyed counselling students through the good and the not-so-good times, and there, too, he developed lifelong friendships with many of those students.

The Amherst College connections with Williston are numerous, especially in the early years of Williston Seminary. There are many of these stories connecting the two institutions throughout this book. I was also working at Amherst College for approximately ten years while Bob was the Dean of Students. We did not really know each other during that period. I was in the Comptroller's Office and in the Computer Center, which were not his thing, so perhaps that was one reason we did not develop a closer relationship.

I believe it was Emily Snyder ('56), a spouse of an Amherst graduate, a graduate of NSFG, and a Williston Northampton School Trustee who, along with a close Amherst friend and NSFG and WNS employee, Charlotte Turgeon, suggested that Bob Ward would be a wonderful candidate to fill the position of headmaster at Williston.

I recall some of the initial concerns that were raised when he became a candidate. Some issues were public and some just whispers behind the scenes. It was almost a written rule in the old world of private school heads, that they must be married and usually of the protestant faith. You have to recognize that the head of school usually was expected to do a lot of entertaining in his/her house, which was often a significant structure, well-appointed and beautiful. Why, you ask must they be married? So the wife could make peanut butter sandwiches for the students! Seemingly sarcastic, but nevertheless true. Also, it fell upon the spouse to take care of the planning for guests and, sometimes, cooking and serving meals when the head of school entertained at his house.

About this time, the mid 70s, the expectation of the spouse serving the school was fading out. It was becoming more common for faculty wives (I say "wives" because this tradition did not apply to men) to be working outside the house. And thus, the women did not have the luxury of time as they once had to do many chores for the school.

The other whisper was that he was a Roman Catholic. I believe, at that time, this was a rather rare happening in the traditional "WASPy" school heads' history.

A devasting accusation was made, some 30 years after Bob's death, that he was involved in improper relations with students. It was very shocking to me and, because there was no legal action, I was only left with today's authorities saying it happened.

I would like to quote from a letter to me and Roger Maroni ('74) from the late Glenn Swanson, Class of 1964, a longtime, very admired Williston History teacher and accomplished coach. Regretfully, "Swannee," as he was affectionately known, passed in April 2019. This letter speaks to some difficult issues concerning Bob's life, while also speaking to his wonderful strengths as a person.

GEORGE B. DUNNINGTON

Glen Swanson '64 History Teacher
(Glen Swanson's Memorial Service)

He says,

"I remember Bob Ward well. He was my boss, generous and compassionate man, an inspiration to many, and arguably a man who saved the school. Like all of us he was flawed; however, very few people knew his flaws until over thirty years after his death, and even then, few details became public, and his legacy was virtually expunged from institutions. Those who knew him well will continue to revere him, some with a tinge of regret that they never knew of his flaws.

The concept of Restorative Justice has emerged as a popular means of dealing with unacceptable behavior, from the criminal to the socially unacceptable. For Bob, now dead over three decades, he never had the opportunity to participate in such a process. I am sure he had regrets, felt guilt and shame, and wished he had been a different kind of person. But he died without public humiliation, without ever having said "I'm sorry" – at least as far as anyone seems to know – and without knowing what his legacy would become.

Bob was a good Catholic boy and then man, and I suspect he might have shared some of his secrets with his priest. On the other hand, he was an intensely private person, so perhaps he chose to deal with his God. We'll never know. And while I do not know what to say to his accusers, who suffered for decades and kept silent and who can never erase whatever happened to them, the Bob Ward fans will maintain their loyalty to his memory and all the good he did.

Another window into the soul of a person may best reveal itself in public favor, not the dark private times where we all go at various points. My term for Bob and others like him is Compensatory Behavior. Bob knew whatever his accusers said he did – if he did it – was wrong. His moral compass was true; his behavioral compass, tinged with whatever emotions he had, found him off track. He must never have stayed off track for too long or stayed so far that he was in trouble at the time. Secrets were hidden.

What was never hidden was the favor with which (he) acted as a teacher, a Dean, a Head of School, a mentor, and a friend. I think he was compensating, doing penance for his flaws by seeking ways he could make a positive influence on other people, truly sincere in what he did, what he wrote, and what he spoke. He carried a heavy burden, and he compensated more than what most of us could possibly do.

Many people end up in the dustbin of history because they did nothing memorable or important. Bob Ward should not suffer that fate. Can a balance exist for people like Bob? Certainly not now, but his record exists and cannot simply disappear by removing some plaques and awards.

Can Restorative Justice happen for Bob Ward? Not institutionally, at least in the foreseeable future, but Compensatory Behavior needs to reflect the essential goodness of the man. We as a community acknowledge it."

Bob Ward stories are many, but before I start telling some of them, I will say a few words of our times together.

When he was elected Head of School, the school had been functioning with a committee of four to guide it, of which I was a member. Bob would visit with us while he was finishing out his term as Dean of Students at Amherst College. This time together was very helpful for both the Committee members and for Bob. There were many issues, very important issues, to discuss. This transition of heads was not just an ordinary transition, for the merger had introduced numerous complicated issues.

When he moved onto campus, and into the head's house, Richmond House, we already felt comfortable with each of our styles of leadership. This was hugely important to me, as I had a "take-charge" style of managing the operating functions that were my responsibility, and felt the need to manage every detail. I would often get involved with offices that were not my direct responsibility. Was this good or bad? I think it was mostly good and helpful, and in all cases I was welcomed and respected. Bob immediately sensed this quirk. He also was first to admit he had very little experience in managing the non-teaching functions of the school. This worked to the advantage of the school as well as for each of us.

During the class day, Bob was frequently walking around the campus with his dog and best friend, Aragon, even visiting a classroom (if invited). He was an excellent listener. which allowed the students to open up and talk with him, not worrying about whether the subject was sensitive in nature. This characteristic of Bob's, listening carefully and hearing what was being said, contributed enormously to the healing of the wounds between members of the community.

In his ever-thoughtful way, he also did not want our friendship to be so noticeable to the community that it might appear like we were one. Yes, we had our many meetings in his office, along with the other leaders of the school. Our very respectful relationship enabled us to talk about almost any subject that was not considered personal or private about another person.

Our "business" was often very stressful because the school was now barely surviving, an issue right from our start as a team. I will remind the reader here of other big issues that affected our lives as the head of school and the business manager, including the "forced" retirement of Headmaster Stevens which brought to the fore his ardent supporters, often in an angry, divisive spirit. The merger itself was perfect for each school, especially for the students, but there were deep, somewhat angry feelings by the adults on both sides of the issue—Williston and NSFG. Of significance to the tone on campus was the fact that the plant was so depleted it had a real negative effect on the admission process and, sometimes, on the ability of a structure to function as designed; the human resources were also depleted over many years, mainly because there were little or no funds available for raises, professional training and the like. Alumni giving and involvement was far from its potential. Lastly, the Board of Trustees was not entirely a smoothly functioning group, and thus there were issues there that we had to dance around.

So, what often happened between us was, I would go to Bob's house after I left my office in the evening, a time when we would not easily be seen together, and we could feel free to discuss whatever issues either of us chose to bring up.

Bob was a very frugal person, so he kept most of the lights in the big house off and the furnace turned down very low. Thus, we met in his small, second-floor study where he kept the fireplace burning, using as fuel his many daily newspapers. Fortunately, he read several papers faithfully every day. He lived in this very large house without a personal cook and with limited housekeeping assistance, either his own paid help or as provided for by the school! This plan was of his own choosing.

I got one of many laughs we enjoyed when, one day, I walked in the backdoor of his house, which opened into the kitchen, while he was in the process of "cooking dinner." Cooking dinner, Bob's way, might not be exactly what many of us would call "cooking," or even "dinner." For him, the confirmed bachelor, it often consisted of opening a can of good old Boston Baked beans, and setting the can—yes, the can—directly on the stove burner! His pot may not be from a "Lecreuse" French cooking set, but it worked for Bob's homecooked meal. Then, when the food had heated through, using a pair of tongs, he lifted the can off the stove to place it directly on the table, where it then became the serving bowl. No fuss, no mess, no dishes to wash. That scene could be a symbol of his lifestyle—honest, and with no frills. Another thing I enjoyed sharing with Bob was a nightly martini, which, after a stressful day, helped us to relax. Sometimes we even had more than one! This practice often helped us prepare for an event.

I had to make things happen, but not always in the way I would like to do them, because of the cost (materials and people). So, Bob and I would talk about the priority of the projects and how it would impact campus life. We had to consider issues such as safety, leaky roofs that affected the usability of an area, and definitely "show ability" for applicant visits. Karin O'Neil, Director of Studies, and Tom Evans, Director of Admission were other leaders who I could always count on for rational and sage advice.

One of Bob's first concerns was the need for a new library. This gave us a lot to talk about. Bob was happily the public mouthpiece, spreading the word about the need for a library. In an article in the Willistonian, "Ward announced that phase one of the campaign includes the design and construction of a new library." The headmaster stated that such a facility was his first priority. "While the technological revolution in the area of information retrieval goes forward, he stated, "the resources of a good library—books readily available to students—will continue to be at the heart of a good school." He went on to say, "Many schools have built new libraries in the past decade. We hope to construct a facility that will be functional and economical and our goal is to add to our campus not an architectural showpiece but a resource center that will be attractive, comfortable and magnetic." Bob spoke enthusiastically because, in his own life, he knew the joy it brought him to be in a library.

Bob wanted me to guide the new library through the mechanical pains of birthing. This kind of work was very rewarding to me and it required construction talents I possessed. We experienced several problems in the early phases of our journey to have a new library. I mention some of these in this chapter of my story because the library was truly Bob Ward's fondest desire. Our fundraising attempts were not initially successful, an issue that had plagued Williston from the 1800s. This caused us to delay the final plans and the start of construction. This delay also made it necessary for our architects to re-draw all the structural plans, because in that time period, the building codes had changed and now required us to have the design and constructional materials upgraded to withstand earthquakes. This was not a building code requirement when we started the project. If my memory is correct, it cost the school an additional $150,000 for the revised architectural drawings—precious dollars. Sadly, we really did not have funds for this change. Also, as we were doing borings to determine the proper foundation design in the area between the science building and Memorial Dormitory, we struck water—another heartbreaker. As a matter of fact, it was an underground stream that ran through that area, not very far down in the ground. This gave us yet another challenge, as our plan included a state-of-the-art lecture hall in the basement with seats that were high in the back and tiered down as they went forward to the front. It was this low part of the foundation that was below the water level. Thus, the waterproofing of the foundation was a special engineering project.

Fortunately for us, Roger Clapp—at that time, our anonymous, very generous donor—agreed to be the major donor for the library. Roger Clapp's story is so important that it is also addressed more fully elsewhere in this book.

It was exciting to finally see this new facility emerge from the ground and begin to look like a library. Bob's dream for the school was realized.

I might add, rather sadly, that our fundraising for the library was not really successful, as there were few other significant gifts from our alumni, parents, and friends.

Robert P. Clapp Memorial Library Dedication 1980

The Head of School has many things to worry about, especially since the head is watching over several hundred young people who are all dealing with the myriad issues a teenager must attempt to navigate.

Sue Curry Barnett wrote me about her experience with Bob, which has to be about the worst kind of incident a Head of School could think about. Sue was visiting with Bob when a call came to him. "It is his face that I see every time I think of that incident. The color drained, and he seemingly grew old in an instant. Tears filled his eyes. He hung up the phone. He said three things. 1) 'Wai Wong, a senior, hung himself.' 2) 'I have to get myself together.' 3) 'Please stay here until I get back.'" Sue says, "I don't remember how long he was gone. Aragon (his dog) and I had a long walk. I do remember that a man, strong enough to allow his feeling to show as appropriate, was broken for a brief moment in time. But this was Bob Ward, and he was more concerned about everyone else."

Unfortunately, on Bob's watch, yet another tragedy he had to deal with was a terrible automobile accident in which a senior was killed. So, it was not only financial deficits and deferred maintenance that consumed his time.

Bob had a strong interest in the faculty continuing to nurture their teaching talents and their academic disciplines. Prior to his arrival, the limited finances over the past several years had substantially reduced enrichment projects for the faculty. Thus, Bob began to develop financial incentives, however meager, for the faculty to seek more education and learn new skills. Working closely with the Director of Studies, Karin O'Neil, and the faculty, they developed a new form of school program which they named "Winter Session." Bob said, "the theme was 'mind,' 'hand,' and 'heart.'" It required all faculty and administrators to take part, and they could not choose a project that involved their primary discipline. For example, at the urging of a history teacher, Barbara Moynihan, I was asked to teach a course in hammock weaving. Approximately 10 students signed up for the evening class. Because of time limitations, I built the looms for them and set them up in our home, filling the large living room, dining room, and even the gracious stair landing with my homemade looms. What fun—what a challenge.

Bob's project was to teach students how to read the newspaper using three or four major and local newspapers. The students learned how each paper handled a major news story and why a paper might choose to write a story where another paper might not.

He also opened his house and his kitchen for Brenda Minisci, a school art teacher and potter, and her partner Vini to teach Italian cooking. She and Vini made this a very special experience by taking the students to Springfield, where there was a significant Italian community and where they could find all the finest Italian ingredients for their sauce. Vini was a significant Italian leader in that community and had lots of influence, thereby giving their students a firsthand look at how that community functioned. We all know the basic Italian pasta sauce needs to simmer for a very long time, so, this process began in the early afternoon, filing Bob's home with the most wonderful aromas. As a matter of fact, they were so wonderful that they attracted the full attention of Bob's very big German Shepard, Aragon. Neither a warm stove nor a simmering pot of sauce was a challenge for this beast, so while everyone was gone, up he got onto the stove, to enjoy the feast! On returning to the kitchen to enjoy the delicious fruits of their labors, the crime was discovered. Bob felt very bad for Brenda, Vini, and the students. It was a real heartbreaker for all of us.

We did mention Bob was a frugal person—he sure was. During the energy crisis in the winter of 1976, Bob and I came up with an energy-saving plan that would help get the students involved in our savings program. Very simply, it consisted of a pizza for all the students in the dormitory if their dorm had saved the most energy over the previous month. Well, the Richmond House, Bob's house, was listed as a house in the contest. One night, I stopped by for a visit and when I opened the door, a blast of cold air hit me. It was so cold I was immediately concerned that the pipes in the house might freeze up and burst. I sped upstairs to Bob's study where the door was closed tight, and upon entering found it very comfortably warm. He had the fireplace burning, using his rolled-up newspapers. He even had a machine to roll the papers tight like a log.

I said, "Bob, what are you doing? The house is freezing."

"Oh, I shut off the oil burner the other day."

Worrywart George was not really sure this was going to be a good plan, but Bob did win his pizza before any pipes froze and burst!

GEORGE B. DUNNINGTON

Leo Hartnett Stevens Chapel
Headmaster Ward designated Leo an honorary graduate
Williston Northampton Bulletin Winter 1974 Page 18

The school had a very elderly (I think in his late 80s) night watchman, Charlie Hartnet, who worked his job very faithfully. He would often stop by my office at night and tell me stories about his other job as a local gravedigger, and also his earlier days of loading soft coal into a local factory steam boiler. Bob, while on his nightly walk with his dog, Aragon, whenever he saw Charlie, would always stop and say, "hi," in a very caring way. Bob took a real liking for Charlie. One morning, he brought Charlie to the all-school assembly in Stevens Chapel, where he introduced him to the student body and told the students how important Charlie's job was at our school. He then presented him with an honorary Williston diploma. The students loved this gesture and gave Charlie a standing ovation. This act by Bob was but another small example of how he cared for all employees, whatever their position was at the school.

Headmaster Bob Ward and Business Manager, George Dunnington—Shenanigans

The stressful year after the merger was fraught with anxiety as a result of budget constraints, over staffing, merging of two different campuses' ways of life, etc. We worked very hard on making things better for the community. Bob was especially considerate of the need to bring the community back together, and his thoughtful ways made life on campus much more relaxing. I would not hesitate to say it was Bob's demeanor that saved the school.

I had the idea of trying to generate some school spirit amongst the students by having a Halloween costume party at the dining hall with prizes and festive food. Armand Davey, the Director of Dining Services, was always agreeable to do whatever he might to help the school, so he came through with special food for dinner and lots of Halloween decorations.

In Bob Ward's "Message from the Headmaster," written in the Williston Northampton Bulletin Winter 1973, he discussed some of his dreams for the school, "a dream about the kind of school we intend to be...We want an academic program which suggests by design that learning is a serious enterprise, and only those who take it seriously will be capable of success." And, only in Bob Ward's inevitable way of understanding what a great school needs to include, in its dream list, he wrote, "Finally we need a school in which there is room – and ample room – for just plain fun...We need the grace of laughter, of humor, of just plain fun. In a good school we should be able to pick up, if we listen carefully, the intimation of joyfulness."[53]

In the spirit of his dream list, I suggested to Headmaster Ward that we should join with the students and come to Armand's Dining Hall Halloween party in costume. Bob was a willing participant. After all, the students dressed up for the occasion. So must we!

In his second-floor study where we discussed many heady things, we decided on going to the party as Sam and Emily Williston, the founders of our school, and whose pictures cover one full wall in the dining room.

Williston had a great theatre program, and Dick Gregory was one of the best costume designers and makers anywhere. I approached him with our plan, and he agreed to make Bob into Sam Williston and me into Emily. I must say, I was beautiful! We dressed at the head's house and walked across the campus and made our grand entrance into the now filled dining hall with all the kids in their amazing costumes. Sheer "joyfulness," only to be greeted, by the students, as George and Martha

Washington (and some other famous couples), not our founders, as we had expected. We even gave out buttons, the thing Emily was most noted for making and the basis of the Williston fortune. Perhaps we should have included a little of our school's history in the school's curriculum. Even though many did not know who we were supposed to be, it did set a fun tone for the evening and a real challenge for us for the next Halloween.

Year two: oh, how were we going to top the Sam and Emily act? We were such a "good-looking" couple, perfect in every way thanks to Dick Gregory. After considerable thought, we came up with the idea of the Lone Ranger and Tonto. "Me, Tonto" and Bob as the Lone Ranger. Williston had a great community, part of which was Jerry Rauscher, a parent of two Williston students who had a nearby horse farm and provided riding lessons for our students. My daughter Amy was a student there, and loved the riding program.

I went to the stables and asked Jerry, "Could we borrow two horses for our Halloween stunt? We will be riding them into the dining room."

Somewhat taken aback, he replied, "Have you ever ridden a horse?"

I said, "Many years ago."

Bob replied, "Yes, the horse on the merry-go-round!"

He went on to ask, "Do you know what a horse will do when surprised by a room full of loud students?"

Amy Dunnington ('83) at the Raucher Farm Riding Program

"No."

"They will relieve themselves right on the carpet. It will not be a pretty sight."

Then he realized I was serious. Fortunately, he was willing to go through with this plan, so he explained to me, "We have a couple of old, relatively calm horses, Ajax and Crackerjack, and I think we might be able to make this stunt happen."

Bob and I dressed accordingly: Bob as the impressive Lone Ranger with his silver six shooter, and me as his faithful Indian sidekick, Tonto, with a feather in my long hair and leather vest covering my bare chest.

Jerry and his son, David ('78), loaded the horses into their horse van and drove it from the stables, to down behind the dormitory, Ford Hall/Dining Hall. They unloaded the horses and led them up the very steep hill by the side of the pond to the entrance to the faculty lounge, attached to the dining hall. The lounge was not designed for horses, with its stunning black-and-white, very slippery tile floor. I had no idea how big these horses were until I mounted my steed with the help of Jerry and his son, David holding the reins. Then they did the same for Bob. Now the horses were snorting and dancing around, anxious for their visit to the Halloween party—really? Bob's horse, I mean the Lone Ranger's horse, upon entering the faculty lounge, could not get a grip on the slippery tile floor.

Tonto (alias George Dunnington) in the dining hall

Crackerjack began to slip and act scared. The Rauchers settled him, but unfortunately not Bob's nerves, I am sure! Now, we were ready for our grand entry: we had to crouch down on the back of the horses, because the mighty horses barely fit through the doors. Appropriately, the Lone Ranger should enter first, much like the style expected from a headmaster. The double side doors to the dining room were held open by Armand, and in rode the Head of School—I mean, the Lone Ranger.

You had to be there to fully appreciate the surprise on the student's faces and the noise from them—even the fear of seeing two giant horses in the dining hall. I remember our math teacher, Jack Cody, on seeing the horses next to his dining table, jumped up, and, in sheer fright, ran out of the dining room. You would think horses were not regular visitors to our dining room!

Tonto entered immediately following the Lone Ranger, and we rode down to the end of the dining hall and back. I wanted Bob to get his horse to rear-up and yell, "Hi-ho Silver, away!" He felt he should save that trick for another time. We made it—how, I am not sure. And, thankfully, the horses held their "load." It was a lot of fun, and the students had something to talk about for a long time.

Year Three: Now, the tradition had been soundly established. How do you top Sam and Emily Williston and the Lone Ranger and Tonto? We did really have a hard time trying to think of what the two of us could do again as a team. Several hours were spent in Bob's study. The year was a presidential election year, so I came up with the idea of dressing up as the two candidates, Jimmy Carter and Gerald Ford, and riding into the dining hall on our political parties' symbols, a Democrat's donkey and the Republican's elephant. The donkey was easy to find, as our good friends at the Raucher Farm had an old donkey, called Chooch, but an elephant took a little more effort to locate. This was a time way before Google, but by searching the hard way, via the Yellow Pages, I discovered the Barnum and Bailey Circus was headquartered in nearby Hartford, Connecticut. That was a real surprise, as I somehow thought it was in Florida. I also found out that P.T. Barnum grew up in Bethel, Connecticut, and he even was a state legislator and mayor of Bridgeport, Connecticut. He was called "The Greatest Showman." [54]

P. T. Barnum, Founder of the Barnum and Bailey Circus
(*The News Press, January 21, 2018 Page 20A*)

I called their headquarters and asked, "Do you rent elephants?"

To my surprise they said, "Yes, we will rent an elephant."

I optimistically said, "I need an elephant that can fit through the doors of the school's dining room. Please give me time to measure the doors that the elephant will need to fit through, and I will call you back."

She replied, "I have to contact the trainer, as they did not have their animal's height and width on file."

I wondered why that would not be readily available!

The next call from the circus was, "What do you know about riding elephants?"

A seemingly logical next question. I had to respond, "Nothing, nothing at all."

Then, very disappointingly, the cost for transporting the elephant and the fee for the trainer simply became much more than our budget would allow, and thus that ended that idea. We tried!

Back to Bob's study, and after deep thought we came up with the characters Batman and Robin. OK, what do the "Greatest Showmen" need for that stunt? Motorcycles, of course. I started making calls again, telling the motorcycle dealers, "I want to ride a cycle into the dining hall."

The first person said, "Have you ever ridden a motorcycle?" Sounds a little like the elephant lady. "Do you know how much one weighs?"

No, to both questions. And he said, "You two will end up going through the wall or out a window."

Not to be shut down so soon, I decided to go look at the motorcycle, as we did not want to accept "No." When I went to see a motorcycle, I was shocked when I simply tried to just stand it up straight, off the kickstand. It was so heavy—scary heavy.

We were then led to a place that sold dirt bikes, a smaller version of a motorcycle. We tried these dirt bikes and figured we might be able to ride them in our costume and into the dining room. I found, at the local Easthampton hardware store, Manchester's Hardware, a pair of very heavy long gloves that came up to my elbows, and very heavy, long wool socks. I dyed the wool socks green and spray painted the gloves silver. Mr. Gregory, our personal costumier, helped us with our flowing capes and the rest of the costume. We dressed and mounted our bikes at the Head's house, looking just like Batman and Robin. We started our bikes in Bob's garage by jumping up and down on a starter pedal and, with the engines roaring and smoking, we zipped across Park Street, and then across the campus, down behind Ford Hall, and up the hill, beside the pond, to the infamous faculty lounge, with that very slippery, black-and-white tile floor.

Armand Davy, again, held open the double doors to the dining room and we rode in, motors roaring very loudly, black exhaust spewing out, across the dining room floor area. As we reached the end of our run across the dining room and had to turn, we realized both of our bike motors had stalled as we slowed to make our turn. Batman—Bob—got his bike fired up with little effort for his grand departure. The kids were yelling and cheering him on. Not so for Robin—he was nervous, sweating, and continued jumping up and down on the starter pedal. But to no avail. Robin panicked and jumped and jumped. He finally succeeded to start the bike, thinking the throttle had to be wide open to make the engine start and stay running and not stall—not a good idea.

The kids were yelling, "Do a wheelie, do a wheelie!" Robin had no idea what that was, but, in his haste to get going, he did do a wheelie—as a matter of fact, a *spectacular* wheelie, and while up on the back wheel he flew back across the dining hall, through the double fire doors, into the faculty lounge. In a panic, and not thinking clearly, Robin put down his great green wool socks on that beautiful, slippery tile floor, thinking his feet would be brakes. Oh, no stopping Robin now! Off he went at full speed, through the next set of exit metal fire doors, then through five plastic trash cans, and then another set of doors and out on the lawn, landing upside down with the bike close by.

Robin was very lucky. I can attest to that!

But wait, the story is not over. Batman—yes, our Headmaster—wanted to go downtown to the Easthampton Police Station to offer our "help" on this busy Halloween night to our local constables. Whoa, really? So, we mounted our Batmobiles and rode through town, with our capes flying dramatically, to our local police station, which was in the back of a dark alley and was not a very impressive place. Batman dismounted from his bike and went into the station, looking very convincing in his flowing cape and black mask.

Upon entering the station, he put his elbow on the counter and, in an authoritative voice, said, "We are here to offer you our help on this hectic night for you cops."

There was a new young guy on duty, thus allowing the experienced officers to be out on the beat, keeping the town protected from malicious vandals. Not surprisingly, this neophyte officer thought he had a couple of whack jobs in his office. Can you imagine that? While Bob was doing his thing, I noticed the young man pushing the panic button, and in minutes, police cars descended from everywhere.

I wish I could have heard the radio call in the cruiser, when the voice from the command headquarters, in a rather panicky voice, said, "Batman and Robin are here and want to help us!"

Oh, really. Thank goodness I knew many of the officers—or, thank goodness they knew us.

Oh yes, we think we have the energy to do one more Halloween stunt. I must say, Bob Ward really enjoyed having fun with the students doing our silly stunts. It was very hard for us to come up with another idea that was as good as the previous ones. Part of the difficulty was trying to find an act that involved two people, as we really wanted to continue to be the Bob and George show—you know, the school's leaders.

Year Four: we decided on two characters from the movie *Animal House*, a popular movie at the time. We were to be John Belushi, or Bluto, and Tim Mathison, or Otter. Naturally, our fearless leader was to be Bluto with his white, Greek-like toga, and I, with my army tan outfit, would be Otter. This show necessitated a little more work for me. I went to Ford Hall Dining Room entrance and again, carefully measured the width and height of the infamous doors leading into the dining hall. From there, I went to the school's grounds maintenance garage and measured our various tractors. After selecting the tractor that would best fit my measurements, I drove it up to the garage behind the head's house and secured the doors so this clandestine construction project would not be discovered. Around the tractor, I diligently built a cake shaped out of chicken wire, then stuffed the holes in the wire with crepe paper, making it look similar to the cake in the parade in the 1978 movie. The movie cake said, "eat me," but our very own Belushi was a little uneasy with that wording, so he decided on the words, "eat it." Perhaps they were more appropriate for the Headmaster and Business Manager of the school.

The time came when we both very carefully climbed into the top of the cake. It was cramped and I had poor visibility to drive the cake. I started the tractor and the cake, with us inside, headed across campus to the infamous faculty lounge. Fortunately, my careful engineering allowed us to fit nicely through the doors to the dining hall with only inches to spare. We took a deep breath, and in we rode. The students immediately went absolutely crazy with shock and excitement.

Yelling and screaming. They quickly recognized the scene being from *Animal House*. Innocently, or stupidly, we did not remember the scene from the movie, or perhaps we never saw the movie, but it was this cake that actually started a huge food fight. Well we, the Head of School and the Business Manager, triggered off the biggest food fight in Williston's history. Bob Ward recognized things were completely out of control and he quickly climbed out of the cake and tried desperately to stop the food from flying about the dining hall. We had to quell the chaos! The entire faculty also tried to stop the food fight. What had we done? Now, Armand Davy and his faithful crew ended up cleaning up the mess we had unwittingly caused—food on the ceiling, the floor, and the walls. The dining

Animal House's Bluto, (alias Headmaster Ward)
and Otter (alias Business Manager George)
(Roger Maroni '77)

hall crew should have received a medal of honor for having to clean up after us. They, in their special way, never complained and even enjoyed participating in the "fun."

There was one final Halloween extravaganza after this, using *Star Wars* characters. Bob Ward was a great sport as well as a great head of school.

Back now to Bob Ward, the Headmaster. I always admired Bob's way of talking to a "hostile" audience without raising his voice. He would start saying a few words, and soon have the audience listening and under control. One such incidence happened when our security person, Bob Cary, called me.

It was late, after midnight, and he said, "The students in Ford Hall have removed every single one of the dining tables, chairs, and serving utensils, down to the basement and on the stairway."

I wondered, "What will they think of next for a prank?"

This one sounded interesting and very challenging, for we needed to be able to serve breakfast to all the students, not just those who lived in Ford Hall. And it certainly was not going to be easy to move all those very heavy tables and chairs back upstairs to the dining hall. I decided to call Bob Ward and the Dean of Students, Bob St. George, for assistance.

Bob and Bob went through the dormitory and told all students to come downstairs and meet in the now empty dining hall. They all, a little blurry eyed, dutifully came down and sat on the floor, with a few chuckles and some very concerned looks. Bob began by explaining how what they did was going to mean some students would be very inconvenienced by not having breakfast; also, if the staff had to move the tables and chairs back, it would mean some other important job would not be worked on.

Then he simply said, "Let's all work together and move all the stuff back to where it belongs and go to bed."

It all happened with no fuss. A seemingly small example of Bob's way of getting others to understand what should happen—no yelling, no threats.

At the time of Headmaster Philips Stevens retirement, a group called the Board of Overseers, Phil's close friends, became very angry and even somewhat rebellious. They had received information that Philips Stevens was asked to retire, infuriating several of the members. I knew some were actually thinking they could get Phil Stevens reinstated, as most of the members were Phil's friends. Bob knew he had to deal with this issue directly.

Bob asked the Board of Overseers, "May I attend your meeting to update you on what is happening on campus?"

He felt this meeting was important, as we needed all the help we could get to bring peace to our community, The Williston Northampton School. Bob knew this was not going to be a pleasant meeting, but in his inevitably thoughtful way convinced this group that we needed them, and at the same time explained they, as a Board, really did not have a meaningful function to perform. They listened thoughtfully and soon thereafter, they willingly disbanded.

We had some very difficult discussions, one of which concerned our ability to keep the doors of the school open. This of course, we never shared with anybody. The deficits were significant from the very beginning of our tenures. The deficits were not just on paper but were real – we did not always have the necessary cash to pay our bills!

The finances of the school could hardly have been worse and still have a functioning school. The Treasurer's report in the Williston Northampton Bulletin for the school year ending June 30, 1971, the year before the merger, showed a deficit of $51,534. The financial condition was somewhat explained in the Treasurer's report: "The total operating income for the year was $1,168,654.52. This was a decrease over that of the previous year, due primarily to a drop-in enrollment and an increase in scholarship aid to students."[55]

While the published amount of the deficit was significant, it was certainly grossly understated. The school had clearly been cutting expenses for several years, to the detriment of the overall well-being of the school. We knew the physical plant was in extreme disrepair and the maintenance expenditures were way below what they certainly should have been for the proper care of its physical assets.

The report showed, "Repairs and Maintenance (Buildings, Grounds and Equipment) $63,949.33." The article continues, saying, "The operating expenses for the year were again high. Faculty salaries and labor costs continue on a steady rise. Non-profit independent schools have been hit very hard by inflation and lower enrollment. However, we must continue to hold up our high caliber of academic excellence, but we continue to build an increasing deferred maintenance item."[56]

The Treasurer's report did admit to the fact that deferred maintenance was an issue. They also spoke about salaries continuing to rise because of inflation. Here again, we knew that the salaries were very low and not competitive with other independent schools, for both the faculty and the support staff.

Failure to properly provide resources for both of these items significantly impacts the admission of new students and was likely one of the reasons enrollment was declining.

Accounting methods before Bob and I joined the school were difficult to understand, as the income and expense categories did not always reveal what was charged to the accounts. Hence, some of my comments about the numbers, before I was the school's Business Manager, I cannot exactly verify.

Bob and I talked very seriously of how we might go about closing down the school because of the lack of necessary funds to make the school a viable institution. This was very scary and something neither of us wanted to do, but the enormous deficits were real. Fortunately, Bob Ward was the kind of leader who was not going to try and hide the large, very shocking deficits from the Board of Trustees. He fully supported me when I told him what I thought needed to be done in order for the school to survive. He also had the courage, and felt it necessary, for the faculty to be aware of what we were doing to ensure there was a future for us all.

To help to better understand the enormity of the crisis, I will offer a few numbers for readers to consider.

In the fiscal year 1969 – 1970, the school reported a surplus of income over expenditures of $66,051, and in 1970 – 1971 they showed a surplus of $232. [I was not able to reconcile the surplus shown in the auditor's report, $232.61, with the School's Treasurers deficit of $51,534.06.] These numbers were, in my opinion deliberately "cooked" to make others think things were not really that bad.

In fiscal year 1972 – 1973, my financial report to the Trustees reflected an operating deficit of $465,045! A number closer to reality, but still less than I knew was required to accomplish a small portion of what really needed to be done. How did we make it through these cash deficit years? Simply stated, we borrowed from the Unrestricted Endowment Funds, Plant Funds, and fortunately we had a few significant gifts.

We were making major improvements to the physical plant, primarily using our own, new, skilled staff. This made Tom Evans and Debbie Hayward, our Admission Office leaders, very happy. And, I do think, it eventually helped increase our enrollment. The subject of the finances will be discussed more fully later in the book. It was very shocking to read.

Even though we did not have many major donors on the Board, we did have a Board that believed in Bob and me, so that was also extremely helpful in our turn-around efforts.

Bob asked me to meet with him one evening so he could discuss some concerns. Well, this gave me pause. What was wrong? Was he going to leave Williston? We met up in his study, the place where we solved all of our problems, or tried to.

He said to me, "George, I want you and I to agree that we will not leave the school in the same year. While the school is certainly functioning at a satisfactory level, it is still in need of tender care. And, if we happen to both leave at the same time it would likely create serious issues in the management of the school."

Bob cared deeply for the well-being of the school and this action certainly illustrated that concern. That request seemed very reasonable, and also made sense to me. Therefore, I assured Bob I would not leave in the same year he decided to leave.

I believe it was in the very next year (1978) I received an offer from Dr. Lee Hall President of the Rhode Island School of Design to be their Treasurer. Deciding whether to accept the offer had many complicating and troubling factors that would need to be resolved. The first issue for me was that their faculty was unionized and had major disagreements with the President. They were threatening to strike. Dealing with a strike would present many difficult issues for me, especially being new to the campus. Secondly, the elderly treasurer had been there for a very long time and was very set in his old ways. The college was having financial issues and wanted me to accept the position very quickly. And, of course, as with any major move it would have a serious effect on my family. I knew I had to talk immediately with Bob about this "opportunity," and that weighed heavily on me, for our relationship was very deep and meaningful. And I cared a great deal for the welfare of Williston and its constituents. When we met, Bob was as kind and thoughtful as I had expected him to be when I told him of this offer. We talked and I shared my concerns. He asked me several helpful questions. After our talk he wished me the very best as I went about making my final decision. He reached out to me and gave me a copy of Robert Frost's poem, "The Wood-Pile." What did that say about my leaving? While reaching out to his friend, Mr. Frost, for insight into this issue was not at all surprising, it was however difficult for me to understand the message the poem had for me.

I cannot recall if I sought Bob's help in understanding what Frost was implying, but I did search for others who had offered various interpretations.

On "The Wood-Pile," comments J. Donald Crowley, "The Wood-Pile" is thoroughly typical of many of Frost's mature nature poems. At once narrative and dramatic, the poem seems astonishingly clear even on first encounter. There at its center are the solitary speaker, a familiar figure, and his story, this one—Frost's others—told in the inevitable simple, straightforward, and calm, almost laconic language that characterizes dozens of Frost's other narrative lines."[57]

This was far from my reaction after reading the poem. I was not a reader of poetry, but while working at Amherst College I did listen to Frost read some of his poems. It was nothing short of beautiful, sitting in the balcony of College Hall and looking down on this rather elderly bard as he read some of his own writings.

So, what was my friend, Bob Ward, trying to say to me by giving me this poem? Was he trying to say, "*I paused and said, 'I will turn back from here. No, I will go on further—and we shall see'?*" Was this my dilemma—should I take the new job, or stay at Williston? Then Frost says, "*It was a cord of maple, cut and split And piled—and measured, four by four by eight.*"

Was this precision, 4 X 4 x 8, representative of all the work I had done to make Williston what it was at that time? Did I, in fact, make the many changes my way?

"*No runners track in this year's snow looped near it. And it was older sure than this year's cutting, or even last year's or the year before.*"

Was this saying to me, that I had worked very hard for many years to build my "Wood Pile?"

And then Frost writes, "*What held it together on one side was a tree Still growing, and on one side a stake and prop, These later about to fall. I thought that only Someone who lived in turning to fresh tasks Could so forget his handiwork on which He spent himself, the labor of his ax, And leave it there far from a useful fireplace To warm the frozen swamp as best it could With the slow smokeless burning of decay.*"

By "turning to fresh tasks," was I going to forget what I had accomplished at Williston? Indeed, this poem left me wondering about all the possible meanings and more. Bob, you needed to take me up to your study and give me a lesson, for I do not believe I was going to *"leave it there far from a useful fireplace."*

Williston was part of my heart and soul and still is. So, I chose to stay at Williston. This dilemma was a subject of several discussions with my wife, Ann, and our children. Ann was always most supportive of my various employment ventures.

Graduation at Williston has always been very special, with seniors saying tearful goodbyes to their friends and classmates, and to their special teachers. Headmaster Ward, in his very special way, left words to the graduating class that were always meaningful. In his talk to seniors of the Class of 1979, which were especially meaningful to me, as I knew this was Bob's last graduation, and my outstanding partner and friend was leaving me, as well as the students.

Of course, Bob could not leave without a quote from his friend and poet, Robert Frost, who said, "education is what you have left after you've forgotten all you Learned."[58]

His farewell to seniors was:

> "I wish you the courage to be warm when the
> World would prefer that you be cool.
> I wish you success sufficient to your needs; I
> Wish you failure to temper that success.
> I wish you joy in all your days; I wish you sadness so
> that you may better measure joy.
> I wish you gladness to overbalance grief.
> I wish you humor and a twinkle in the eye.
> I wish you glory and the strength to
> Bear its burdens.
> I wish you sunshine on your path
> And storms to season your journey.
> I wish you peace—in the world in which
> You live and in the smallest corner of the
> Heart where truth is kept.
> I wish you faith—to help define your living
> And your life.
> More I cannot wish you—except perhaps
> Love—to make all the rest worthwhile."[59]

Bob sadly left Williston and returned to his beloved two-acre home in Kent, Connecticut to be with his parents. He constructed himself a separate area of the house where he could live his own life. He enjoyed working in the yard, planting trees, and writing and lecturing on Robert Frost. He also had the idea that he would like to teach high school English again. His leaving should not have been a surprise to me, as he had said from the outset, "I plan to stay only five years and then let someone else take over where I left off."

Even after he had retired, I remembered him telling me about the lovely river that flowed behind his property, the Housatonic. He talked about how beautiful it was and how "each day," they opened the dam by the upstream power plant and let the water rush downstream right behind Bob's house. He explained it was a wonderful experience to go tubing down the stream with this fresh gush of water.

So my children, Susan, Amy, and Geordie, and our good friend Roger Maroni ('77) packed a lunch and decided to experience this trip using our inflatable boat. We unknowingly made several bad decisions; first, we remembered Bob said it would be a quick trip and so we left the water and our lunches in the car. Second, we believed him when he told us the water was released every day at a certain time. Thirdly, we did not take any personal spending money, not even a dime to make a phone call. And fourthly, we never realized the river went through woods so deep that, in fact, there was no sign of habitation. So, we went forth with great joy, anticipating the rapids and all the thrills that would come with that kind of venture.

We began our exciting excursion with the river being so low we had to walk and push our boat. After nearly an hour went by, we kept thinking they really would open the dam and we would be flying down the river to Bob's house! It did not happen, and I got a little concerned as I had no idea how far down the river Bob's house was. We were getting thirsty and hungry. I tried climbing the very steep river walls, and soon found out there was nothing up there. We continued on, paddling and walking, getting more and more concerned.

Then, from the side of the river came a voice, "Hi George."

Whoa, who is this, out in this never-never land? It was Ken Heath ('67), the Dean of Day Students and French teacher. He was an ardent nature lover, and he was at that time hiking the Appalachian Trail and had stopped for lunch.

We were shocked, and asked him, "How far is it to Bob's house?" He had no idea, so I asked, "Do you know how far Kent School is?"

He was not sure, but assured us it was down the river. Soon, we heard the noise of a car, so I went up the steep embankment to a road and found out we were getting close to our destination—thank goodness, for we were all very tired and starved.

We finally did meet Bob and told him our tale, and then he told us, "I found out the dam was not released every day!"

We enjoyed hamburgers cooked on Bob's grill and told tales of this harrowing experience.

Sometime later, I received a call from Bob and he asked, "May I come up and chat and maybe have lunch? I will meet you at Pitcher House."

For some reason, I do not remember being surprised or concerned about his call.

We sat in the kitchen and he started talking: "The doctors have discovered I have stomach cancer." He went on to say, "It appears to be very serious and the doctors are not sure what the next procedure will be."

Well, this was a terrible piece of news. I sensed from the way Bob talked to me that he knew it was extremely serious. Not long after our meeting, I learned that his cancer was terminal and he did not have long to live. I went to Kent, Connecticut and visited him at his parents' house. Hospice was there, and Bob was weak but sitting up in his chair.

We chatted and then he said to me, "I can hear the pitter-patter of little feet in the coffin. I want you to know I have prepared three envelopes."

One was for the person who ran the town of Kent, a very good friend of Bob's who was a member of the Town Council. He even ran for a few years unopposed by either Republicans or Democrats, Bob's party. The second envelope was for a longtime friend whom he had taught at Loomis Chaffee, and later continued his friendship when he went to Amherst College, where Bob was the Dean of Students. He became a Supreme Court Judge in Arizona. Bob was honored to be the main speaker when he was granted his judgeship. The third letter was addressed to me.

Bob asked, "Please do not open your letter until I have passed."

When the time came to open the letter, Bob had asked me to speak at his memorial service in the Kent Chapel. Public speaking was not my favorite thing to do, especially when I knew the chapel would be filled with his numerous friends and it would also be a very emotional moment for me. It was both a surprise and an extreme honor to speak for my special friend; I survived, but remembered very little of what I had said.

I was also asked to speak at a memorial service for Bob in the Alumni House on the Amherst campus, his alma mater. I choose to share happy stories, as Bob always said he wanted his death to be a fun celebration of life. Honoring this wish seemed to be easy for the many speakers that day, as we all laughed very exuberantly, just as Bob had asked us to do in celebrating his memory. The hall was filled with Bob's many friends.

When Bob retired, he gave me a Robert Frost book of poems and inside the cover he wrote the following note to me.

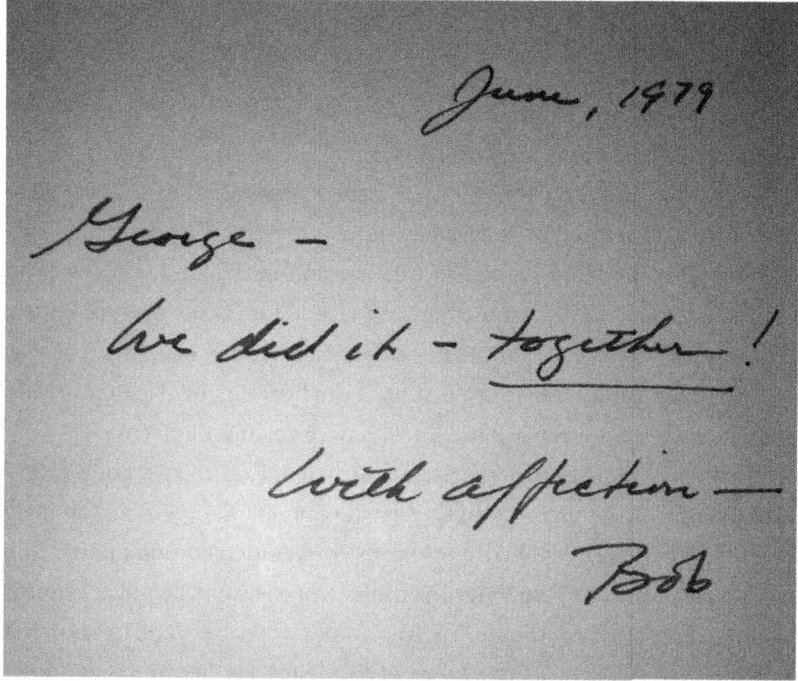

Yes, Bob was a very special and caring friend to me, but most of all I personally think he saved Williston Northampton School. For that, the school owes him a deep sense of gratitude.

Christopher C. Corkery, Headmaster 1979–1984

When Bob Ward made his announcement to leave Williston as its Headmaster to pursue other adventures, he was in fact following his original commitment, which was to spend approximately five years at the school.

Much effort went into selecting the members of the search committee that was tasked to find a new Headmaster. They, like any other search committee, had a few issues that needed to be addressed by a new Head of School. Thus, the search firm tasked with finding qualified candidates had to consider what the school's own search committee defined as necessary attributes.

Karin O'Neil, a longtime, well-respected faculty member and administrator who served on the search committee, said, "It was time in Williston Northampton's history when the school was struggling with its identity."[60]

This was a significant challenge for the new head. Another issue was to put into place a 150th Planning Committee. This was an involved project that attempted to look ahead 10 years, setting goals and pathways to attain those goals. Thus, a new Head certainly needed to have an extensive background in the independent school education.

There was another task for the new head that was not well known, and by its nature was kept confidential. When Mr. Ward left the school, he suggested to the Board of Trustees that there needed to be some serious upgrading of the faculty. He said that it was a job he simply did not feel comfortable doing, and he apologized for that shortcoming.

I believe few leaders would be comfortable doing some of these necessary but unpleasant tasks. Again, doing that job humanely and yet effectively required years of school experience, and the conviction of knowing when you are right. Chris Corkery accepted that directive, and I am sure he did not particularly look forward to doing the "annual faculty review," addressing some long-time shortcomings of the faculty. I believe he, too, came to the same conclusion about the quality of the faculty as did Headmaster Ward. The issue of having some staff and faculty not carrying their "full weight" is a perpetual concern of a person running a school. Schools, like Williston, with a long history, can find itself having faculty who have not been staying on top of their discipline or may have even reached a point in their career when they should be considering retirement.

Chris was well respected by his faculty. Head of the Athletic Department and longtime football coach, Rick Francis, wrote, "While Chris had a background in prep school football coaching, he never second-guessed my decisions with regard to the Williston program, keeping his opinions to himself. I always felt that I worked with Chris, not FOR him, and enjoyed his friendship. He was a totally unpretentious leader, and I was sorry when he left Williston."[61]

While I did work a year with Head of School Philips Stevens, he had been asked to leave at that end of 1973. If one considers that, Chris was the third headmaster for me to work with at Williston. Each head, as would be expected, had his own visions and goals for the school. Fortunately for me, they all worked well with me, respecting me and giving me full responsibility for the finances, human services, dining program, physical plant, and summer programs. And, most importantly to me was that I was always deeply involved in all major school decisions.

Shortly after Chris and his wife, Nancy, moved into the Head's house, Richmond House, my wife, Ann, and I invited them to our house to have a welcoming dinner. The evening began as a leisurely time together, getting to better know each other while enjoying cocktails and dinner. We had prepared a formal dinner, to be served in our dining room where the windows of the beautiful Pitcher House looked toward the adjacent John Wright dormitory. Soon after being seated, I could see several students come running toward our house, carrying another student. They all came up on our porch adjacent to the dining room. Immediately I went out and saw a terrible wound on the student's leg, with a huge hunk of fatty tissue hanging down. His friends told me this was the results of the boy running through the John Wright's plate glass, exterior door. We called an ambulance, and I rode with the student and medics to the Cooley Dickinson Hospital in nearby Northampton. Fortunately, we were met at the emergency entrance by Dr. Tarantino, a surgeon and a school Trustee, who quickly took charge and cared for this student. The student recovered with the help of several stitches. So, upon returning to my house, I said, "'Welcome to Williston,' Chris and Nancy."

Each year, the head of school would write a letter of reappointment and make a few brief comments. Below is the letter Chris wrote to me on February 28, 1980. As this letter may be difficult to read, I will excerpt the contents here.

> *"Dear George: I don't think it is necessary to point out to you the high regard I have for you, both personally and professionally. It has been a much greater adjustment for you to learn to work with me than the other way around. I have always relied on able people like yourself*

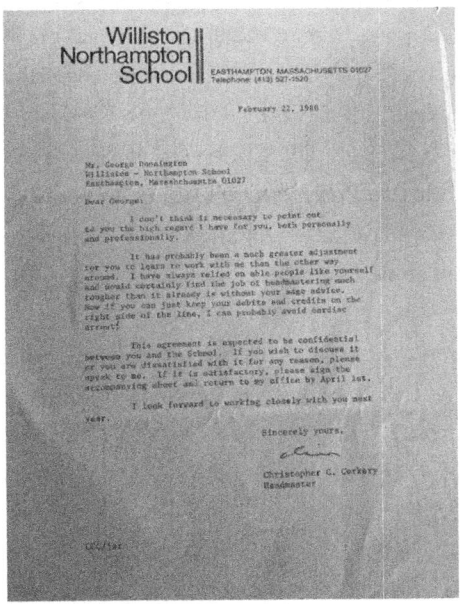

and would find the job of head mastering much tougher than it already is without your sage advice. Now if you can just keep your debits and credits on the right side of the line, I can probably avoid cardiac arrest!"

There were several happenings going on in private secondary schools across the country which also challenged Mr. Corkery, the Dean of Students, and the faculty at Williston. One involved the increase in the use of drugs and alcohol on campus. To make it worse, the legal drinking age was 18, the age of many of our senior students. There seemed to be an increasing variety of new kinds of drugs—amphetamines, LSD, pot—and some forms were very difficult for us to readily discover when searching for this contraband.

Stories, not necessarily truthful, about drug usage on campus came to the Board of Trustees. Some Board members thought this was a more serious problem at Williston than at other institutions. They also mistakenly thought illegal drug use could be easily stopped. There was no denying drug use was serious and an issue that had to be continually dealt with using education and discipline. Mr. Corkery, as Head of School, was criticized, often behind his back or by Trustees who really did not understand how complicated it was to stop the usage of illegal drugs, especially since the use of drugs was a major issue with our neighboring schools and colleges in the whole Pioneer Valley. Charlotte Heavens Bruins, ('47) was one Trustee who strongly felt Chris was not doing enough to stop the drug problem. She had a daughter attending the school, which likely gave her access to many students and their drug stories—some true, some exaggerated, and some likely false.

In the September 10, 1979 *Willistonian,* Mr. Corkery said, "The key to a healthy campus is strict discipline, henceforth the discipline system of last year will not be changed. He regrets having to enforce punishment to its fullest extent..." [62] Chris went on to say, "One reason for saying he regrets strict enforcement was his concern that students lose time out of school or may be dismissed permanently. We all know kids can make very dumb mistakes in judgement. To partially address a one-time mistake, we did have a 'one chance policy' which included time in the Health Center, counseling and evaluation."

Discipline by itself was, in my opinion, not going to stop the use of drugs and alcohol. This was a very distracting issue for Mr. Corkery to have to deal with, especially as it infiltrated into the Board, often in exaggerated forms.

The other national issue that was continuing to confront our schools, as well as colleges, was the recruiting of minority students. Their lack of adequate academic preparation and sufficient amounts of financial aid were issues that challenged our schools. Chris was personally involved in the independent school's effort to develop programs way back in 1964. It began as Independent School Talent Search Program, and that became the well-recognized program, A Better Chance (ABC). So, in keeping with his deep convictions, he focused on trying to attract more minority students to Williston.

The problem of adequate financial aid continued to challenge schools. Mr. Corkery wrote in *The Bulletin* in the Spring of 1982, "Many business managers and board treasurers say that the pressure of inflation on tuition, maintenance, salaries and educational programs, make the financial aid budget a legitimate target for reduction. (Fortunately, this is not the case at my school.)"[63]

Chris had a real understanding about what a private day and boarding school required from its teachers. Quoting him from an article he wrote about teachers, "The faculty of any school are the principal human and pedagogical resources." He went on to say, "We want men and women who are not merely looking for a job, but who are willing, no eager, to buy into a way of life...I believe those who teach today in independent boarding schools have a higher calling. I do not mean to be mystical about this, but only someone with a calling would put up with regular sixteen-hour days, three institutional meals a day, dormitory housing, endless preparation and correcting of papers and the myriad other things that occur in that sixteen-hour day—and all for the princely sum of $14,500 a year. So why do we do it?" asks Chris. [64]

Teachers care, and their actions can and do make a difference. Some teacher involvement is very significant, even life changing. Some involvements are everyday, parent-like, guiding changes. I surely got major personal rewards from my interactions with the students.

This was all very true, and Williston had, for the past several years, tried to increase their faculty salaries so that they were more competitive with other similar schools.

Cathleen Robinson (Brown), 1974 – 2001, wrote: "I served on the 150th anniversary committee, a committee of trustees and faculty, and our mission, on the 150th anniversary, was to plan for the next ten years…Many people on the Committee questioned, 'how can you plan ten years ahead?' That didn't stop Chris and his robust expectations for Williston Northampton. When asked to jot down our dreams upon hearing them he shook his head in disappointment. 'Your dreams are so small and conservative,' he said." Cathleen continues and comments, "But trustees and faculty alike had been through the turbulent 1970s when economics drove a number of boarding schools out of business. Under Headmaster Ward and Business Manager George Dunnington (your author), Williston had survived, in no small measure to their guidance." She goes on to say, "He was a champion of the faculty and salaries rose 43 percent during his tenure, lifting us out of the bottom of the boarding schools we competed against for quality teachers."[65]

She went on to say, "Chris Corkery told us to believe in our worth as a school and to dream big."

This, I believe, speaks to one of his initial objectives of giving Williston its identity.

As time went by and Chris had his annual reviews with each member of the faculty, those needing improvement were undoubtably told what they needed to do to make them better teachers, better coaches, better dormitory parents. Such recommendations for improvement might have included going back to college and getting a master's degree, taking some enrichment courses, etc.

These discussions, as would be expected, created some dissention and unease with those teachers affected, and some did talk negatively about Chris with a few Trustees. This added to the dissention on the Board.

Chris worked hard to get some new Board members that would bring real talent and treasure to the Board. He was successful in recruiting William Schreyer, President and Chairman of the Board of Merrill Lynch in NYC. Mr. Schreyer arrived at his first Board meeting, landing on

Sawyer (football) Field, next to the Williston Pond, in the Merrill Lynch helicopter.

Mr. Schreyer served as President of the Parents Association and the Executive Committee. In his talk at the Parents' Association meeting, he focused on Chris Corkery's earlier message concerning "value added" at Williston. His daughter, Drue Ann, attended Williston and also lived in Pitcher House with my wife and me.

From observing his daughter as she went through Williston, he could see "value added," about which he adds, "I am referring to the relationships which develop between students on one hand, and students and faculty on the other. This is where value added picks up an added dimension."

Chris really enjoyed observing how the school's faculty and staff interacted with the students and how they gave the students their full share of the Williston experience—"value added."

Sadly, it was at Mr. Schreyer's first Board meeting that the Board decided to ask for Chris's resignation. This apparently upset Mr. Schreyer and ultimately, I believe, resulted in Mr. Schreyer resigning from the Board.

Chris had also been acutely aware of the need to increase the annual fund. With the help of Tom Kelley, Director of Development, the annual fund had been increasing, albeit slowly.

Chris said, "A successful Annual Fund is absolutely crucial to the fiscal good health of this school."

This slow but steady increase in our fundraising was very encouraging to me as the Business Manager. Later, Joe Lucier ('50), Director of Development, Priscilla Lucier ('50) and Joe's brother, Fran Lucier ('45), Chairman of the Board's Development Committee, worked diligently to make significant increases in annual support. The raising of gifts, both for capital projects as well as for operating needs had been the nemesis of Williston almost from its founding.

From the Bulletin, Summer 1983, the headline read, "Headmaster Announces Resignation" and the article went on to say, "Christopher C. Corkery, Headmaster since 1979, startled the Williston Northampton School community when he announced at a faculty meeting on May 30 that he sent a letter of resignation to William B. Palmer ('49), President of the school's Board of Trustees, five days earlier.

"Mr. Corkery, who will continue to serve as Headmaster through the 1983- 84 academic year, said that, 'he felt that the time for a change was auspicious and that Williston Northampton was in an excellent posture in terms of faculty, budget, student recruitment, and curricular and extra-curricular offerings.' Noting that the essential steps for a successful capital campaign had been taken, Mr. Corkery said a new Head would be able to focus on that project and offered his expertise in making the transition year a smooth one." [66]

Chris Corkery's inference was quite correct, as the launching of a capital campaign was indeed one of the earlier tasks for the succeeding new Head of School, Denny Grubbs.

Being the head of a private school is a very challenging position, as the head is responsible to so many "bosses": parents, trustees, alumni, and faculty. And many of the issues are of the kind that set off emotional hot buttons. It is not difficult to read between the lines when a head of school resigns rather prematurely to realize something did not go as it should have.

Richard Gregory, a former well-respected and admired faculty member, wrote to me on August 6, 2005: "Chris Corkery, who very recently passed away, was an admirable headmaster who ran afoul of probably the worst Board we have ever known. When he sneezed, they kicked him—out." [67]

This feeling was shared by others, and my interpretation of what was happening was that some Trustees were hearing stories from biased school sources and drawing somewhat erroneous conclusions.

"Think big. Dream big. This school is so much finer than anyone around here seems to realize." —Chris Corkery

Selling of the Northampton School for Girls Campus

A School Merger Necessity

As far as the general public was concerned, the merger went very smoothly. Mr. Fuller, as Associate Head at WNS, was generally orchestrating the curriculum matters at WNS with the help of the faculty. Philips Stevens continued as the Head of WNS. Whether or not you had allegiance to either of the previous heads of school, it was obvious the merger ended the careers of these two heads, at the newly merged WNS. Both Stevens and Fuller submitted their resignations effective at the end of the school year, 1973.

On campus, the students, both the girls and boys were fortunately unaffected by these changes. However, there were many concerns in the adult community about how the boys and girls would get along. As a matter of fact, one of the primary reasons that the Whitaker – Bement building was constructed on the Williston campus was so the girls could have a place to escape from the boys and be alone with each other. This, by the way, really never happened—it became co-ed very quickly and functioned quite successfully as the new student center, a badly needed facility on the Williston campus.

A great deal of time had passed since the merger, and it was now time to really increase our efforts and deal with the sale of the campus of the Northampton School for Girls. This was a significant financial hardship and worry, especially for me. It was a substantial piece of property. A brochure for marketing the property was prepared by Nathan A. Fuller, Headmaster of NSFG.

The brochure described the property and showed pictures of the old houses:

1. 20 Acres of land
2. 14 sports playing fields
3. Beautiful Gardens
4. 11 fine old Victorian Homes
5. Full size gym 22,128 sq. ft.

Part of the NSFG's property was in the flood plain and included a very large dike designed to hold back the floodwaters from the Connecticut River. The school experienced serious floods in 1926 and 1936, with the most severe flooding from the 1938 hurricane.[68] This hurricane caused flooding all through the Northampton area. While this structure had a definite purpose, it was not something just anyone would want to own.

The NSFG Board formed a Property Committee to deal with all of the nuances of selling the campus.

The Property Committee Meeting Minutes of September 25, 1970, made several motions, some of which are as follows:[69]

1. The asking price would be $1,500,000.
2. They placed major ads in the Wall Street Journal, The New York Times, and The Christian Science Monitor.
3. The possibility of a split sale was discussed.
4. It was agreed that, if necessary, the Trustees would be prepared to hold the Northampton School for Girls property until the price was right.
5. Headmaster Fuller was appointed secretary.
6. The Secretary was asked to write a letter to Vincent Virgillio, a contact in the Department of Mental Health, indicating that our committee would make every effort to help him sell the property by exerting as much influence as we could on those whom he will have to contact.

About this time, the Commonwealth of Massachusetts was trying to phase out the large, institutional-style, state-operated mental health facilities, including the ones located in nearby Northampton and Belchertown. The "new" thinking in mental health was that a child would go to

Nate Fuller, Headmaster of Northampton School for Girls

a home-like facility and stay for a set period of time, i.e., 90 days, and then be discharged to live with the parent or in a small homelike facility. Whereas, in the old care scheme, it was common to commit a patient to the mental health facility where they would stay for the rest of their lives.

In October 1971, the Massachusetts Legislator passed a bill to buy the NSFG campus for a mental health facility. Everyone from NSFG, as well as the local mental health community, was delighted by this action. It was to be the event that would help the NSFG community to pay off some debts and make the merger fully happen. Soon thereafter though, the NSFG Board of Trustees was informed that even though the bill had passed the Legislature, no money had been appropriated to finalize the sale. It only approved the right to buy the property for a mental health facility. The vote appeared to be a political gesture to placate the mental health advocates. Needless to say, this information was very disappointing for both schools as well as the mental health community.

An Easthampton woman, Mary Brewer, who was the town accountant and known for her very ambitious involvement in town matters, was also deeply involved in local mental health groups. She had two sons who went to Williston, Alan, Class of 1962, and Michael, Class of 1964. Her son Alan may have had some mental health issues, perhaps explaining her passion for a new mental health facility on the NSFG campus. She worked tirelessly, trying to move this sale to a conclusion, so that at least part of the NSFG campus could become a facility to serve the mentally handicapped.

Albert H. Zabriskie, Acting Commissioner of Administration and Finance, [70] wrote to State Senator, Edward M. Kennedy, informing him, "Much work has gone into the planning and programming of this property by the Area Board, Commissioner Greenblatt, Peter Goldmark, Secretary Executive Office of Human Services and the Secretary of Administration & Finance, Robert L. Yasi."

The newly appointed WNS Headmaster, Robert A. Ward, then Dean of Students at Amherst College, also wrote on October 4, 1972 to his friend, The Honorable Edward M. Kennedy,[71] asking for his help. He commented, "I realize that the present state administration may not be readily responsive to interventions by those not of the 'in' party..."

It was very obvious that the sale of the campus was bogged down in

Massachusetts's politics. As time passed, it was extremely difficult for me to understand if anything involving the State would ever happen.

On May 18, 1973, I wrote the Prudential Committee of the WNS Board a memo concerning the sale. Below are some of the points I wrote about:

1. "As of last week, the State Real Estate and Review Commission reported they were in favor of the purchase. The papers reported a price of $600,000, but I have not been able to substantiate this figure."
2. "No one on our staff has sufficient knowledge of the communication channels or the real power points in the State administration."
3. "I have a person in mind, David Harrison, who has both the experience and knowledge to handle our negotiations. He is presently trying to determine the status of the deal and then will talk to us about a fee." Vinnie LoBello Sr. who worked in the business office, was very involved in state politics and knew Mr. Harrison as a well-known state lobbyist.
4. I also discussed why I thought the price needed to be reduced because of new unfavorable zoning regulations for the property, including identifying the wetlands.
5. "The average monthly cost to us to hold this property is increasing rapidly. This average monthly cost will reach $16,000 in July 1973, up from $8,600 a month in fiscal year 1971/72. This represents an average cost per student in 1973/74 of $481.00, which is 13 percent of a boarding student's tuition and 26 percent of a day student's tuition."

The school eventually hired the lobbyist, Attorney David E. Harrison, whom I previously recommended, to keep this project alive and to see that the right government people had the necessary information to help them support any opportunity to fund the purchase. His services were very costly, especially at a time when finances at the school were extremely limited.

I met every couple of months with David Harrison and never came away from those meetings feeling like anything was happening.

Enter College Church

I had been renting the NSFG gym to the pastor of a newly formed College Church, Reverend Paul MacVittie. His congregation was growing rapidly. We rented him the property for about 20 months. He and I talked frequently about the possibility of the College Church buying the gym and the adjacent Logan House. He liked to meet with me at 6:30 in the morning, usually at the local Norm's Dinner in Easthampton. He would start the meeting with a prayer, then try to negotiate a price to purchase only the gym. I explained to him that I would not be willing to sell the gym without having identified buyers for all of the other real estate parcels. Well, this man was an incredibly convincing individual, who worked tirelessly on this deal, and he eventually found buyers for all the properties. His efforts demonstrated both his conviction to his church's expansion and his ability to sell an idea. Remember that the school had voted to sell the property in 1970, and had hired real estate brokers and a state lobbyist, and countless hours had been invested by many other people, including myself, and we had failed to close a deal to sell the property.

The Hampshire Gazette said on January 19, 1974, in an article entitled, "All 12 NSG buildings may be sold within week," "Mrs. Brewer said that various groups, including the Children's Lobby, Children's Aid and Family Services, and the Association for Children, began pressuring state administrators in Boston yesterday to buy the property before it is sold to private investors. 'As far as we are concerned,' Mrs. Brewer said, 'the blame is to ride squarely on the Governor.' Mrs. Brewer said that she first learned of the possible sale of the former Northampton School for Girls Thursday morning, when Dunnington called her and said there was a 75 percent possibility that that the gymnasium would be sold to the church."

At last, there was a real possibility that the property would be sold, and a date was set for the buyers to meet in Florence, a little town just outside of Northampton. The meeting was in what appeared to be an unused storage room over a convenience store. It was a Saturday afternoon, January 19, 1974.

The buyers all showed up and I, all alone, somewhat nervously and full of anxiety, explained for all in attendance my conditions for the sale:

1. Every piece of property must be sold, including that infamous dike.
2. A 10 percent deposit of cash or check must be made today, on each piece of property purchased.
3. The closing date was to be March 20, 1974, at the Northampton Savings Bank, in downtown Northampton.
4. If any one buyer dropped out, or did not pay the balance owed, all sales were off.

This was a rather stressful moment for me, trying to make a $700,000, long-awaited deal to sell the 14 properties.

With masking tape, I taped up on the wall a property map, showing all the parcels, including the dike and wetlands. The church was first, giving me a deposit check for $40,000 and a promise to pay the balance, $360,000. I wrote a receipt and I remember how my hand was shaking with the stress and excitement of finally closing this deal. This process went along rather smoothly until the end. And, yes, the dike was not one of the properties that were marked as "sold" on my wall map.

This gave me some concern, because it really had to be sold, so I said, "Deals off! This dike must be sold."

I knew that owning a dike could be a big problem in the future, as it had legal restrictions with it, i.e., maintenance. After some very interesting discussion by the various parties present, someone agreed to buy the dike. This whole process—the meeting, the discussions—were very civil, all the buyers were respectful of each other, and all parties showed a sincere interest in the future of the College Church.

This news of the sale of the NSFG to private individuals leaked out, and the local press considered it big news, as the State did not buy any of the properties, as was expected.

A headline from the January 20, 1974 *Springfield Republican*[72] reads, "Former School for Girls Won't Be Sold to State." That same article said, "While local citizen groups have indicated that they will pressure legislators into initiating eminent domain proceedings, Dunnington discounted this possibility as 'highly unlikely.'"

The news was hot, with stories blaming the State for not acting and for dragging their feet all this time.

Again, the *Daily Hampshire Gazette* on January 21, 1974 said, "NSFG plan fails...In our opinion, The Sargent (Governor) administration is going to have some explaining to do now that the proposed sale of the Northampton School for Girls property to the State for a mental health center has fallen through. After a delay of more than two years, the owner of the complex—the Williston Northampton School in Easthampton—has decided to sell the buildings and land on Pomeroy Terrace to private interests. It is surprising that the school has been so patient with the state bureaucracy for so long. The incredible delays that plagued this project may be without peril even in a state bureaucracy that is not noted for its efficiency. The legislator approved a bill that would create a state mental health center at the NS(F)G property more than two and a half years ago and voted $1 million in special funds to carry out the project. It was widely agreed by specialists in the field of mental illness that the plan for NS(F)G had great merit. There were long delays in having the buildings appraised at the outset and more recently there were greater foot dragging in agreeing on a final price with the owners."

In still another headline by the *Daily Hampshire Gazette* dated January 21, 1974, "Angry reaction in wake of sale of NSG," the article reads, "All 12 of the former Northampton School for Girls buildings sold to private interests Saturday, despite a vote of the State Legislator more than two years ago to buy the property. Dunnington added that he thinks the private buyers plan to use the property for apartments and single-family homes...Benjamin Rici, president of the friends of Belchertown State School (a mental health facility), called the weekend sale of the property 'a tremendous blow' to progress for the mentally ill and retarded citizens in the area."

The Daily Hampshire Gazette on Wednesday, January 23, 1974, headlines, "State official arrives hoping to save NS(F)G buildings for a health care facility," which reads, "The 20-acre, 12-building property was sold to four local real estate investors and to the College Church last Saturday for $700,000, despite a vote by the legislature more than two years ago to buy the land for a mental health facility."

Before the College Church bought the property, a very strange thing happened to me during this rather desperate process, when the President of the Williston Board of Trustees, Frederick K. Daggett ('25), called me and said he had some connections that might help sell the property to the State of Massachusetts. He gave me only an address, no company name, in Providence, Rhode Island. I dutifully traveled to Providence, went to the address provided, and then to the fifth floor, in a building located in the center of the city, which was a law office. There was a group of approximately seven or eight people, including the Massachusetts Secretary of Human Services and a representative of the Governor's Office of Massachusetts. There was some discussion and a rather clear agreement by the Massachusetts State people to look into the matter of the State buying the NSFG property. After the meeting, I went downstairs and across the street to meet a friend, Christopher Corkery, at a bank. I told him why I was at the office.

He said, "George, do you know whose office you were in?"

I said, "Not really."

He then said, "That is Raymond Patriarca's office, and he is the head of the Patriarca crime family and the mob don." He said, "George, do not mess with them, it can be really bad."

"'Really bad,' you mean like concrete boots at the bottom of the harbor?"

I was somewhat upset by this information and when I got back to campus, I called Ted Daggett and told him what happened.

He said, "I thought that was possible."

Thanks Ted!

In my position, I was always very concerned about the "town/gown" relationship, especially as there were many important people in town behind the NSFG campus becoming a mental health facility, as well as the fact that the facility was being proposed to help children in need. Fortunately, for WNS, all the news reports placed the blame for the sale going to private parties squarely on the Legislature and the State bureaucracy.

It sometimes seemed to me like there was an uncontrollable fire back at home while I was dodging reporters and renegotiating the Saturday deals. First, I got a call from one of the buyers and he said, "The State wants to buy one of my buildings at the same price as I paid you, do you care?"

I said, "No, I only want the agreed-upon money at the closing."

Then another investor called and had the same deal, only for two properties.

Later, I was at a Board of Trustees meeting at Babson College, where I was a Trustee. The meeting was on the Babson campus, in Wellesley, Massachusetts. The meeting room was on a lower level of the Commons building, in a walkout area where a road came down a hill for the dining hall trucks to make deliveries. I was looking out the window, and I saw two State Police cruisers pull down the drive right near the window where I sat. They parked, and then two large black limousine cars pulled in with State Troopers opening the doors. Upon seeing this impressive show of power, I thought we must be having an important State dignitary here to be our evening dinner speaker. Soon thereafter, someone pounded loudly on the door outside of our meeting room; it was not just a friendly knock, but a pound. I still did not connect these two happenings. Jesse Putney, the Babson College Treasurer, and a no-nonsense kind of guy, went to answer the door.

The people outside the door tried to come into the meeting room, and Jesse firmly said, "No. Who do you want to speak to?"

They said, "George Dunnington. We are here from the Governor's Office."

The entire meeting was halted while Jesse came over to me and quietly asked, "Do you want to talk to them?"

I replied, "No."

He told them they were not welcome and closed the door. I am sure the other Trustees present must have wondered what Dunnington was up to, because of all this attention. I watched the State officials all drive away. I wondered to myself, will the sale of the NSFG campus ever end?

As was customary, on a cold winter evening, in our house on the campus, my wife, Ann, my children, Susan, Amy, and Geordie, and the two students who lived with us were peacefully playing 33 RPM records on the turntable by a cozy fire in the fireplace. I kind of remember it was a *Johnny Mathis* album. Suddenly, there was a loud knock at our front door.

I wondered who this could be, especially at this hour, and so I asked my daughter, "Susan will you please go to the door and see who it is?"

When she attempted to open the door, it was pushed open hard, and three people came barging into my house with a very bright TV light on and a large camera on the shoulder of one person.

The reporter shoved her microphone into my face said to me, "Mr. Dunnington, tells us why you did not sell the NSFG campus to the State Mental Health Department."

I politely said, "I will talk to you tomorrow. Please leave."

The Great State of Massachusetts Performs

Again, I thought to myself, could this possibly get any more upsetting? Well, the simple answer was, yes!

Richard B. Covell was on the Board of Trustees of the School and was also President of the Northampton Savings Bank. When I told him about the closing and the exchanging of checks and cash, he offered his bank as a meeting place. He also agreed to clear checks for me. All the parties showed up, as well as the press, and also the school attorney, William E. Dwyer ('20). He was an elderly man; you could describe him as "very old school." He sat there, and I do not think he ever said a word as papers and checks were passed back and forth. Also, the State had sent an attorney to the meeting, looking very unprofessional and rather shabby. He told me he was authorized by the State to buy a couple of the NSFG properties. He had previously talked to the people who had made the 10 percent down payment and had agreed to pay the balance owed on the properties at this meeting. I had agreed to this switch of buyers prior to the meeting. I did stipulate that no one could profit by the change from the original buyers, unless it was WNS.

This change of buyers involved me giving back a couple of deposits and then making out a bill of sale to the Commonwealth of Massachusetts.

A good friend and a Williston graduate Class of '46, Gene Berman, and a prominent Springfield attorney had advised me not to take a check from the State of Massachusetts until I was sure it would clear the bank. This seemed to be a strange bit of advice, especially since I always thought the State was rather powerful and good.

Well, when the State's attorney handed me the checks, I said, "I need to see if Mr. Covell, the Bank's President, can determine that these checks are funded."

Upon saying this, you would have been amazed at the cameras flashing at me as the reporters asked me questions. They said, "What do you mean you're not accepting a check from our State Treasury?"

They were clearly implying that I was a terrible person for doing this. We all sat around and waited, a little uncomfortably, for several minutes.

And finally, Mr. Covell returned to say, "These checks are not funded."

So, what my friend Gene Berman had warned me might happen, had happened. These checks were worthless, or in the vernacular, they bounced.

We all waited, rather exasperated, for an hour or more, before the State's attorney returned, saying he had been able to get the money transferred to the proper account. Again, being a little reluctant to just accept these checks as presented, Mr. Covell again went downstairs in the bank and determined that they were now valid.

Following all the commotion of the closing, a funny, but rather sad story happened. After most people had left the Bank. I said, to the shabby-looking State's attorney, "I have, for your safekeeping, four large shopping bags full of keys to all the buildings and rooms on the NSFG campus."

You may be able to imagine what a mess that was—there was no campus key system; a key was made uniquely for each lock as needed.

I went on to say, "If you need help in figuring out which key goes where, I will be glad to arrange for someone to help you—or someone you designate?"

He simply took the four bags from me and put them straight into the trash bucket. He could not care less. I was absolutely shocked at his actions, knowing the cost of re-keying and the importance of being able to open doors.

Then I said, "I have a fantastic night watchman, who is a local farmer and looks like Paul Bunyan. I have never had as much as a window broken in the last several years while he has been our night watchman. I think, it would be very important for you to make sure the State's properties are properly protected."

He replied, "No thanks, that is not my job."

As if on cue, shortly thereafter, thieves broke into one of the recently purchased State buildings and stole all the copper pipe and fixtures. So sad!

Well, this really did close out a very difficult and strenuous time for both the schools. But the sale cleared the air of some distasteful rumors. It was especially helpful to me for several reasons; first, it relieved me of having to deal with the numerous associated real estate tasks; secondly, it meant that I did not have to worry about maintaining and protecting the property; thirdly, it eliminated many of the necessary associated expenses, such as heat and insurance for the property and debt services related to the mortgages.

I made a final report concerning the finances of the sale of the Northampton School for Girls Campus to the Prudential Committee on March 20, 1974.

Sale of Northampton School Campus Reconcilliation of Closing Money March 20, 1974[73]

Selling Price			$	700,000.00
Deposits Received	$	70,000.00		
Deposits Returned		(5,000.00)		65,000.00
			$	**635,000.00**
Paid at Closing				
Mortgages Paid	$	207,770		
Fees		45		
Interest		1,116		
Taxes Escrow		4,922	$	213,853
Net Cash Received				421,146
			$	**635,000**

All our debts related to the sale of the NSFG Campus were paid off and the net proceeds were entered into the WNS Plant Fund. It was a long, arduous struggle beginning in 1971 when the State Legislature voted to buy the campus until 1974, when I was able to actually deposit the sale checks.

Admissions—A Critical Story at a Critical Time

ENROLLMENT, WHICH TRANSLATES TO TUITION, IS THE LIFEBLOOD of most independent secondary schools. I believe most people do not think of that when they talk about a school and its admission office. In many schools, such as Williston, the income from tuition is approximately 70 percent of total resources, a very big part of its annual budget.

An old business adage says that when sales are heading down, you should increase your advertising budget, not reduce it. Schools often do not follow that sage advice. Instead, in bad times, schools often trim all expenses, including the admission department budget of personnel and advertising. That is exactly the wrong thing to do. School admissions are the same thing as product sales. When sales slow, it's time to invest in the promotion and the product to make it better, not worse. It appeared to me that while budgets at Williston got tighter and tighter and enrollment was falling, nothing was done to enhance the admission office.

There are many factors that can make recruiting students very difficult. Unfortunately, schools have no control over at least two of those factors: economic recessions and birthrates.

Over the years, Williston Seminary, Williston Academy, Northampton School for Girls, and Williston Northampton School all shared one enormous problem: trying to constantly maintain their enrollment level over time. Real harm and suffering was felt by all those schools when their enrollment dropped. Going clear back to the founding of Williston Seminary, there clearly was a history of this phenomenon.

During the period when Samuel Williston was active in the running of Williston Seminary, (1841 to 1874), he personally covered most of the deficits resulting from lower enrollment from his own funds. A report from the Trustees in 1862 "shows that a crisis is imminent." The report gave, as a possible reason, "The depressed state of the country, owing to the civil war…An examination of the catalogues for the last fifteen years (in that time period) shows a diminution of English scholars of about 70 percent. This decrease was ascribed to the increase of public high schools, normal schools and scientific departments in colleges. The local causes named were <u>reduction of the number of teachers as an economical expedient, the lack of appropriations for apparatus, etc.</u>" [74] (The underlines are the author's) The cost reductions clearly indicate that cutting budgets for faculty and equipment is not always the best way to build enrollment.

In July 1886, Rev. William Gallagher became the sixth principal of Williston Seminary. He also was the first principal "to occupy the Williston's house, and henceforth, this homestead became the residence of the principal, in accordance with Mrs. Williston's bequest (the head of school presently resides in the Richmond House just across the street from the Homestead.)[75]

When Dr. Gallagher arrived, he found a condition which he did not create but was expected to improve (that sounds like a very familiar situation that faced Head Robert Ward in 1973). "Mistakes had been made by those who had the management of the affairs of the school. Mistakes had been made here and loss resulted. But the school suffered more from misjudgments than it suffered from mistakes. Mistakes can be repaired. Misjudgments persist."[76]

"For the time the school was continued on hope, and the drafts on the bank of hope were large, endangering credit."[77] The "drafts" of the 1960s were also frightening, and were likely providing the working capital necessary to function. Loans such as these were not, in fact, working capital, and the school could not pay these debts until the mid 70s, a real burden to the Ward/Dunnington administration.

When Headmaster Robert Ward and I started to dig deeper into the school's condition, I believe there were, in the 1960s, many misjudgments and mistakes that had been made. Also, I could not find any evidence of a real plan for the school's management to follow that would increase enrollment or increase gifts. And perhaps one of the biggest misjudgments was the virtual elimination of funds to establish a competent internal labor force, one of the qualities that could help clean and repair the buildings and the equipment. This had a direct impact on the admission office's attempt to sell the school to prospective students. Why the Board of Trustees was not made aware of this significant depletion of assets I do not know. Perhaps they were but did not have the finances to help, nor did they try to seek gifts to change this mistake.

It was not until the Northampton School for Girls (NSFG) Board merged with the Williston Board in 1972 that this terrible mess was brought to the fore. The Board finally became fully aware of the effect the physical plant had on recruiting new students.

These needs were driven home to me almost immediately and I fully accepted that challenge, for I also appreciated the importance of the plant facilities in the admission process.

In 1972, Headmaster Philips Stevens asked a member of the French department, Tom Evans, to be Director of Admission. Tom was young, energetic, and always had a wonderful, uplifting attitude. Tom hired Debbie Hayward as his assistant, who focused on the girls' admission. She was also young and attractive and very welcoming. Finishing out the team was their administrative assistant, "Secretary" Barbara Ouelette. It was a pleasure for me to work with this team. I fully understood the importance of this office and what it meant to the success of the school and was anxious to provide whatever help I could.

In preparing this recollection, I wrote to Tom and asked, "What was your worst nightmare when showing the school to perspective students? Encountering the longhaired hippies, or showing the run-down buildings?"

Tom replied, "Both and more. It was a permissive time, e.g., we [the school policy] allowed smoking outdoors, even for freshmen! Every building entry was littered with cigarette butts, and half the time to get in I had to part the sea of grungy looking kids in hoodies, puffing away, in a mist of smoke. 'Send us your kids, so he/she can look just like these studious kids!' Or the Saturday a.m. dorm tour, with the residual smell of the pot the night before. I went to Bob [Headmaster Ward] about all this, saying, 'I need a school I can sell to kids, and parents, too! And I need a faculty who when I encounter them on tour, will take a few very positive moments to extoll the school's virtues, and not snarl at me and say they're just too busy.'"

Tom went on to comment on campus tours, "Every single family got probably three hours of my time on campus, and I didn't enlist lots of kids to help with tours. I didn't use student guides as much as most schools did/do. Why? Because I knew that what we could encounter on tours, I might be able to handle more diplomatically than a sixteen-year-old kid. So, when I did use kids for tours, like Roger [Roger Maroni, '74, an unusually dedicated, helpful student], I picked them really carefully."

I personally attended most of the financial aid meetings. Unlike some schools that could say they met all accepted students' needs, our aid budget was very limited. This committee was very competently headed by Ken Heath ('56), the Day Student Dean and French teacher. I was on the committee, for I had the financial background to help in the decision-making. And perhaps because Wilmot Babcock, the Business Manager, was previously in charge of financial aid awards. Babcock was also the coach of the swim team, which, as I have previously noted, was his first love. Earlier, I reflected on mistakes and misjudgments of the past. Mr. Babcock was guilty of both. In that position, he recruited swimmers, providing them with financial aid whether they fully qualified for it or not. Most private schools did not, as a policy, grant athletic scholarships. They followed a national financial aid application form to determine the recommended amount of aid. Babcock seemingly did not employ the national financial aid model—a bad misjudgment.

I personally know this, for at one of our financial aid meetings, Ken Heath brought to the meeting a swimmer's aid application and said, "He does not qualify for any aid, and he has a big grant."

I was asked to call the parent of the swimmer and explain that the student/swimmer did not qualify for any money.

He, the boy's father, rather forcibly replied, "My finances are none of your business! My son got a swimming scholarship. He was one of the best in New Hampshire."

I cannot say for sure, but I believed he was not going to send his son back to Williston if he had to pay the prescribed tuition. The Financial Aid Committee rationalized that it was certainly not the student's fault, and maybe not the father's either. We ultimately gave an award so the student could finish his senior year at Williston.

Tom Evans said, "People blamed me for the decline of the swimming program, when the real reason was that we finally got honest about giving out aid."

Again, in trying to fine tune all the things that helped us enroll students, we listened carefully to what Tom and Debbie had to say. One of the things that was mostly out of our control was the school's location. At that time the Williston campus was situated just north of the most run-down part of Easthampton.

Tom said, "WNS is a great school that always performed way over its head, but wasn't seen that way. *Half* of my admissions battle was the reality that Route 141 from 91 came in through the seedy side of town, past the Majestic theatre, a failed movie theater then showing adult movies— the titles were in bold type on the marquee right on the main street leading to Williston and the bars! Would *you* send your kid here?"

The town has changed dramatically for the better since then, becoming a haven for artists with very attractive places to live.

Another change that Tom made was to try to discourage weekend interviews. He said, "Also in my last two years, I discouraged weekend visits whenever I could. I had done an informal study of enrollments over the prior four years, and discovered that the majority of struggling or expelled kids had come to interview and tour on weekends. My conclusion: they came from families where dad's job and convenience came first, not the actual match of kid's needs to school's program. So, my message to parents was, come during the week when you can see us in action and really feel the pulse of the school. So occasionally, families came to *us* on the weekday and saw Deerfield [an elite boys' school not far from Williston] or others on the weekend, putting *them* at the disadvantage. I do think that improved the quality and commitment of both kids and parents."

Following Tom Evans as Director of Admission was another French teacher, Bob Blanchette, who in 1976, at the urging of Headmaster Ward, took the job. I wrote to Bob Blanchette to get his comments on his time working in admissions.

He responded, "I had been at Williston for four years, had no admission experience, and could not imagine how I would make such a transition so quickly. I knew the school was struggling financially and the enrollment had been dropping, but I had lots of respect for Tom Evans who was hard-working, personable, and perfect for the admission job. I believed he was doing the best anyone could possibly do under the circumstances. I was scared to take on that responsibility, but Bob Ward convinced me I could do it. I trusted Bob, so I said yes. "

Debbie Hayward worked with Bob for the first year, which was very helpful, and when she left, he hired Anne Duncan Ritchie in 1977.

Bob said, "Anne turned out to be a star. Barbara Ouellette [stayed on] as our secretary/receptionist. She was excellent as a hostess to all the families who visited, but it was impossible for her to do both jobs. Anne and I came in evenings and weekends to catch up on correspondence to inquiries and interviews." He went on to say, "We could not travel as much as we should have…"

Knowing how industrious Anne and Bob were makes me wonder why we did not add staff to the office, as I believe it would have helped to recruit a few more students. Bad judgment? More likely, it's quite possible that we couldn't spare the money—who were we fooling?

Bob Blanchette and Tom Evans expressed similar issues confronting the admissions office. Bob went on to say, "Other challenges included the long, beat-up corridors of Mem [Memorial] dorm, the smokers who would fill the entry to the dining hall on rainy or cold days. Also, the financial aid budget was limited when I started in 1976; we had only three boarding girls and five boarding boys in the ninth grade."

On a positive note, Bob says, "But despite all the challenges, I believe we convinced a lot of families that we had a faculty that genuinely cared about the kids, a curriculum that was diverse, interesting, and challenging, the courage and talent to offer a very impressive array of courses in winter session, an administration that was personable, interacted well with students and visitors, and was committed to improving the school, and a student body that liked being at the school and supported one another in good times and bad."

Bob Blanchette continued, "Without a doubt, the most enjoyable part of my admissions days was the Friday afternoon financial aid meetings—Anne, Ken Heath (head of the financial aid committee), you (your author), and me, and Bob with a bag of chips and at least one six pack of beer. After a long week filled with a wide array of responsibilities, those meetings offered a release, a chance to take a deep breath and laugh a little."

It is easy to fail to realize how much pressure is on a conscientious worker when she/he knows their job is critical in the success of the school.

Bob said, "I woke up every day feeling the weight of the future of the school on my shoulders, worried about succeeding. It was not true, but I believe that edge, that fear of failure, kept me motivated and sharp no matter how difficult the challenges may have seemed. I am really proud of what we accomplished over those five admissions years and the many that preceded them and followed them. Bob Ward was a courageous, forward-thinking leader, and he relied on you [George Dunnington] to get the school back on firm financial footing. You did that, and left the school far better off than it had been in 1971, when it was teetering on the edge of a cliff. Numerous other schools closed their doors in the early 70s, but Williston gathered together a group of intrepid individuals who bonded, survived, and eventually prospered. This is quite a legacy."

I also wrote to Anne Duncan Ritchie, Director of Admissions for Girls, seeking her comments on her time, 1977 to 1982, at Williston.

She wrote, "WNS was a different place than it is now in terms of recognition in the independent school world. We were constantly up against other schools which were better known, more 'legacy' oriented than we were, and showed off fancier buildings and athletic facilities. We never had enough money…in spite of this, I loved our financial aid meetings. George, Bob, (Ken) and I would sit in my office and talk about kids, money, no money…which kid? How much money? Please, George, we need more. Lots of schools had the same problem—lots of schools still do. We had the problem *and* we had humor." Anne goes on to say, "One of our biggest challenges during this time was becoming known in the 'feeder school' world…We targeted those schools aggressively…By the time 1982 rolled around, I was quite sure we were finally *on the map*."[78]

The gauntlet was thrown and landed squarely on my desk – the campus must be made to look better. And, as quickly as possible. I knew

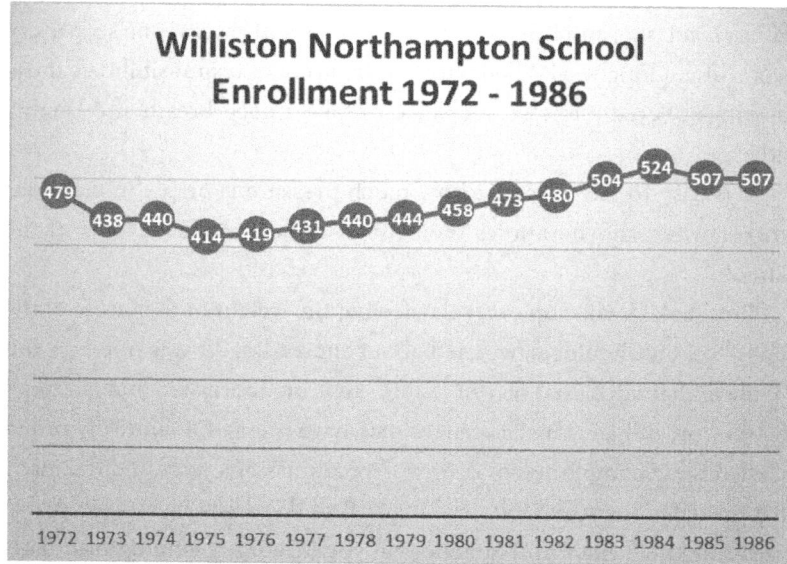

that from the beginning and with very limited resources, we worked extremely hard every minute of every day to help the admission people and the school to present itself in a better way.

As time went on, things changed, hopefully for the better. The atmosphere on campus evolved. We did away with student smoking where it could be seen. Campus buildings improved bit by bit. With every passing year, new students arrived with less of the 1970s tie-dyed look and Vietnam War era mindset. It took a long time for that to wear off, but it finally did. Things on campus became more preppy—a bit more formal. More of what most protective parents were looking for in a boarding school.

While Williston was changing its image and the admission office was enrolling stronger students, the enrollment numbers held steady, showing a 5.8 percent increase from 1972 to 1986. But most importantly, the quality of the new students was increasing and thus making admission to Williston more competitive.

Early Alumni Issues

I HAVE CHOSEN TO MAKE A FEW COMMENTS ABOUT THE SAD STATE IN which we found the alumni functions at WNS in 1972. Hopefully, these reflections will give the reader an appreciation of the pressing challenges we had ahead of us in this very critical department,

In 1972, Westcott E. S. Moulton ('27) was the alumni secretary and an enthusiastic cheerleader for the school. It seemed to me in the earlier days of private schools and colleges, alumni secretaries were mostly interested in "glad-handing" with alumni, not doing much in the way of trying to press for financial support. This old-style alumni secretary might have been helpful in schools and colleges who had already developed a "habit of giving." In many wealthy schools, giving was virtually a tradition. That simply was not the case at Williston. And, to make matters even worse, the alumni files were of poor quality; the information was incomplete and graduates were missing from the records. Hence, it was difficult for us to even contact our alumni.

An example of what appeared to me to be questionable reporting of alumni giving is a report of Mr. Moulton's in the 1972 Bulletin: "Alumni contributions, amounting to $137,971 from 1671 alumni, achieved a participation rate of 57.8 percent. Although participation was down for the second consecutive year compared to our high of 76.5 percent in 1968, it was a very fine showing. The national average for alumni participation in colleges and schools is still below 30 percent."[79]

The reader should know that it is, in my opinion, virtually impossible to achieve a giving participation rate of 57.8 percent, let alone one as high as 76.5 percent. Our findings indicate the alumni files were "doctored" by eliminating alumni that were not giving. These numbers were great to show, however, I wondered who would believe them besides Philips Stevens.

To cite another report from the Development Office they reported, "Annual Alumni Fund (unrestricted) gifts of $40,712." Unfortunately, there was no report on percent of giving. The report also said, "...alumni annual giving this year (1973-74) was slightly less than the previous year."[80] In reading several reports from the Alumni Office they often say, "annual giving was slightly less the previous year." Hence, your author was getting on a seriously sinking ship.

Charlotte Turgeon joined the alumni office at the time of the merger (1972) as the Associated Director of Development, coming from a similar position at NSFG (Northampton School for Girls).

In her role at Williston she had two primary functions. The first was to help in the alumni office, especially to try to update the contacts with the girls/alumnae from the Northampton School for Girls.

This was a very critical task as the NSFG records also were not complete—not by deliberate action, I feel, but because of lack of adequate staff. Also, with a significant change to an old school with lots of tradition, a number of the women had become disenchanted by the merger. Secondly, she was to assist Headmaster Robert Ward (a single man) with his necessary entertaining for Williston.

Charlotte knew Mr. Ward from his Amherst College days when he was a student there, as was her son, and also when he was the dean of students. Charlotte's husband, King Turgeon, was the head of the French department at Amherst College for many years.

In reading my memoirs you will note from Williston's founding in 1841, Williston and Amherst College had close ties, especially with teachers and administrators, and in this episode the tradition continues.

While Philips Stevens was head of Williston, he held some alumni meetings, but toward the end of his tenure the meetings seemed to have dwindled in number as well as in attendance.

Wes Moulton continued in the alumni office when Robert St. George assumed the position of head of the alumni relations office. Again, there was much fence mending to be done. Some alumni were definitely not in favor of the merger, Some of the women felt Williston, the "gruff" boy's school, was going to just swallow up the girls' school with all its special, lady-like customs. Mr. St. George was a longtime history teacher at Williston. He was perfect for the job at that time in the school's history. He had a very calm demeanor, was well spoken, and, perhaps most importantly, he seemingly could remember the names of nearly all the students/alumni of his long tenure.

Bob Ward, Head of School, was also a very thoughtful and calming person, an excellent speaker, and a person who never showed an unpleasant side. This combination of leaders was exactly what was needed to try to heal the wounds created by the merger and the divisiveness that was generated by the sudden retirement of Headmaster Philips Stevens.

Mr. Stevens' many years as head of Williston made him a very popular head of school.

We immediately put a huge, but humble effort into attempting to reinvigorate the interests of the alumni, men and women. Because of severe financial limitations, we focused on nearby major areas of alumni concentrations. These cities included NYC, Boston, Washington, and Philadelphia. In spite of our attempts to get the word out about the meetings, the turnout was less than encouraging, but we did make a few good connections. And we persevered!

Our alumni parties were wholeheartedly planned on a shoestring. Our call for help was enthusiastically answered by the staff and faculty all joining in to help. Because of the budget, these trips were, whenever possible, made in one day—no expensive overnights. The faculty that came along were extremely commendable to endure this stressful program, and they did it truly for the good of the school. Some of our most beloved teachers—Jack (Doc) Gow, our highly regarded biology teacher; Ellis Baker ('51), a dedicated theatre and English teacher; Dick Gregory, outstanding costume designer, English, and fine arts teacher; Glenn Swanson ('64), better known as Swanee, a favorite history teacher; and Karin O'Neil, teacher and administrator are the names that come immediately to mind. They were also favorite teachers among the alumni/ae. Our mode of transportation was the school's rather old and uncomfortable athletic vans. The onboard crew, in addition to Headmaster Ward, Bob St. George, Charlotte Turgeon, and myself, could accommodate six more faculty. This trip was always a little stressful—actually very stressful to me. I was a worrier; it was part of my job.

I recall, on one particular ride to NYC, I asked Charlotte, "May I see the list of expected attendees?"

I wanted this so I could be prepared to meet and greet our guess. She gave it to me, and I started reading it, then was slightly surprised said, "Charlotte, I did not know Bill Williams ('45) was in the NYC area?"

He in fact did not live in the city. Charlotte had brought the wrong list of attendees! Charlotte was a great trouper; she was often trying to do to many things, and this often meant organization was certainly not her strong suit.

Charlotte Turgeon, in her other role as Bob Ward's personal party planner, on the road or on campus, became enormously helpful in this period of explaining to the alumni/ae and parents the benefits of the merger.

She was also a real help to the school in her other role of being a highly recognized professional cookbook writer and chef, specializing in French and Italian cuisines. She did give all functions a special touch of class with her exceptional appetizers, also saving us lots of money. Charlotte made all the hors d'oeuvres for the evening in the Headmaster's House's very dated kitchen. Yes, this was a lot of work, but Charlotte never complained.

As an example of our frugality, when we went to NYC, I rented two adjoining rooms in a hotel, where we could hold our function with the alumni. We brought all the refreshments (wine and hard liquor) packed in our suitcases—our "pretend" overnight luggage! This always made me a bit nervous, bringing alcohol to our room and not buying it through the hotel as, I believe, was the expected thing to do. And, of course in NYC, the bellhops always wanted to help and always wanted a tip. This they made abundantly clear to we who preferred to be our own bellhops.

Yes, I felt very guilty, but not so much so that I wanted to buy the beverages from the hotel.

It was always very uplifting when, in addition to a few other alumni, some of our more involved and dedicated Trustees would attend. One event I recall was attended by Dan Cain ('64), Bill Palmer ('49), Bob Tullis, a parent of three students, and Guy Palmer ('53), all very successful people and impressive leaders in business. After we had a very pleasant evening talking with the ten to fifteen alumni, it was late and we were all starving. We had not eaten a real meal all day.

With Charlotte's national reputation among the restaurant community, she volunteered to see if she could get us a reservation for dinner at a well-known Italian Restaurant. She made a call only to discover the restaurant had closed for the evening. She then identified herself and talked to the owner. He immediately responded and invited us all over for dinner. That was very impressive to me, as it was extremely gracious of the restaurant owner to open for us—for Charlotte. Since French and Italian cooking were her specialties, the owner was honored to have her eat at his place. It was excellent food and a fitting reward for our long, hard day's work. I especially enjoyed these scrumptious dinners, as I always asked Charlotte to order for me. She did all the ordering in Italian, and since I did not speak any Italian, when the dinner came out it was truly a surprise—and always very delicious.

Our ride back to campus was very late and, on a full stomach, made for easy sleeping. My recollection was that Bob St. George, bless his soul, did most of the driving—thank goodness!

We did this low-budget form of spreading the word and introducing the newly merged schools, as well as our new Headmaster, Robert Ward, for a few years. At the same time, the Headmaster was seeking ways to upgrade the whole alumni operation. In addition to the traditional, basic alumni operations, fundraising and development became an important emphasis. To accomplish this, he searched for a person with experienced leadership—and he also increased the office staff.

The turn-around began with the arrival of Donald Lightfoot, Class of 1966. He left his college, Washington and Jefferson, where he had been involved in the admission office and the alumni development office. In January 1977, Don became Director of Development and worked with the associates already in place, Dan Griffin and Charlotte Turgeon.

While this is but one short story of how we were trying to turn around the alumni office and its functions it certainly illustrates the phrase, "you have to start somewhere."

I hope you can see some of the hardships we endured, and perhaps get a chuckle reading of our adventure to the big city. Most of this "happening" for me must have been in the fine print of my job description.

Williston Northampton School Health Services

YOU MAY ASK WHY THE FORMER BUSINESS MANAGER WOULD include a story about the "Infirmary" in his history at Williston. I believe the fresh, more up-to-date professional health practices marked a significant turning point in the delivery of student health.

When I first arrived on campus, to increase my understanding of the school I investigated every part of campus life. I went to the "infirmary" and talked to the nurses about how they handle student issues. This practice I was told about: "If a student had any personal medical problem, the nurses called home." There was no involvement of the student—no privacy.

While at Amherst College, their College Health Center decided to join with the University of Massachusetts Student Health Services. This decision significantly upgraded and expanded the medical skill sets available to Amherst students without a corresponding cost increase. From this experience at Amherst College, I learned from the doctors, "we want students to feel free to come to the health center for any reason. And they should expect confidentiality and compassionate care." That was simply a concept that, at Williston, was not fully appreciated or practiced. My wife, Ann, was also a RN at UMass, and this connection was very informative and helpful to me. Almost immediately, I started to upgrade the health services. In addition to the dated healthcare services of the nursing staff, the building was, not unlike the other campus buildings, very run-down and unwelcoming—not comforting.

The "Infirmary" was under the direction of Dr. Henry Donias, a member of the Williston Class of 1924 and parent of two graduates. He reported to the Business Manager, Mr. Babcock, my predecessor. "Doc," as he was affectionately known, had his private practice in his house just across the street from the campus. He faithfully served many faculty members and I do not believe he sent many bills for his services. Ann eventually became co-director of the Health Center. She told me, "Dr. Donias was known to be an excellent diagnostician, and this was of great benefit to the Williston students' well-being."

The nurses in 1972 had served many dedicated years at Williston and were nearing retirement. Interesting to note, there were many rumors about how an athletic team went to the nurses regularly and received vitamins and special attention. I confronted the doctor about this, and he confessed to this practice and noted it was his boss Mr. Babcock who asked him to do this for his infamous swim team's success. This "special" treatment was not something I felt was appropriate, but fortunately, I did not take any action against the doctor, as he was a loyal alumnus, a parent, and a most dedicated school doctor.

I was lucky to very quickly employ a nurse who believed in this more up-to-date way to deliver medical services to the students. The new nurse also confirmed, "Doc had great diagnostic talents and loved working at the school." The health center became a very important part of the overall school program, offering many services and reaching out to the students.

I heard stories about how students, in the past, had found themselves or friends in a dilemma—for example, drinking too much alcohol. The action pursued by the student's friends was often more in response to a school rule. Rules ranged in severity, up to and including dismissal. So, the health and well-being of the student was not always considered first, and thus the action was not always in the best interest of the student. This possibility led me to let it be known that in situations of this nature, student(s) could call me and no one would get into trouble. This happened rarely, but one time I did get a call telling me a student was intoxicated and passed out down the hill behind Sawyer House, a dormitory on the Main Street campus. When I went there, the ground was covered with snow. The student was freezing cold and non-responsive. I struggled to bring her up the frozen hillside, and I brought her home to Pitcher House where my wife, Ann, decided to take her immediately to the health center. It took us a while to bring her temperature up. This clearly could have been a life-threatening situation, had a student not made that critical call.

From a "Take Two Aspirin" Philosophy to a Total Person Care Health Center

The philosophy of the Health Center was known to promote good health, physical and emotional, with an emphasis on education.[81] For the first few years of my tenure as Business Manager, the "Infirmary" continued to report to me. I was fortunate to engage a nurse, Heidi Bruingaus, RN. She supported and practiced the philosophy of total care and education. It was a very stressful position, living in the building and being on duty for way too many hours. For sure, there should have been more nurses to do the health-related nursing that was truly required. After losing a few more very good nurses, we entered a rapid improvement of the health services when Liz Blanchette, RN, became our nurse in charge. She lived in the building with her husband, Bob Blanchette, our Director of Admission. He was a most dedicated supporter of Williston. Ann Dunnington, RN, and Pat Davy, RN, both worked with Liz until she left in 1977.

In 1978, Ann and Pat started a whole new health care concept.

Pat wrote, "We changed it to Health Services so that we could educate the students on their health and how to care for it, and treat the total person, not just the physical but the emotional and spiritual." When I asked Pat about the physical facilities, she said, "We changed the concept to include a more relaxing environment and to that end we had areas to study, rest, or stay overnight if need be. Students felt safe and welcomed, and that was missing in the infirmary model."[82]

Each year, Health Services became a more important part of the life of our students. With the support of Headmasters Christopher Corkery and Denny Grubbs, the Director of Studies, Karin O'Neil, and eventually, with Ann and Pat's leadership, the professional staff expanded to include more professional counselors, who were at the school every day, with several more nurses. The health center became an integral part of the school's philosophy of looking after the whole student's life while at Williston.

The success of this important school program made me pleased that I was part of this movement.

Williston Welcomes Computers [83]

IN 1972, COMPUTERS WERE STILL IN THE EARLY STAGES OF DEVELOPment. Very few of the smaller schools and colleges, including Williston, had one. Also, interestingly, the small hand-held calculators were very powerful and expensive. They were clearly not computers, and many faculties would not allow students to use them—I believed they felt their use was "cheating."

Having previously designed and implemented the computer centers at Amherst College and at Wesleyan University, I had a good idea how we might acquire some computing power at Williston. Even with our very limited resources, I planned to acquire a Digital PDP-8 and have three terminals, two in the Schoolhouse on the second-floor computer room, and one at the Easthampton High School.

Jack Cody, our math teacher and designated computer instructor wrote, "The system consists of a PDP-8 computer, 12K core memory, DECtape drive and controller, and two terminals. Until this year, we have worked with a single terminal connected with the UMass computer."[84]

The high school was very anxious to have a terminal. They could afford to rent a terminal from us, which in turn made it more affordable for Williston.

We had a couple of faculty members interested in using the computer, but primarily Jack Cody and Alan Lipp, both math teachers, were most involved. As you may know, the computers of those days were nothing like our laptops of today. You had to actually write the code, i.e., in FORTRAN or another language, what we called a high-level language. Programing/coding every step of your problem required some unique abilities. There were few, if any, "Apps," and machine language, though difficult to use, was practiced only by the real computer nerds. As you might have guessed, those unique skills *were* found in our own students.

1973: Math teacher Jack Cody and Business Manager George Dunnington and a Digital Equipment Corp. Representative, explore the PDP-8
(Spring 2006/ Bulletin From the Archives by Richard Teller '70 Williston Archivist)

One particular student stands out, and that was Paul Henchey ('74), an exceptional student. He was the son of a very popular faculty member, Richard Henchey.

Paul could make our computer really "hum." He wrote me, "The first computer I used was the Dartmouth time sharing system. Jack Cody had a teletype terminal in his math classroom that was connected to the college in New Hampshire via a low-speed modem. You dialed a number on the telephone and when you heard the whining sounds on the line, you stuck the handset into an acoustic coupler with two rubber gaskets for the earpiece and mouth piece. A student named John Fine showed me how to use it."

He continued, "Yes, my exposure to computers at Williston did help set me off on my career working for several software companies, mostly in the area of healthcare management. In those days there was little formal training available, so my self-directed learning at Williston and Harvard made me into what passed for an "expert."

Paul is now President of Henchey Information Solutions, LLC. I might add Paul also worked for me, hauling construction materials into the Schoolhouse and up to the third floor during its renovation. He was not afraid of manual labor, as he also laid many decorative cobblestones on the campus.

Computers were, to students, almost like a disease; they could not stop using them and would work many hours solving problems. Seeing this attraction to computers gave me a lot of personal satisfaction. *Wow* does this remind me of my grandchildren and their addiction to their iPhones.

There were several other students who also made the computer more useable to the other students. To mention just a couple, there was John Fine ('73) and Bill Koszewski ('87). Bill went from Williston to Brown and then to Microsoft. He now owns his own software company in the state of Washington. The academic computer system was very popular, and we upgraded it to the more powerful DEC, PDP 11/24.

To further enhance our computer's instructional capability, I was able to get a local adult education firm to rent space in the old Plimpton Library to teach computer programing on one of the early desktop computers developed by Digital Equipment Corp. The firm had approximately 20 units, and part of our rental agreement stated that our students could use the computers during the day.

It was time to hire a person with the computer and software skills who had the sole task of servicing all the computer users. In July 1982, I hired Gloria Granfield to fill that position, allowing us to expand the computer systems from the Business Office to the Admission Office and the Development Office. My computer experience was such that I fully understood what computers were capable of doing, and therefore I had designed application systems that the programmer could use to do the coding. This skill was not necessary when we contracted for the already designed systems. It was a skill helpful in evaluating the predesigned systems.

At Williston, we did start introducing computer applications in the Business Office. At this time, it was deemed expedient to rent a software package from a company, Quodata, out of Hartford. They specialized in school software packages. Thus, they maintained the software and assisted us in the conversion to their systems. The Business Office used packages for payroll, student billing, and accounts payable. Initially we choose a PDP 11/44 computer and ultimately upgraded to PDP 11/84. Quodata hired Lesley Harrison, a former Williston Coach, dorm parent, and an assistant to me in the business office. Having her work on our account was very helpful.

Interesting to note: Ralph Miller ('77), our electrician and the school's grounds crew, successfully ran cables underground, from the homestead to the Schoolhouse computer. While it was my idea to do this, it certainly was Ralph's talents that made it happen.

A few words of "computerese" to help put these prehistoric days in perspective:

1. The computers used removeable disks called RK07.
    a. It held only 28MG of data. A typical flash drive now holds 16GB of data, which is 16,384 MG of data—or 584 RK07 disks!
    b. The PDP-8 used ¾ inch magnetic tape to store data.

While I was not a programmer, I did like doing systems design. Another business manager, Nick Bakker of Thayer Academy, and I ran a summer program for business managers at Northfield Mount Herman School campus. I designed a rather involved model of a school (business areas primarily). Fortunately, we had a very capable programmer at Williston who worked part-time and who programmed the model I designed. Mount Herman had 10 or 15 terminals that we were able to use. I offered the course, and 10 or so folks signed up to take it. Several of these people were so fascinated by the model they wanted to work late into the night and even chose to miss our planned fun activities. Their model had several variables that could be tested: faculty salaries, enrollment, endowment size and return, dormitory space, tuition, etc. Nick and I gave out awards at the programs closing dinner. These awards were based upon the students' model school's balance sheets and profit and loss statements. Computers were as great an attraction to these adults as they were to the students of the day.

The Easthampton High School had a dial-in capability to our

administrative computer. As previously stated, this helped us to pay for the cost of our computers, but this service came with some big headaches. The students at Easthampton High had limited times when they could access our computer. However, like many students, once allowed on the computer they had to explore all its capabilities. That included trying to access our mainframe computer and getting into confidential information. That proverbial challenge is pretty much the same in today's world.

To try to protect the privacy of our system, Gloria limited the number of times a single user could enter their passwords to three. After three attempts to guess at a system's password, a bell would sound on our computer. This was very disturbing for Gloria to deal with, as she had to call the teacher at Easthampton High School and have him get the student off the teletype. We eventually banned a few students, but, being a public school, the parents of those students filed a complaint. While I sympathized with the public school, it eventually contributed toward ending the sharing agreement.

I was very pleased with the computer implementation at Williston, both academically and administratively. It grew and became much more sophisticated with time.

Summer Programs— A Major New Happening

IN 1972, THE SCHOOL WAS BLEEDING RED INK; ENROLLMENT WAS down, as were the number of gifts. There did not seem to be any plans to make significant programmatic changes to try to turn things around. My observations possibly could be negative, as I was observing a headmaster who was forcibly facing retirement and had been dealing with difficult school merger issues. There were signs that the school's difficulties had begun several years before I became the Business Manager. There were no signs that Philips Stevens was fighting to save the school. Wilmot Babcock was prepared to retire, and I believe looking forward to it. Again, it was hard for me to observe and understand how Stevens and Babcock managed the school. I saw evidence of Babcock being content with his job as it was, not wanting to add any extra work to his plate.

Expenses were already cut to the bare minimum, so I knew I had to try to find other sources of income that would be compatible with a school such as Williston. Having been in the school business for many years I listened to people attempting to better utilize the campus facilities on a year-round basis. Even during the regular academic year, the utilization rate of classrooms and other physical plant facilities was sinfully low. Tradition was a real roadblock to change.

Thus, I began to think what we could do to bring additional income to the school. We had physical assets sitting idle off season with that potential, such as tennis courts, ice rinks, residence halls, playing fields, etc. With the admission office trying to attract new students while having to look at the horrible appearance of the physical plant, I was looking at that same issue while trying to get people to rent the campus.

SCHOOL DAYS

Fortunately, on my first venture to rent the campus I was able to get The American Field Service organization out of Vermont to operate a two-week training program for their students to prepare to spend time in Chile. This was a wonderful way to start. First, it was small enough that we could house them entirely in John Wright dorm; we had classroom-like spaces and could feed them in the nearby, new, attractive, Whitaker Bement building; and my house, Pitcher House, was also in the adjacent area. On most nights, after a hard day's work, the staff had cocktails on my deck and enjoyed sharing time together. Armand Davy, our dining hall director, did an outstanding job of feeding the (college age) students and staff. They really appreciated this special treatment—not just dormitory food. Remembering back to my Amherst College days, a retired college president, Charles W. Cole, Amherst '46, had been the United States Ambassador to Chile. He also had been a Williston Academy Trustee. I asked him to come and talk with the students, and he was delighted to do so. What a great experience for AFS students. While this camp was not a big program, it was a start.

We then reached out to many sports programs, including hockey, soccer, and cheerleading. We continued our summer school and added a theatre camp. While these all went well, they did present a disruption to our faculty families, whose homes were in the dormitories. They were great to tolerate all this new noise and commotion.

The big challenge, as well as a big money maker, was an adult tennis camp operated by noted celebrity coach, Nick Boleteri. He had camps all over the country and catered to the "rich and famous." Thus, air conditioning was essential, a big expense and a gamble that the camp would continue and thus pay for this capital improvement. Nick Boleteri paid the whole cost of installing a large air conditioner to cool all of the Whitaker Bement building! I installed A/C window units in all the rooms in John Wright. He also bought rubber tennis courts to be used in the hockey rink in the event of rain. At the time, our clay tennis courts were a plus and people liked playing on them—easy on the feet, and a cool surface. Our grounds crew did a marvelous job at maintaining the clay surfaces. We hired a few students to tend to the court maintenance during the day and between games, i.e., sweeping the white lines and the clay surfaces. Surprisingly, Boleteri only appeared on campus once or twice!

This camp was eventually sold to Ed Fondiller, a younger and very demanding person.

Penney Mitchell, our switchboard operator and college counseling secretary, became the summer camps coordinator and endured the demands of Ed. We hired a lot of students in this camp to set tables and bus the three-daily, restaurant-style meals. Also, to make the beds every day and change the linen. This helped our students to earn money to attend Williston or college. I was very proud of them; they were great ambassadors for Williston.

Ed's complaining was endless; "the base boards were not dusted," etc. Penney told me a funny story: "Ed wanted fresh bagels from the Bagel Company in Northampton. Armand refused to get them; Ed offered to pick them up daily. Armand refused to cut them. Yup, I cut them every morning early, for about a week."[85]

It is easy to see that operating summer camps is not without its problems, both big and small. Fortunately for me, we were able to do all the staffing from within the school.

I believe Williston Academy ran a summer school for many years, but as far back to the late 50s, I could not find any sign of this happening in the annual audited financial statements.

Looking at the chart on page 183, showing income and expenses for all summer programs in the period from 1973 to 1986, it appears that they did not bring significant "profits" to the school. I'm not sure this is as clear as the chart makes it seem. These numbers are not truly representative of the full monetary benefit to the school. For example, we kept some part-time employees employed and we employed a number of students, which enabled our dining services to serve a larger number of diners with approximately the same expenses. Also, my accounting practices did not accurately reflect the distribution of all cost to their respective cost centers.

One interesting issue I had to solve was how to keep the summer students working through the whole summer—no vacation time for them. I came up with the idea of paying bonuses to those students who completed the camp season. That worked for most of the students and the school.

It may be easier to understand why the previous administration did not want to venture into the summer camp business when you consider

SCHOOL DAYS

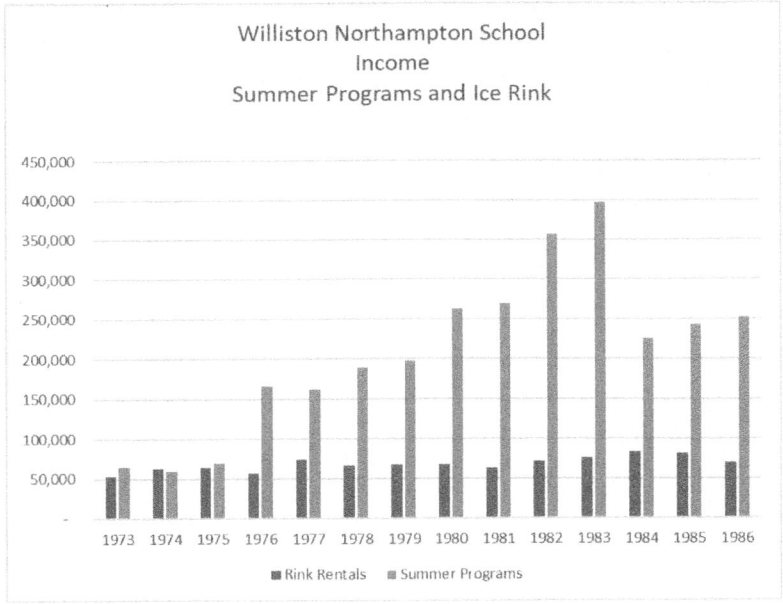

all that had to be done to accommodate the various needs of each program. For example, what had to happen in order to have ice for hockey when it was 85 degrees outside? One major problem that happens when you have ice on the entire rink floor and it is hot and muggy outside is that you have fog inside, fog so thick you cannot see inside the arena. Hence, it was necessary to install a giant dehumidifying system: a big expense and a technical challenge. You also need to consider what happens to the ice if the ice making does not stop for a period of time during the year. Briefly, what happens is that the ice keeps on freezing deeper into the ground, and at a certain depth it eventually spreads out under the rink foundation. This can lift the foundation walls up. A quick answer is that the ice making must stop for a month each year to stop the perma-frost. As this brief story illustrates, you can see the decision to enter the summer camp business also means you will have to make a significant investment into the physical plant. I will say, even though the investment was for summer programs, most of those investments made the school a better, more competitive institution.

The near-full use of the campus in the summer was, for sure, a historic undertaking. Yes, it had its challenges, but we were lucky as all of our employees fully supported the idea and helped ensure its success. Also, we have to thank all the faculty and administrators who lived in the previously very quiet dorms for tolerating the many, many kids running around their homes.

Legal Challenges and Campus Security Duties

Musings on a Colorful Career

TO ADD TO ALL THE PRESSING ISSUES WE WERE DEALING WITH IN the early 1970s—falling enrollment, merger issues, budget—all of a sudden, we were faced with a noise pollution suit! Yes, a campus neighbor, Mary Young, brought the suit as we were planning to add two more tennis courts to the long-time established clay courts behind John Wright Dorm and the Stevens Chapel. There were nine clay courts that had been there for years and, at the end near the Chapel, there was also an unused area. Enough land for two more courts and a bang board, which had been in existence for many decades. For those who do not know what a bang board is, it is a large wood wall against which you practice hitting tennis balls. Naturally, because you're hitting balls against a board, it makes a noise. Our plan was to remove the bang board and add two new clay courts. The suit alleged that the new tennis courts would make more noise than the balls had made hitting against a bang board. Noise pollution—really?

Ridiculous, as this may seem, Mrs. Young was able to drag out the court battle for over two years. She represented herself in court—therefore, she had no expensive lawyer costs. She was able to go to Boston and avail herself of free government legal services for town government people. Unfortunately, we had to hire real lawyers. A very active alumnus, Gene Berman, Class of 1942, had his firm provide us free legal services for all the preparatory work and only charged the school for the actual time his attorneys spent in court. While this arrangement saved us precious money, it did take valuable time away from other pressing matters that I had to deal with. After many years of haggling, we finally prevailed in court and were able to build two new clay courts. The addition of these two extra courts enabled us to operate that very successful summer tennis camp. We still needed to finance the new construction and, as luck would have it, when I was working on the Galbraith athletic fields, I observed some good quality clay in the ground. When I showed it to the tennis court contractors, they were happy to dig it out and use it to build our new courts. It saved us some money.

Mary Young, our litigious neighbor, was not willing to give up after our battle. Now she charged us with violating the Wetlands Act. In this area where we were planning to build the new courts, there was a slight depression in the ground that we filled in. Hard to believe, but it had to be dealt with in a legally prescribed way. We did that and prevailed, but again, using more of my precious time and money.

Our tennis court legal issues were not over. When we began planning to build more badly needed, new courts on Sawyer Field near the pond, we faced a legal challenge from the town-appointed Head of the Wetlands Commission. The Wetlands laws were a hot, new, newsworthy item for all people to deal with, as they introduced many changes as to how we could use our earth's landscape. We needed these new tennis courts, as it was difficult to have competitive matches with other schools on a campus with only nine—and later, 11—courts.

The process of getting a favorable vote from the Wetlands Commission was a sad story of local politics. At the meetings, I pled our case and the Board had a lot of heated discussion, but ended up voting against the school's application. Again, more of my time was forcibly devoted to this legal issue. Fortunately, the town leaders were on our side on this issue. As a result of this, all of a sudden there was a new member appointed to The Wetlands Commission—a true holy terror. I have no idea how they could have found this person, but I guess small town politics has its ways. At my next meeting, he harassed the Chairperson until she broke down in tears, walked out of the meeting, and quit. Soon, we had a favorable vote to proceed.

Next, we had a faculty member charge the school with sexual discrimination. This was real shock for me. I was sitting in my office diligently working during a school break, thus very few people were around.

SCHOOL DAYS

Suddenly, into my office walked this rather heavy, hardly able to walk man who asked for me. I identified myself and he presented me with a legal notice that essentially said, "the school discriminated against a female faculty member because we would not let her live in a boy's dormitory," meaning Ford Hall.

My first reaction was that this was absolutely insane. Not surprisingly, this was a very difficult diversion to deal with on top of all that was happening in trying to keep the school's doors open.

I had no choice but to assume the leadership role in planning out our strategy before the Massachusetts Commission Against Discrimination (MACD). I met with all the relevant faculty and administrators—Phyllis Beekman, Director of Studies, Robert St. George Dean of Students, Karin O'Neil, Dean of Faculty, and others.

Unfortunately, it happened that the school's attorney, William Dwyer, was a graduate of Williston, a Trustee, and a rather elderly estate lawyer with no experience in legal discrimination matters. These kinds of issues did not happen in his practice. I spent time with all our people involved in what became known, by our accusing teacher's name, "the Barbara Carlin case." I carefully went over and over everything that we knew to be facts, including the fact that school faculty member positions were in jeopardy as the school was overstaffed from the merging of two sets of faculties. Ms. Carlin, a young single lady, never asked to live in Ford Hall, a boy's dormitory. As a matter of fact, she personally said to me, "please do not put me in a dormitory." So, to help her, I had offered her housing at the now empty NSFG campus. My personal kitchen furnishings were still in the house where I first resided for her to use. So, she got her wish not to live in a dormitory, as many faculty were required to do.

Remember that your author never had any legal experience. At the hearing, in the Springfield Court the first thing that happened was that I was declared a "hostile witness." Having never spent time in court I was not familiar with the judge's declarations. Also, the school's attorney William Dwyer ('20), did not fully understand this happening and was completely taken aback.

I stood up and asked, "Why am I being declared a hostile witness?" and was immediately told to sit down.

This quadrupled my already heightened anxiety. I was later told that as Business Manager, it was my duty to defend the school—therefore I was hostile! Indeed, I was! Next, the plaintive attorney asked to have all my witnesses sequestered. Again, I had no clue what this meant or why it happened. Our attorney was equally surprised. Remember that our accusing faculty member's attorney was employed by the MACD and we were sitting before a MACD judge. Our attorney, Mr. Dwyer, became visibly upset. It seemed to me he was having some medical issues. I was beyond furious and demanded he ask for an immediate recess. That did not happen until after I was attacked with "leading questions," permitted when addressing a hostile witness.

Finally, I told Dwyer, "Do it now. Get a recess."

Immediately I went out and made a panic call to Gene Berman. He was a very busy person, but he always took my calls—thank goodness. He immediately sent over one of his lead attorneys, who coincidently had been previously employed by MCAD. What is good for the goose is good for the gander! He ended the disaster for the moment by demanding a postponement of the hearing. This legal process went on for over a year and included several court visits, causing me much stress. Even though Gene Berman did not charge us for much of his time, it still cost the school precious dollars. When we went to court for the final time I stupidly acted like a wise guy and, when asked how much I was willing to pay Barbra Carlin for her lost wages (she was asking for three years back pay), I said, "Nothing." This was not a good thing to do, but I was most upset with this whole episode and lost my patience. I believe we paid her one month's pay as opposed to the three year's pay her attorneys were asking. We prevailed, but not without pain. It was my opinion that Barbara Carlin was overly encouraged to act against the school by some of the very radical women in the Northampton area. Knowing her, I was disappointed and surprised by her actions.

Campus Security

I guess I should have read the fine print in my job description. If I had, perhaps I would have read that campus security was not only an administrative function, but that I was responsible for it. In fact, I *was* security. Security issues did keep me busy for a while. We had two night watchmen who were only qualified to do that limited function and little else.

Watchman Ross Stanwood was a handicapped veteran and was under "care" of the Northampton Veteran's Hospital, a very interesting character to say the least. Here are a few Ross stories, which students at that time may remember.

He lived over the kitchen along with two other kitchen workers. Not a nice place, I soon realized, especially when the exterminator made his monthly visit to the kitchen just below his room. After spraying the critters, the termites discovered they could escape upstairs to the workers' rooms. There they went, en masse.

In those days, the means of communicating with the night watchmen was a good old fashioned two-way radio, a rather large, bulky instrument which they carried on them. I faithfully kept mine beside me when on duty, even by my bed, much to Ann's dismay. Ross was affectionately called "Lurch" by the students, because of the way he dragged one leg. Ross was a very faithful and diligent employee, so he felt compelled to call me almost every night, about 2:00 a.m., to say, "I am having my Table Talk blueberry pie at the nearby 7/11." I really did not think this was urgent, and Ann really hated being woken up. I finally convinced him it was not necessary for him to communicate that information.

On another late night, Ross called me to say, "There is a fire under the railroad bridge (near the hockey rink)."

I replied, "Check to see if there are any of our students under the bridge (a frequent hang-out)."

He came back, "I do not see any students," spoken in a very nonchalant way. But he continued to say, "There is a car upside down and burning."

"Shit, I will be right down!"

I called the police, and while I was dressing Ross came back with, "I can see two bodies."

How is that for a fast wake up? The ambulance came and took the two gentlemen to the hospital.

My final Ross story. I received a call from Tom Smith, the dorm master at the nearby John Wright Dorm, and he said, "George, Ross is dead in the basement by the oil burner." Immediately I ran over to the dorm and went to the basement. Indeed, I found Ross on the floor looking very dead, a very worrisome site for me to see. Fortunately, with a little shake, he came to life after having had a good sleep.

We had a break-in at the Building & Grounds Headquarters, and many of the master keys had been stolen. This was a very serious problem because it was so expensive to replace the keys and to re-key all the doors, and, of course, a security dilemma of the worst kind. In my walks around campus, I rather discretely asked some students if they had heard anything about this. I did get one clue. School was going into recess, so when all the students were gone, I took my master key and went into the suspect's room in Memorial Dorm and discretely removed the hinges on the student's locker and found all the missing keys. Whether this was legal for me to do, according to school rules, might have been questionable. So, I decided to get a search warrant, thus ensuring nobody could question us when the student was dismissed.

The police called a local judge with whom I spoke, and she said, "Is this student a minority student?"

After a few other questions, we went to her home and picked up the warrant. With our very helpful local police, we thoroughly searched the room and secured the booty. Being such a serious offense, the student's parents were called, at home, by Dean St. George. The parents came and picked up what was in the room. Unfortunately, this dumb mistake caused him to be dismissed from school.

Students can be amazingly brilliant and amazingly dumb. A police cruiser was making its regular rounds up behind Stevens Chapel and John Wright Dormitory, and in the unshaded window of the dorm was a very bright grow light shining on some very healthy marijuana plants. The officer drove next door to my house (Pitcher House) and told me what they had observed. I walked over and knocked on the room door, and the two girls wondered what I wanted—duh. I removed the plants for safekeeping.

While I was attending the refreshment and dinner part of the Trustee

Meeting at the head's house, an enjoyable break after a hard day's work, I received a call from the Easthampton Police.

They informed me, "We have a very belligerent student here at the station, and we had to arrest him for fighting with one of our officers."

Really! That was very shocking to hear, so I left the meeting and went immediately to the station. Upon arriving in a side room, I found a physically huge local Polish police officer holding the student by the top of his head as he continued to swing at the officer.

I said, "May I talk to him alone, to see if I can reason with him?"

The officer said, "I know we almost never arrest your students, but we had to because he was so belligerent. Now the law makes him our responsibility, and I am not supposed to let him out of my sight."

Surprisingly, this student even gave me a hard time. I wanted to take him back to school and let Dean St. George deal with him. In order for this to happen, I had to go through a long process of signing papers, relieving the police from further responsibility and making me the responsible person. Sadly, but deservedly, he was driven to the airport by Mr. St. George and sent back to his home in Ohio the next day.

Yes, there is still more. I received a call from the Easthampton Fire Department asking, "Do you have any Petrik acid on campus? This an unstable chemical and can easily explode, in your labs."

I went over to the Science Building and asked the Science Department Head, Jack Gow, if he had any Petrik acid.

"No, but Eve Couderc (chemistry teacher) might have some in his chemical closet."

Sure, enough Eve had a good supply of the old unstable stuff sitting in a bottle on the shelf. Soon after I reported back to the fire department, they told me they had to refer the problem to the Springfield Fire Department, as we do not have a bomb-removal vehicle. A short time later, the Springfield Fire Department arrived with a fire truck and another truck pulling a big round bomb carrier. Wow! This was exciting for all the students to watch, as the firemen carefully carried out this dangerous chemical.

After leaving with the Petrik acid safely in the bomb truck, Eve said to me, in his rather pronounced French accent, "That was silly. I have used Petrik acid for years."

One evening while standing at the kitchen sink in Pitcher House and looking out the window, I saw three people running very fast across the lawn and across Park Street, through the main campus gate by the gymnasium. This was looking rather suspicious. I called the police, and they said to come on down and we will go there and find out what is going on.

I replied, "Sure I will come right down."

So, when I got to the station two officers were by their police cruiser and one let me into the back seat. Off we went, I mean *really* went, extremely fast, and as we approached the gate, we saw our people of interest standing by the side of the gymnasium in the darkness. The officer in the front seat jumped out of the car and took chase through the gate, down and over the walking bridge over the Williston Pond. With me still in the back seat, we went "flying" down to the next-door Sawyer Field and entered the gate on to the nice, green, slippery grass. The cruiser, because of its speed, proceeded to spin around before it came to a stop. The officer in the front seat jumped out and started the chase, not remembering George was securely locked in the back of the car! No door handles for the "bad guys" in the back to get out. After a yell or two, I was let out and ready to help in the chase, so, I commenced running across the athletic field in hot pursuit of a single culprit. Suddenly, I realized I was going to catch this bandit. Well, that gave me momentary fright. I asked myself, "Do I really want to catch this runner? Could the runner have a weapon—a gun?" So, confronted with this frightening issue, I decided to jump on the person's back, knock the person down, and run like hell if necessary. Well, we both ended up sliding across that nice green grass, me on top. Suddenly, I was shocked to find it was a girl—and one of our students. The popular thing to steal at that time was scales from our science labs to measure out contraband, and although I suspected this might be the reason for their escapade, none were found. I told her to get up and go, and we would deal with this at another time.

Back to our chemistry teacher, Eve Couderc—our renaissance man, as he was referred to by Robert Ward, our head of school. Not only was he a good science teacher, but he also was an excellent art history teacher.

I had observed him driving students to field trips in the school van and was not entirely comfortable with his "renaissance" driving skills. I talked with Mr. Ward about this concern, and he was troubled about how to handle this issue sensitively. Mr. Couderc liked to take students on short field trips. Saying, "no driving," to him would be strictly an arbitrary decision. There were no incidences to base the decision on, but, on the other hand, we certainly did not want to put our students at risk.

Not too long after struggling with this dilemma I received a call from the Holyoke Police Department, saying, "Your van went through a stop light and was hit by a car on its side, and it rolled over. The driver and the students are in the Holyoke Hospital and have been treated."

I immediately called Headmaster Ward and we drove to the hospital. When we arrived, we were very relieved to find Eve Couderc and the students only had bumps and bruises. The van was another story; it was totaled. I believe Eve Couderc decided not to drive students again.

To be sure, I did not get bored. Rand Alexander, a young new faculty member just out of Dartmouth College was taking his Economics class to NYC to see the stock exchange. On leaving the big city, he side-swiped a NYC dump truck.

When he got back, rather late at night, he called me and said, "George, I just wanted to tell you we had an accident in the city."

I replied, "Was anyone hurt?"

"No."

"Did it do much damage to the van?"

"No, some scrapes on the side, but I could not close the van's sliding door completely."

"Did you report the accident to the police?"

"No."

So now I became slightly agitated, thinking we would for sure be on the NYC hit-and-run list. As the school's paid worrier, I was sure we would have to go to court in the Big City and face a huge fine.

Well, if you have ever tried to call the NYPD, I can attest to you it is a major undertaking. After several phone calls, I finally did get the precinct that had jurisdiction over that area of the hit-and-run accident. I proceed to tell the desk sergeant my sad story, and he replied in a gruff voice, "Do you know how many accidents we have here in one day? I will tell you, we have more in one day than your whole state has in a year! Don't bother us, please."

Whoa. Shocked and relieved was I.

A private independent residential school has somewhat of a family atmosphere, with faculty and students living together in dormitories. Many faculty live in school-owned apartments and houses with all their home repairs done by the school and even their utilities paid. On many school breaks, faculty would often leave campus for their own homes or to visit family. During breaks, the campus was pretty quiet with just a few administrators and faculty left. On one of these breaks, a student from Germany was staying with the Millers (school Trustee and parent of four students) in Southampton. We always tried to help students find local lodging when vacation travel costs became financial hardships.

Dave and Ruth Stevens were faculty who very much enjoyed their escape to their home in Mattapoisett, MA. One of their sons, "Buddy," stayed in their school home, Sawyer House. This student came over to Pitcher House and said she wanted to come in and talk.

She had befriended Buddy and said, "I can't locate Buddy and I think he was in the house. I am concerned."

I said, "I will go into the house and check to make sure everything is OK."

When I entered and got to the kitchen area, I unfortunately found him slumped over the table with drug paraphernalia, and he was dead. I called the police, and they came immediately. Now, it was my duty to call his parents, Dave and Ruth, in Mattapoisett.

When I reached them, I said, "I have some sad news for you," and then continued to tell them about their son."

Ruth said to me, "George we can't possibly come up to Easthampton, will you contact Mitchell's Funeral Home for us."

Shockingly I said, "Yes, of course," being rather surprised by this response; I could only think if it were my son, I would have driven back as fast as I possibly could.

Sadly, this was not the only story with a similar ending. This one illustrates how young people can make very bad decisions, something Headmaster Ward cautioned the students about on more than one occasion.

It was late at night, just after midnight, as I recall, when I received a call from the Easthampton Police Department.

"Your students have been in a very bad accident on the road to Northampton. Three are in the hospital."

I immediately went to the hospital and talked with the Emergency Room doctor. He said, "One of your students, a boy by the name of Peter Edgerton, is in very serious condition and may not recover. The other two are girls and are badly banged up, but will recover."

I immediately called Edgerton's parents' home in Brookline, Massachusetts.

By way of background, Mr. and Mrs., Edgerton had, that very evening, attended a play at the school in which their son Peter had a lead role. After the play, the parents went up to Peter's room in Ford Hall to celebrate Peter's role in the play and to say goodnight. Then they drove home, approximately a one and half hour ride. So, it was very late when they finally got into bed. It was at that time when I reached them on the phone. Distressed and sad, I was very anxious about the gruesome news I had to deliver.

"Mr. Edgerton, Peter has been in a very serious auto accident when he and some friends were driving to Northampton. Peter was so seriously injured he may not recover."

Mr. Edgerton said to me, "We cannot possibly drive back to Easthampton; we just got back and are in bed."

A little taken aback from his response, and just to make sure he understood the gravity of my statement, I said, "Mr. Edgerton, Peter may die (the word I did not want to say), so I think it would be very important for you to come to the hospital immediately."

Soon thereafter, while waiting in the emergency room for the doctor to report again (I am, in school jargon, *"acting in loco parentis"*) he now informed me that Peter had passed. Someplace in this episode I called Headmaster Ward and filled him in on what had transpired so he could set into motion the things that needed to be done on campus.

Again, feeling terrible having to deliver this horrible message, I called Mr. Edgerton. "Mr. Edgerton I am sorry to have to tell you, but Peter passed a few minutes ago. Can you come right up to the hospital?"

He replied, "No!" and asked, "Can you handle the matter and have his body sent to Brookline?"

And, in shock again, I said, "I will contact the undertaker and arrange for his body to be sent home."

The rest of the night, Bob St. George, Dean of Students, Head Bob Ward, and I tried to track down the other students who were in the car and try to find out what happened. It took us a while, as they had dispersed on campus and did not want to be found knowing what they had done was in violation of school rules. They, of course, did not know how serious the accident had been. When we located them, the students were reluctant to tell the whole story until we told what had happened. A student from Old Saybrook, CT had gone to her home, knowing her parents were on vacation, and took her parents' small compact car to campus and hid it near the school. After the play, late at night, after the Edgerton parents had left the campus, she and, I believe, five other students crowded into this small car and were driving toward Northampton when she failed to negotiate a curve in the road and crashed into the side foundation of a house.

To address the needs of grieving students, Headmaster Ward chartered a bus, and a large group of students and faculty went to Brookline, MA for the funeral services. Indeed, a sad day for our school.

It was now time for me to stop being "George the Cop," the only security person on campus. The school needed to have a full-time, trained security person. This person needed to be around at night to keep a watchful eye on the campus and to talk with the students. I was fortunate, in 1973, to hire Robert Carey, a UMass student. We talked about what I expected of him, and I believed Bob would do well. He, too, stayed in touch with me using his walkie-talkie, however not as frequently as had been the case.

He did say to me, "I will most likely stay on as your Security person for only three years." At the time, I did not worry about this, even though I was disappointed. Well, he retired in 2014! Thanks Bob!

Soon, we had our first joint effort to rid the campus of "burglars." Barbara Kaak, our bookstore manager, came to me and said, "I think someone is getting into 'my' store at night and taking things." She went on to say, "I have watched very carefully every day to see if anyone looks suspicious."

I have never met anyone like Barbara, who knew her store inventory almost by memory. One side of the bookstore was a wall of windows covered by heavy drapes. Since she suspected the vandals were getting in the windows somehow, she baited the trap. Every day at closing, she would check all the windows and, sure enough, she found one had been unlocked. She informed me, and George and Bob sprang into action. George decided he would hide in the small storeroom which was just off the main book store floor, accompanied only by his trusty walkie-talkie and wait. Bob was to stay near, but out of sight. Soon I heard the window open, then some voices, and then people crawled in the window and entered the store. Wow, suddenly my mind envisioned some bad guys from Springfield. Were they really big? Did they have a weapon? With my adrenaline going crazy, I searched around the floor for a weapon and found a four-foot 2 X 4 that was used to hold the books off the floor. Clutching this tightly, I burst out of the closet with the 2 X 4 in both hands over my head and slammed it with all my power onto a heavy table. Besides wrecking my hands, I scared the life out of the intruders.

I said, "Hit the floor and do not move."

Unfortunately, they were our students, and Dean St. George was left to deal with them.

So ends a few stories from Williston's Business Manager in the early 70s that, I believe, may enlighten the reader to some of the issues that a residential secondary school has to deal with. Perhaps it illustrates that I had to function way outside of what might be a typical Business Manager's job description.

A Few Faculty Stories that Made the Business Manager's Life More Interesting

Perhaps you remember that soon after I arrived on campus and moved into Pitcher House, the new Headmaster, Robert Ward, was still living and working at Amherst College. This was a time when the faculty were going through much stress resulting from the merger and a change of headmasters. I felt it was important to do some relaxing social events to help ease tensions.

My wife and I were also getting to know the faculty and we enjoyed having parties at our very comfortable campus home. Hence, we often entertained the faculty, administrators, and their support staff. I remember fondly the Christmas party with Santa Clause and a big "get warm" party after faculty member Kevin O'Connor led the faculty and administrators through his Outward-Bound course on the school's Southampton acreage in the cold, snowy woods. And, when everybody was tired and frozen, we all went back to our house to get warm by the fireplaces and enjoy some libations.

I am sharing a few faculty stories for your enjoyment and to help you see how Williston is somewhat like a big family that worked very hard to educate and care for the students. As a very cohesive group, we not only worked together, but we also played together and helped one another when necessary. Enjoy!

A prominent and unique faculty member, Eves Couderc, taught chemistry and lived with his wife, Irene, in a school-owned, single-family home in downtown Easthampton. In a kind way, I would say they were both a little eccentric. This story begins at 5:30 a.m. on a cold and snowy morning. I received a call at the house from Irene, who, in a very distressed voice began scolding me because the grounds crew had not plowed her driveway so she could get to work at the top of nearby Mount Tom.

In the middle of a major snowstorm, her personal work schedule was not the first thing on my mind. I was trying to make sure our kitchen help could get to work and feed our hungry students, and trying to make sure all the grounds crew were at work plowing and shoveling to make sure the campus would be up and running on time. Your author and school Business Manager in the early years of his tenure also worked on the snow removal team. So, at 6:30, I was driving a truck, plowing school roads and driveways, and as I was driving by the Schoolhouse, I saw Irene trotting down the center of Payson Avenue in the deep snow, headed toward Mount Tom. Dedication? Craziness?

Did I drive her up the very snowy, steep mountainside? I did!

This story brings us to visit with Irene's husband, Eves Couderc, busily lecturing in his chemistry laboratory. I am not sure of why I went to see Eves, but upon entering his lab he was deeply engrossed in an experiment that was happening in front of his students. It was now in flames. That was not the only thing in flames. His lab coat was also on fire, and he was busily slapping out the flames with his bare hands without ever missing a word in his lecture. The students did not seem alarmed at all, like it was an everyday happening. Perhaps it was. As the school's Business Manager, I acted cool, like the students did. After the fires all subsided, I left, yes, wondering whether this was a frequent happening? Is this something I should worry about?

At the time a very new faculty member, Cathleen Robinson (Brown) came to Williston after working in a Catholic school as a teacher and religious leader. Why she arrived during Christmas break, I cannot remember, but she did, and she had very little money and no car, an absolute necessity. Not a good situation, when there were few people on campus to lend a helping hand. To make matters a little more difficult, her apartment in John Wright Dorm was still in the final stages of refurbishing.

So, I said, "Cathleen, don't worry, you can stay next door in my house, Pitcher House, as my family is on vacation."

It was a very large house and I told her she could watch the TV in the second-floor family room. My wife, Ann, was not a TV person, so we had an old, temperamental TV where you had to use pliers to turn the channels. Cathleen dealt with this and settled into our house. While relaxing in the TV room, suddenly there was a knock at the door. Startled and surprised, she went to the den door and there was a man/student. What I had forgotten to tell her was that a student from Thailand, Vut, was also staying at the house on the third floor. This issue was easily dealt with and house sharing was fine.

A word about Vut. He was a family friend, and because of the cost to travel to and from Thailand he spent most of his vacations at our house.

Now back to Cathleen. It just happened that Glenn Swanson, history teacher and a kind soul, was on campus and happened to have an old, well-worn car, a Maverick, which he sold to Cathleen for $500. After acquiring the car and being very anxious to drive it, she realized she did not have enough money to register it. This was embarrassing to her, and so at the time she never told anyone. The car sat behind Pitcher House, your author's house, through several large snowstorms until Cathleen received her first paycheck and could afford to register her car. Finally, she was ready to take her first drive, but the car was now totally covered in snow. She began digging, unburying the car with the help of Glenn Swanson. I also joined them. As more of the car became visible, we could see one tire was completely flat. On seeing this, Cathleen was upset but we assured her we could easily change the tire for her. We opened the trunk to fetch the spare tire—and it too was flat! Now, poor Catheleen was in tears. As Swanee (Glenn) was trying to remove the tire clamp, the tire fell partially through the rusted trunk floor. Swanee and I started to laugh so hard we could hardly stand up. This was not funny at all for Catheleen. Needless to say, we finally got the car on the road for her to enjoy.

Perhaps another Catheleen story would be in order now. We had a new student from Mexico who arrived at school by way of Switzerland. When the billing office clerk was settling his bill, he gave her a check in the amount of $6,000, much more than the actual amount due. To make this more shocking, he asked for the change. Wow, said Ellen, our Accounts Receivable clerk.

"We do not usually give students that amount of cash back, especially without the parent's specific directions."

I got involved, and said, "I need to call your parents and get their specific instructions to give you this money."

He replied, "My parents only speak Spanish."

Knowing that Catheleen spoke fluent Spanish, I asked her if she would help by calling the parents. She was a little reluctant and nervous because of the nature of the business that had to be communicated, but she agreed. Sitting in my office, I reviewed with Cathleen what I needed to hear from the parents. She gathered up her courage and made the call. Immediately, she started communicating in fluent Spanish, big smiles, very positive gestures, and after what seemed to me to be a very long time she suddenly paused.

"George," she said, "This is the maid I have been talking to, and she cannot help us."

Catheleen was finally able to talk with the mother and we were given permission to give the student the money. Not business as usual, especially for the office clerks who thought $6,000 was like a fortune.

We had just hired a couple of coaches right out of college. Fred Hill was an outstanding Lacrosse player out of Syracuse University and was going to be Williston's Lacrosse coach. He was inexperienced at coaching a real team and frequently had issues being the coach. For example, he would go to the field with two dozen Lacrosse balls and come home with six. So, bussing to an away game meant he had to do a lot of planning, or I should say, he should have done a lot of planning. The team bus arrived at the school to pick up the team with all their gear, sticks, balls and helmets etc. They drove away. After a short while, a few Lax team members rushed into my campus office to ask about the whereabouts of the bus. Remember, in those days, there were no cell phones, so we could not reach Coach Hill while on the road. Upon his arriving at the opponent's school, the Coach realized he did not have all his team members. So, he called me to tell me his tale of woe. It was too late now to get the rest of the team, so I guess you had to call that a self-inflicted handicap!

Another Fred story for the road. Our illustrious coach was driving his rather old car home from Springfield to campus and it was snowing very hard. When he got to Exit 17 to Easthampton off Route 91, he decided to leave his car in the yard of a group of apartment houses just off the exit. Ten or so days later, I received a call from the Holyoke Police Department.

"Do you have a person on your campus by the name of Fred Hill?"

I thought, *oh no,* and replied, "Yes, why do you ask?"

"His car has been illegally parked in a private driveway for about ten days."

I walked over to Memorial Dorm to his apartment and asked, "Freddie where is your car?"

At first, he had no clue at all. So, I reminded him, and then drove him to retrieve his car.

The last Fred story. While I am not really trying to pick on Fred, as he was a good person and I liked him, he provided some interesting stories. I had a second home in Mystic, CT, about 100 miles from Williston. Immediately across the street from my house lived two boys who also went to Syracuse University and played Lax with Fred. The scene is set. I was in my garage, working diligently in my shop on a house project when all of a sudden, I was brought out of my deep concentration by a loud CRASH! A Lax ball came flying through the glass garage door window, spraying glass everywhere. When I walked out the side door, who was there to greet me and embarrassingly to confess? Fred Hill.

He shockingly said, "I cannot believe it is you!" Nor could I believe it was him.

Mr. Gregory, a talented multi-disciplined teacher was the dorm head of the senior dorm, Ford Hall, for many, many years. Built into the genes of senior students are "pranks." As an old Navy man, sticking to the rules at all times was his *modus operandi*. This, in turn, invited retaliatory pranks. Dick Gregory wrote in a letter to me about one memorable such prank.

I was home late one evening and got a call from Dick saying, "I can't get out of my room to do the evening check-in of the boys. Both my apartment doors are securely locked."

I replied, "I'll be right over to see why you cannot unlock your doors."

It was simple; the seniors had super glued his locks so you could not possibly get a key into the lock. Simple problem? Not at all. With the help of some substantial tools, I managed to take the door off the hinges and let Dick free to do his nightly check-ins. I left the lock problem to our maintenance person, Ernie Willard to solve the next day.

For those who do not know Dick Gregory, he was very musical and started several musical groups including the Caterwaulers, a very popular men's student singing group. He wrote in a letter to me sent long after he retired, "I played the tuba in boarding school and in the Yale University Band. So, when the then Head of School Philips Stevens decided that his school ought to have a band, to rival his admired Deerfield Academy's band, he bought me a tuba and put me in charge. I remember at one football game, putting the bell of the tuba on backwards, so that I could face the kids in the band and still have the sound of my instrument broadcast over the field where it could be heard. I stood up—and fell over backwards! Afterwards, when anyone asked if they had seen the game, the answer was always about the sight of me, on my backside."[86]

When I was all involved in seemingly crisis after crisis, I was not always aware of what the faculty knew or surmised about what was happening in the life of their school. In another letter from Dick Gregory to me dated August 6, 2005 he wrote, "In your letter you mentioned the gallantry of the faculty, back then, to keep rowing against the wind. Well, I don't think that most of us understood how stiff that wind was. We saw things. We coped with deferred maintenance and declining I.Q. scores and onslaughts of dope and the eighteen-old-drinking age (when I was trying to run the senior dorm). We saw you astride a snowplow and Bob Ward painting a staircase in the Science Building. But it was not until things began to turn around, in the 1980s, that we began to realize how close we had come to extinction. And we might well have, had you and Bob not been there."[87]

Although I was involved in these previous stories, to be fair, I will now tell one that involves me directly. When I left Williston to take up my new position at Milton Academy, a few of my friends prepared a booklet: "This Book is Dedicated to the Memory of George B. Dunnington Jr." From the book: "In the early years of the rebuilding of WNS, George worked hard. He spent long hours talking to people, balancing the old check book and bringing summer camps to campus. As Karin O'Neil tells it, this was one thing George was very proud of, the summer income for WNS. George stood up in front of the faculty at the first school faculty meeting of the year telling them about the summer income of WNS. He was so excited about the direction that WNS was taking. He told about having an adult tennis camp and a hockey camp for the younger set. As George grew eloquent about the benefits that our admissions would reap from the hockey camp, he concluded:

'…and furthermore, it gave us the opportunity to expose ourselves to several hundred little boys.'"

"Need we say more?"
(A Williston Cartoon book prepared by various Williston friends,
"This Book Is dedicated To The Memory Of George B. Dunnington Jr. June 1986)

Another story from the same booklet. "George's job did not end at 4:30 pm. You could find him around the campus most of the time. The boys from Longmeadow (looking for the chick from Longmeadow) did not know this. Nor did they know that climbing up on the roof of John Wright Dorm would not save their hides. Up on the roof went George, in the middle of the night, to chase off two lovesick boys from Longmeadow, as the Dean of Deans cheered him on."

SCHOOL DAYS

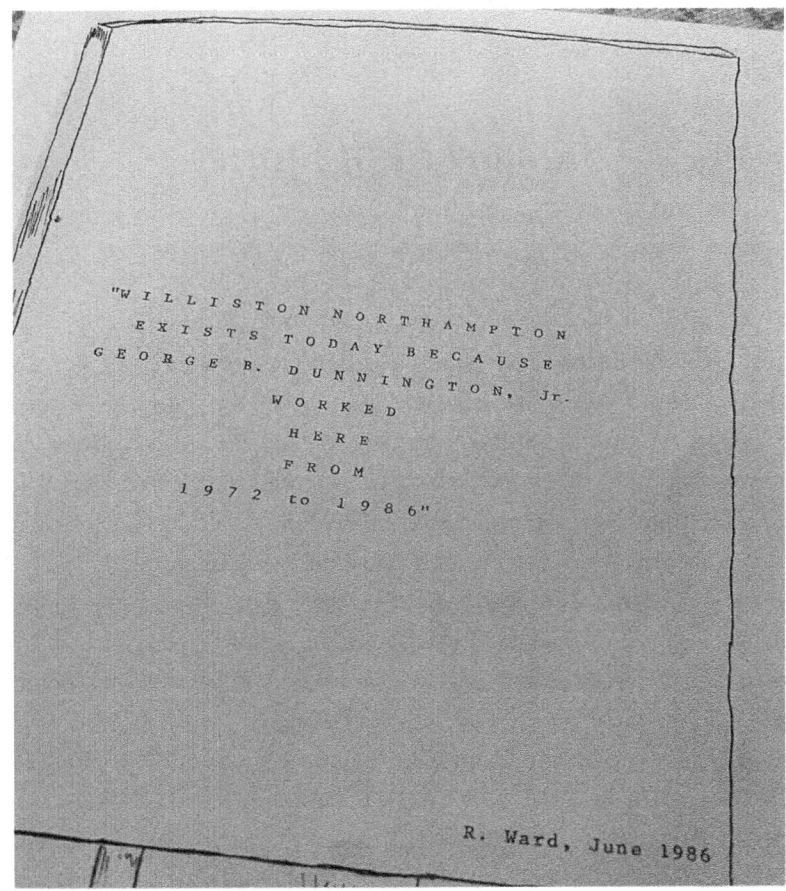

(From a cartoon book prepared June 1986 at the time of my Williston and going to Milton Academy)

"Had they no heart for young love the Business Manager and Dean of Deans?"

Retired Headmaster Ward wrote on the first page, "This Book is Dedicated to the Memory of George B. Dunnington Jr." It was very touching note and personally very meaningful. Bob Ward and I both knew we had a great team to help us. I especially thank the faculty for their help in what was a very difficult struggle to save the school.

Support Staff Stories

When thinking of Williston, a private independent school, one may not realize how important a role the staff plays in keeping the programs functioning in the best way possible. I have always had an appreciation for the work that is done by the hourly workers, especially when they do a good job, be it cleaning the floors, plowing snow, cooking a dinner, bookkeeping, or doing clerical work. All very important jobs.

On arrival at Williston, one of the first things I did was to travel around campus and meet the staff doing their respective jobs. I was sorely disappointed to find that the buildings were not clean. I believed it was because of lack of qualified supervision. The housekeeping staff had never been trained, and equally important, their equipment was old and often did not function. I was also upset when I saw the condition of the equipment that the buildings and grounds folks had to use. It was simply deplorable.

These people also suffered because they were not paid fairly and were the ones who seldom seemed to get a raise. They were the ones who had borne the brunt of the school's financial hardships. Why, because they were scared to death for fear of losing their jobs.

There was no employment handbook for any of the employees that assured them of their benefits or explained what was expected of them. In many cases, the benefits were not equally available to all employees.

Heading up the Buildings and Grounds Department on my arrival was Ernie Willard, a very kind and hard-working person. And, because of the way the school was run, budgets were so inadequate that it was virtually impossible for him to do the expected jobs. (He also had too many jobs to try to do.) He retired in 1975 after ten dedicated years. He was a big help to me as I improved the management of the B & G functions with more supervisors and higher performance expectations.

Yes, things were pathetic and often unbelievable. The management of the school used the workers and let them suffer more than their fair share. I say this knowing the faculty were also at the bottom of our competitor schools' compensation rankings.

Perhaps a couple of stories will serve as a way to tell some experiences of our workers.

Ford Hall Dormitory had always been a boys' residence hall, until I chose to make it a dorm for a summer girls' camp. One late afternoon I received a frantic call from a lady at Ford Hall saying, "Your janitor was in the girls' shower room while the girls were showering."

"What!"

Immediately I hustled over to the third-floor shower with all the girls just outside yelling and laughing as I went into the bathroom. Sure enough, our custodian was mopping the floor. I yelled at him asking what he was doing in the shower room filled with a bunch of girls. It was then, very shockingly, I realized he was blind! This story ends sadly, because I simply could not have a blind janitor, even though he had apparently worked there, a boys' dorm, for years. I also can't believe I was the first person to discover this problem.

Supervision and training were almost completely lacking for the custodial and maintenance personnel. Armand Davey, Director of Dining Services, did an excellent job at training his kitchen and wait staff, but that was the exception.

Making a visit through all the buildings, it was quite common to find the custodial help watching the "soaps" on TV. On several occasions while watching the floors get vacuumed, I noticed the floors were just as dirty as they were at the start. From my going-away cartoon book, I can't help including the illustration concerning the school's vacuums. It is such a true story albeit sad.

The vacuums were either so old or in such bad need of service they simply did not "suck." I remember getting very upset when I took a vacuum away from the custodian and looked at the bottom. There was no belt to drive the beater! Likewise, I found many of the vacuum hoses were simply plugged up. These issues again reflected the lack of training, a common problem that should be part of the everyday tasks.

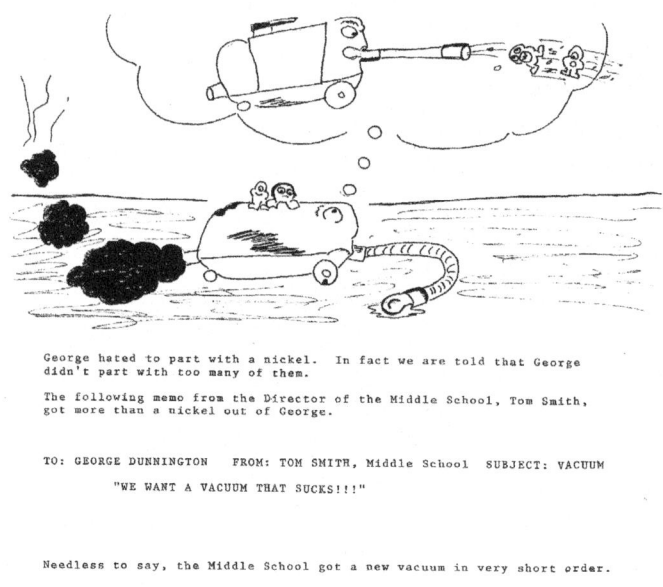

George hated to part with a nickel. In fact we are told that George didn't part with too many of them.

The following memo from the Director of the Middle School, Tom Smith, got more than a nickel out of George.

TO: GEORGE DUNNINGTON   FROM: TOM SMITH, Middle School   SUBJECT: VACUUM

"WE WANT A VACUUM THAT SUCKS!!!"

Needless to say, the Middle School got a new vacuum in very short order.

(This cartoon is from a book of George stories presented to me on June 1986 on my leaving Williston for Milton Academy)

The way the workers were treated was shocking to me. Ernie Willard was a good person, worked very hard, and did whatever Mr. Babcock asked of him. I continued my visits to the various dorms with him. One time when we entered Swan Cottage, a small dorm for boys, just under the main stairway was a janitor sitting on a chair sound asleep. Since this happened with the Business Manager, his immediate supervisor present, it of course embarrassed Ernie. So, surprisingly, he went over grabbed the janitor and whacked him in the face. That event really upset me. However, similar happenings, perhaps not as bad, were seemingly a way of life.

The workers simply did not have any equipment that was new or even in decent condition.

The following story was an embarrassing one that also happened to me. I got a call from a local downtown insurance agent and he said,

"George, Ernie cannot get his pick-up truck started and it is in front of my store, in the street."

I went and got a set of jumper cables and went to try and help. I opened the driver's door of Ernie's truck and in doing so, it fell completely off the truck and onto the street. I was so embarrassed, I picked the door up and threw it into the back of the truck. We started it and drove it back to campus. The condition of this vehicle was typical of much of the other equipment and school vehicles, and it concerned me deeply as I knew it was going to be a costly problem to rectify.

Lack of proper personnel training showed up almost everywhere. One particularly bad example happened in the dining room. It was quite common for the janitors to think that the more cleaning materials used, the better it was. "Mixing them together" was still better. As I was entering the dining hall for our evening dinner with my family, we started coughing and many of the students were doing the same. To really clean the carpet the janitor had mixed two cleaning agents together, creating a dangerous gaseous solution. This sort of incident led the Federal Government to issue safety regulations for hazardous materials, a new regulation that required better skilled supervision.

Armand Davy did an amazing job working with the social service agency down the street from the school that trained disabled/mentally challenged workers. He always had several trainees working in the kitchen, and he found they did a great job and at little or no cost to the school. This does remind me of a funny and rather scary story that happened in downtown Northampton. My wife, Ann, and I were walking down the sidewalk along busy Main Street when from all the way across this busy rather wide road I heard, "Hi Mr. Dunenger! Hi, Mr. Dunenger!"

I looked up and heading across the road, all excited, wanting to greet me were three handicapped folks from the kitchen staff. I was worried they were not paying attention to the traffic and could get hit by a car. I ran toward them saying, "Go back, go back, I'll come over." I made it over and had a chat with them. It was so special for them to just be able to talk with me outside the work environment.

Williston also had two very dedicated, challenged workers on the grounds crew. Dougie Brin was a very competent driver of the school's very old payloader, used for snow plowing and moving dirt around on the campus. One day, Doug came over to my office and asked to talk with me. What had happened was that he heard that I had planned to install a curb along the side of the road that circled the grass in the front of the gym. So, he offered me this piece of advice.

"Mr. Dunnington, if you put a curb around the road by the gym, I will not be able to plow the snow off the road because I will hit the curb and break it up."

I replied, "Doug you are absolutely right, I never thought of the problem you would have plowing snow. Thanks so much for your advice."

Given Doug's limitations I was very impressed how he understood how what I was about to do would hinder his work. I was only thinking it would look nicer and keep the cars off the grass. I was very impressed by his thinking and the fact he was comfortable coming directly to my office to talk directly with me.

I had another great experience hiring a person who was, at the time, receiving welfare assistance which subsidized her hourly rate. Yes, that fact saved the school money, but I had a good feeling this woman had more potential than she believed. She told me my Assistant Business Manager,

Douglas Brin In 'His Payloader'
(Williston Northampton School yearbook "Log 1978" Page 130)

Ariam Hintlian hired her to begin at $2.10, as our Assistant Switchboard Operator. She recently reminded me it was the old type switchboard with the wires you plugged in and out. You know, the Ruth Buzzi type from *Laugh-In*. She grew with the job and was eventually in charge of the switchboard and all related functions. This person was Penny Mitchell, who took on more challenges and earned more money. She became Don Lightfoot's secretary in the College Counselor's Office. Her biggest challenge came when she coordinated all the many summer programs and made sure the dorms, playing fields, hockey rink and dining hall were ready for the camps.

She writes in this memo, "The final memory is of a business manager who saw something in a struggling mom and gave her the chance to grow. You will never know the feeling I got when I got a letter from the welfare department that I was deemed self-sufficient and no longer would receive help. The greatest day in my life. You (George Dunnington, Business Manager) gave me and my children the right to dream, and we did. I can never thank you enough and I pray you include this in your memories."[88]

Yes, I will Penny, and thank you for your kind words.

There were great inequalities in the way the Williston workers were compensated. The only equality was that their pay checks were all very low, and in my opinion barely at a subsistence level. To attempt to address some of these issues I decided, in the early 70s, to hold a Christmas Party at the Headmaster's rather plush home for all the support staff. Armand Davy, Director of Dining Services, prepared a sumptuous feast, one that made everyone attending feel very special. All the folks dressed in their "Sunday best," very impressive, and everyone was in the full Christmas spirit. To make the folks feel that Williston really appreciated their service to the school, I recognized the many who had been employed at Williston for five or more years with a financial reward. While I am not sure I can exactly remember my formula for determining the money each would receive, I believe each person received one dollar for every year of service, and also for every five years of service they got an additional five dollars. The "ceremony" went like this; I would read the person's name and talk a little about the person and his/her years of service. Headmaster Ward would then shake their hand and give them the money. (How meager was the reward, and looking back, it was even embarrassing.) One special person to receive recognition was Herve Pepin of the Williston Class of 1919. He was the manager of the grounds crew, tending to the many athletic fields and tennis courts. He retired in 1973 after thirty-eight years of faithful work. He also had two sons attend Williston, Neil ('48) and Ronald ('44).[89]

Ellie Banas, Secretary to the Dean wrote me on December 24, 1984 a thank you letter, from which I quote below;

Dear George,

The staff Christmas party was a high success and as usual you were a great Master of Ceremonies. There seemed to be an atmosphere of peace and contentment among the group. You seemed very relaxed and this set the tone for a very pleasant evening.

Needless to say, the excellent food and the bonuses given to the senior members of the staff are always the highlight of the evening. Monetary remuneration is always appreciated but more important to me, is the way in which it is presented. Making one feel that he/she is a contributing factor to the successful operation of the school is very gratifying to all.

Thank you for one of the most pleasant evenings I have had while at Williston.

With sincere appreciation,
Ellie Bana

This letter clearly expressed what were my hopes and expectations for this ceremony. I cannot remember when we began this party or how many years Bob Ward and I did this before moving it to the dining hall.

Perhaps one of the most important things I accomplished while at Williston was the writing of "The Employee Handbook," a complete and thorough handbook that stated clearly to all employees (faculty, administrators, and staff) what was expected of them from the school as their employer, and in turn what the school expected from them as an employee. I could not have accomplished this significant handbook without the help of a Babson classmate, Jack Simpkin. I had known Jack when I worked at Amherst College in the 60s. He was, for many years, the Head of the Smith College Personnel Department. In the personnel department he was responsible for the several unions, staff, and faculty. He was also the father of Steve Simpkin ('74) at Williston.

For the first time, the often discretionary employment-related decision that were made by the school's management were narrowed down and made more equitable. This was a huge undertaking for both me and my secretary to be sure the written regulations were helpful to all employees. It was also necessary for me to meet with various work groups and review sections of the book as well as answer their questions. I recall, because many other similar independent schools did not have formal employee handbooks, Williston's Handbook served as a guide for them to write their own. This time period was when the business functions of the private, independent schools were becoming more professional.

I was most fortunate to have had several very competent and caring secretaries, and I am sure their experience in my office was involved in many tasks that would not likely be typical of a secretarial job in a traditional for-profit business. Each secretary had a lot of interactions with the students, and it was a part of their job they especially enjoyed. This practice was something I promoted. As an example, my first secretary, Terry Faiver, (see a wonderful Terry story in the section about the McCormick Estate) was from England and had worked for a Babson College friend who was founder and President of Lestoil in nearby Holyoke. He gave Terry a glowing report, and thank goodness for that. She was able to help me settle in and keep a very busy pace with a variety of tasks. She handled many of the travel arrangements to get our foreign students to Williston and back to their distant homes. In the early 70s, we had many students from Venezuela. While there were many private elementary schools in Venezuela, there were few quality high schools. The fact that the public schools were not competitive caused parents to look outside of their country. There also was some unrest in the country (funny to say that in 2020), which made Terry's job more difficult. Both the parents and Terry did not like using the Venezuela airlines for several reasons, but the government wanted the students to fly their airlines.

We also had a significant number of American students living in Saudi Arabia, and they also had some issues with routes. They all lived in what

I called an American compound, but there were some restrictions as to their travel. I remember a Manchester Dormitory student who talked with my secretary and told her she wanted to bring a real Christmas tree back to Saudi Arabia. She asked me to help. The girl and I went into the nearby woods and chopped down a beautiful fir tree. I rolled it up tight and tied it well and it went all the way home with her. It was a big attraction there. This could never happen today.

As you might expect, many school problems ended up in my office, either directly or through my secretary. I hired a custodian to clean the Language Building and the Art Studio (Railroad Station). He had a master's degree in geology from the University of Alaska—I thought that was strange. While peacefully working at my desk, in blasted Brenda Minici, an art teacher, with tears in her eyes telling me, "That janitor just threatened me with a knife!"

Brenda could be a very demanding person especially when it came to her workspace, but what exactly happened this time I was not sure.

I said to my secretary, "Please call Sargent Ramsey at the Easthampton Police Station and ask him if he could meet me at the office."

Meanwhile, I went over to the Railroad Station and brought back the janitor. When the Sargent arrived, I told the janitor to sit in my outer office with my secretary and we went into my inner office, closed the door and discussed what happened. As a result of our discussions the janitor agreed to leave the school.

After the Sargent left my secretary said, "Thanks, George, for leaving me alone with this guy and his knife."

I never thought about the possibilities of that.

A great thing about the Williston support staff was that they really cared about the students and many students sought out their kind words and motherly/fatherly advice. Susan Snyder, my secretary in the early 80s, wrote me on April 14, 2017 a few words that illustrated this point.

"I recall Paul Reggie ('82) from Louisiana. Such a nice kid. He stayed in touch by sending me Christmas cards. He had two children who would be in high school by now. Several years ago, he passed away. His wife informed me and continues to send me Christmas cards."

Truly a long-term relationship, of which there were many.

Susan goes on to say, "You also built a bridge between the nonacademic staff and the WNS team. In your 'reign' (tongue in cheek), you treated your staff with respect and welcomed them into your office, your life. We all knew there was a split between the highly educated faculty and the 'keep the place working' staff…Your 'staff' seemed committed to you, especially after you evened the playing field with…retirement, etc. You were always approachable and truly enjoyed your staff, especially the 'colorful' ones…I loved my years at WNS with you. It's where my life changed from marriage to motherhood to confidant to part of a bigger team. It made me who am today, and I feel lucky I had such a great experience in my first 'big girl job.'" While this is all very flattering to me, I include the stories because the workplace tone I attempted to set was the same for all employees, not any single group.

One of the school's most beloved motherly counselors was Bernice "Bonnie" Crowthers, affectionately referred to by the students as "Grandma," who ran the school Snack Bar. She always found time to talk and share with the students as they visited the Snack Bar. Her conversations were thoughtful and very sincere, thus the student went away feeling better for the chat. I always thought she was an incredible asset for the school.

There were so many wonderful stories to tell I could fill another book with them. Each and every one was important and meaningful. Looking back at my time at Williston, I feel that working with the staff and helping them appreciate that they were important in the success of the school helped us through this crisis period.

Pitcher House—A Dorm—Our Home— A Reason to Love My Job

Pitcher House was very special place for me and my family, special in many different ways as well as for each member of our family.

First, a few words about Pitcher House's physical structure. It was built as a luxurious private home with five fireplaces, a large dining area, a huge living room, a spacious hall, and a luxurious stairway to the second floor.

The second floor had four bedrooms, all with fireplaces and two baths. The third floor, where the students lived, had two bedrooms and a bath.

Our family, my wife Ann, Susan, Amy, and Geordie lived on the first and second floors. The students officially lived on the third floor, but the

The "Old" Pitcher House, A Beautiful Residence of Mr. Pitcher, Class 1891

fact of the matter was the students lived throughout the house with no restrictions—it was truly their home to enjoy.

I am going to write selfishly from my own personal experience, because it was so special to have the girls live with us. As business manager, I did not have regular contact with the students, as a teacher would have in a classroom, even though many would visit my office or in the dining hall.

A word about how our home became a Williston "residence hall" each year for two or three girls. Soon after we moved into the house to live, Deborah Hayward, Director of Admission for Girls, came to talk to me about a new student, Monica Kawarick ('73), that had arrived late from her home in Brazil. Deb felt it was very important for Monica to be comfortable in the dormitory setting so she could focus on her studies while adjusting to living at Williston. She asked if my family would consider having her live with us. Ann thought it would be a good idea, and thus began our time being dormitory parents for students that might benefit from our special circumstances.

My daily Williston routine would generally include walking home from my office and gathering our family together and going to the Dining Hall for dinner. In the Dining Hall we often sat at tables with five other students, our assigned table. Then, I would return home and often read a book with the kids or play with them. At around 7:30, I would return to the office for two or three hours. When I got home, in the evening, it was common for my kids to be in bed or to be in their rooms doing homework. The Pitcher House students, at around 9:30, would visit with friends or gather at the kitchen table, enjoying each other's company. This was also a time when we could talk about how their day went or discuss other issues they may have had on their minds. We often sat by the fireplace, in the living room, and listened to 33 RPM, vinyl records. Incidentally, I have just cleaned up a lot of those very old records and I am enjoying them again.

We lived a lot like a big family, and my older daughter Susan ('83) would hang out with the students. To make life a little more interesting, we raised a couple of litters of sheepdogs which were also very much at home with all of us. Our first dog, Agnes, was purchased from Jean Miller

('36), a Trustee and mother of five students. Because this breed of dog was very expensive, she made a deal with me so I could afford to buy one. Our family had to raise two litters of dogs, and Jean would get the pick of each of the litters. She had a large kennel on her property in Southampton where she raised dogs and boarded them.

Ann was a registered nurse, and she, too, spent a lot of quality time with the students discussing issues that were of concern. I often felt this was a wonderful and special resource for the students. Ann was a great mother to our children and this motherly instinct often carried over to the students. Our children and the students frequently brought other students to the house to enjoy our company.

I was always available to talk with the students, whether the discussion concerned their schoolwork, struggles they might be dealing with, or issues with a teacher or an academic subject. I also wrote student comment cards for the Dean of Studies and their parents about my impressions of how the student was doing in school, with extracurricular activities, and life in general. Before sending this home, I always shared my thoughts with the students. Also, in addition to performing my expected dorm head duties, we did have a wonderful time as an expanded family.

A few personal stories to share that present how many of the girls felt about living with us. Ann and I talked with each girl that asked for the opportunity to stay in this dorm, especially since there were only two or three beds available. This also gave us a chance to consider whether the fit was going to be beneficial.

Nina Goodrich ('74) was very special in so many ways, as a super special person, as an athlete, and as a student. When we talked with her, she shared some very personal stories including some struggles she had had prior to attending Williston. This greatly enriched our relationship.

She told me a story about one of her favorite teachers, Mr. Couderc. He said to her, "I understood that girls weren't as smart as boys, so he would understand if we didn't do as well in Physics. We were #1, 2 and 3 in the class."

Can you just imagine how this comment would be accepted in 2021?

Nina goes on to say, "Ann (Dunnington) and I spent a great deal of time together. She was a real mentor for me. I also remember you helping me with my college essays. You told me to write about it the way I talked about it. That has been good advice throughout my career. My Williston memories are very positive. You and Ann were a big part of that. Thank you. You treated me like a friend. I also remember you both being friends with your kids, and I have tried to do the same with mine."

Another resident, Linda (Malgeri) Wellner ('79), said, "The teachers at Williston lifted me up from the debilitating low self-esteem I had when I arrived. You and Ann were a part of that support that helped me have the courage to carry on and get a Bachelor of Science degree. Living in Pitcher House was the best living situation of my many years at Williston. It was so wonderful to come home from classes and find Ann at the kitchen table ready to chat…It was so comfortable in that house and many things that happened there shaped my goals for my own future home…Ann used to leave a small vase of flowers in our room to greet us when we first arrived in the fall. I now do that for guests who come to my home. Also, the dinner parties you used to have that included us were an inspiration to me as well. I had such parties my entire life." Finances put a lot of pressure on Linda, so she went immediately to work. "I applied late to UMass as a computer science major. The excellent reputation of Williston and my grades enabled me to start that program as a sophomore."

Ann and I were always aware of our opportunity to share with the students, as it was a real pleasure and very rewarding. Perhaps it is because my wife has passed that I feel so wonderful writing about the students that shared their experiences with Ann.

Linda goes on to say, "I loved Ann. She was and remains one of the most important people in my life. We used to talk about life and philosophy for hours in the time after school before you arrived home. Some of her views about being open and honest with one's children helped guide me in being a good mother. She was a good mother to me. I have good memories of you too, George. I remember your talents as a carpenter and your silly jokes. I don't remember if you mixed gin and tonics or martinis, but I thought your skills as a cook and as a bartender were awesome fun. I remember you driving around campus in your red jeep and the close relationship you had with Roger Maroni ('74)."

This next story I tell is about Anne Mehr ('80), because she, like all the other girls, was also very special. We have stayed in close contact over all these years. Anne starts off her note by saying, "If it were not for Pitcher House I would not have stayed at Williston. Pitcher House defined Williston for me. The 3rd floor of a beautiful three-story Victorian home served as home away from home for me for two years. Two bedrooms and one bath on the third floor was shared among two or three Williston girls each year. The Dunningtons—George and Ann, their three children, Susan, Amy, and Geordie, became my family away from home. Their two English sheepdogs, Agnes and Benjamin, were the Pitcher House Greeters, greeting everyone as soon as you walked in the backdoor after classes or practice. I confided in George and Ann about my teenage angst and asked advice about boyfriends. The girls and I became friends and Geordie was the terror and tease that every little brother should be. My flat mates and I often shared preparing and enjoying lavish dinners on the weekend with the family, dining in the formal dining room (red wine and all), and lounging in the living room by the fire listening to vinyls of Joan Baez, Carly Simon, George Carlin, Jackson Brown, Cat Stevens, and James Taylor."

A few fun stories for you to enjoy.

I remember taking two Pitcher House students, and Amy, Geordie, and Romney Mosher, camping up to the Williston woods in Southampton. This was a beautiful wilderness that had a very cold, fast-running stream. The fun began by seeing (not me) who could lay down in the freezing cold stream for the longest time, our version of an Outward-Bound test. Then, we assembled our tents. I am not a camper, but Geordie, our dog Benjamin, and myself were in one tent. Amy and Romney were in another, and the two Pitcher House girls, experienced campers, were in another. All was fine, in spite of a little nervousness from the younger folks. As the very quiet and beautiful nighttime settled in on us, we could hear an animal cracking the branches as it walked nearby our tents. This immediately brought Benjamin, our dog, to full attention, and he expressed his concern with a very deep and powerful growl. He woke up all the campers, and I am sure they were all imagining "Bigfoot" was out there. Even with all this excitement, we finally all got back to sleep.

Halloween was a big trick or treat night, and Nina Goodrich ('74) decided to make my daughter Amy a costume. It was a big UNICEF box that she could get into and walk around the neighborhood, collecting candies. We reached one house, the Strongs, and they had a huge old house, where every year they set up an elaborate, scary walk through their house. Amy wanted to go in with Nina, so she got out of her box and left it by the sidewalk. When she returned, very unexpectedly, her UNICEF box had many coins in the bottom!

Another Williston tradition was Winter Carnival. Each dormitory would build a snow sculpture, which would be judged. So, Nina Goodrich ('74) and others from the house decided we would build a huge whale. I cheated and took the school's big payloader—snow plow—and made an absolutely enormous pile of snow in the front yard of Pitcher House, larger than any other dorm could possibly have made. After making the pile of snow, we carved out the huge shape of a whale, including the mouth and the tail. Nina got some purple dye and we colored the whale. The finishing touch was when we ran a garden hose up through the head, and thus our whale could blow water out of her spout.

We had lots of fun and delicious dinners in the very gracious dining room. At our table we could seat 12 diners. What do think one of the favorite menus consisted of? It was fondue, all kinds, with three fondue

Thar, She Blows

pots bubbling away emitting an awesome smell of brandy and cognac. It was legal, said the school, to cook with wine—it was not legal to drink it. Well, leave it to the girls to find recipes containing alcohol. I do not believe they used a measuring spoon to determine how much would be good. Lots of fun and delicious fondue!

The midnight raid of the Pitcher House ladies. In the lower level of Memorial Dorm was the school Snack Bar. Armand Davy, our dining hall director, was always on top of protecting his delicious Snack Bar goodies from students illegally entering and raiding the Snack Bar. His security included the best motion detectors, etc. Well, as his immediate "boss," we often talked about keeping food and the like secure. My inquisitive mind had to know exactly how the security systems worked. With this highly guarded information in hand, I led the whole Pitcher House gang secretly out of the house and sneakily went across campus and down to the Snack Bar. First, employing the top-secret security information, I shut off the alarm system. Next, being an old drug store soda-jerk, I began making banana splits, hot fudge sundaes with delicious whipped cream, chocolate fudge sauce, bananas, and strawberries, all on top of huge scoops of vanilla, chocolate, and strawberry ice cream. With our sweet tooths satisfied, we now returned to the house and had a celebration of our mischievousness. I do not believe Bonnie, the Snack Bar Manager, nor Armand ever figured out what had happened.

Patty Corkin ('75), another wonderful Pitcher House student, wanted to bake a carrot cake for a friend's celebration. Ann, my wife, always was ready to help, and especially this time as Patty had never baked a cake. They managed to make a very delicious smelling and scrumptious looking carrot cake. Well, you know a cake has to cool. Where? A good spot was on the back of the stove top. Cooling nicely and smelling very delicious. Enter Agnes, our big sheepdog, to check out those special smells. She did just that, and ate the whole cake! When Patty discovered the empty cake pan, she was just about in tears.

Ann said very compassionately, "Don't worry Patty I'll help you make another one. Maybe better than the first."

So, they busily worked to mix the batter and made another delicious carrot cake. They waited patiently as the cake cooked, and its amazing aromas wafted throughout the house again. Ding! went the stove timer, and excitedly Patty removed her cake from the oven.

She asked, "Where can I put this cake where Agnes can't get it again?"

Ann suggested she put it way-up on top of the refrigerator. There is no way Agnes is going to get it way up there! So, we all went off to do our thing while that beautiful scrumptious cake cooled. Patty could hardly wait. Well guess what? The refrigerator was next to the kitchen cabinet countertop, and apparently, not a challenge for Agnes. She jumped up on to the kitchen counter, a stunt we had never seen her perform before. Once on the countertop, it was easy for her to put her feet up on the top of the refrigerator and happily enjoy the second cake. I am sorry, but I cannot remember what happened after that, except to I know Patty was most upset.

One of our favorite things to do in the Fall was to load up the school's flatbed truck and drive to the beautiful town of Amherst to Atkin's Farm Stand, with its miles of apple orchard. Each of us would, at the stand, get a large bag and head out to fill their bag with the various kinds of apples, MacIntosh and Cortland. Naturally, while picking we were always eating the apples. There was a challenge—not just any apple would meet our standards, but only the biggest, reddest apple that was on the very top of the tree. You probably know the one I am talking about. This challenge never phased our kids, as there was always one that could climb the tree with little effort.

Now, for the best part. Back to the farm stand, where they were always baking hot, sugar-covered donuts that had amazing, mouthwatering smells. If that is not bad enough, they had the freshest squeezed cider to drink with your warm, sugary donut. What a wonderful outing, even though some of us did not feel too good after eating so much. The other fun things were that I often invited students from foreign lands to go to the orchards, where they likely never had such an experience.

On another outing I took my daughter Susan and four of the students and we went to our house in Mystic, Connecticut to go for a sail in my 26' sailboat. We sailed over to Watch Hill, RI and I cooked dinner on the boat's tiny alcohol stove. We enjoyed the evening together as we were rocked to sleep by the soft waves splashing against the boat. I cooked breakfast, which of course always tastes better when you are out on the ocean taking in the sea breezes. It was a new experience for most of the students, but they all took a hand at sailing the boat.

It was not uncommon for the Pitcher House students to bring friends to visit and talk. So, there was often activity at the house. A none-speaking deaf student, Kenny Glickman ('73), came over to "talk" with me. He grew up using sign language and did not read lips, so his attempt to speak was difficult for me to understand—I would get nervous and struggle. What he wanted me to do was to call his girlfriend and be the interpreter. Well, this got to be too much for me, so I called Ann and said, "Please help Kenny." She was amazing at listening to his girlfriend and trying to tell Kenny what she was saying, employing her lips and her hands as best as possible. It was so nice that Kenny came to our house for help.

I once taught cross-country skiing as a Winter Session course. In those days, we had the good old fashion wood skis that needed waxing. To do so, we used an old flat iron to melt-in the wax. Teaching this task was part of the course. The cellar in Pitcher House was a great place to teach the art of waxing the wooden skis. It was a tough course for me to teach because it was so weather dependent—yes, we needed snow. But, when the weather was perfect and there was a full moon, we would all go down behind the Raucher's Riding stables where there was a beautiful meadow and lots of gentle hills. I remember this fondly, as we would ski for a while, get hot and tired, then sit down in the snow and look up at the gorgeous, star-studded sky. It does not get any better than that.

As a dorm head I was also the students' advisor. This I enjoyed, as I got a chance to talk about the girls' life at school and their future plans. Also, as dorm head I had other duties like making sure the students were in the house at the proper time after their evening free time. I had a lot of trust in all the Pitcher House students and never had any issues. Except, well maybe, but not really.

This one evening, Anne Mehr ('80) had a "work job," which was to supervise the art center in the evening. She was an enthusiastic potter and could lose herself in her work at the potter's wheel. About the time when she was supposed to be home, she was not. So, I called Bob Cary, our one and only security officer, from our kitchen, using my walkie-talkie, not

Pitcher House Gang 1976
From left to right, Me, my son Geordie ('86), Lisa Hefelfinger, an Agnes puppy, my wife
Ann with Agnes, my daughter Amy ('83), two more Agnes puppies, Ann Mehr ('80)
In front, Susan ('80) and our dog Penny

realizing Bob was just outside the kitchen window. He looked up at me and asked what I wanted.

I said, "Bob, have you seen Anne Mehr tonight?"

Anne and Bob were talking with each other right below the window, and he looked up and said, "She is right here!"

Oh well, as I said, "the students never gave me any issues." I encouraged Bob to talk with the students and he was good at getting to know many students.

When there was a school Trustee meeting and the students were on break, Pitcher House also served as a place for two or three Trustees to spend the night up on the third floor where the students stayed. This was a great relaxing time for me, as the Trustee meetings were very stressful and required a lot of preparation. Likewise, the Trustees had often driven a distance and had to endure meetings all day. So, it was also a wonderful time for us to share an evening drink and talk about nothing special, but perhaps get a better understanding of each other. I was fortunate also because the Trustees seemed to have faith in my work, and I believe they relied on me for honest, straightforward reporting. Without their support, there would have been no way I could have accomplished what I did.

Such a beautiful house in its day, it had been badly neglected by the school for many years. Thus, the luxurious shine of its beautiful craftsmanship was somewhat diminished. The warmth of its occupants and the many visitors simply covered up all wounds of its hard life. To all the girls who lived in Pitcher House, you made Ann's and my life very special.

It was a great pleasure for me and my family to share this house with the students, faculty, and friends.

Thank you all.

Outstanding Williston People
Early 1970s

WHEN I DECIDED TO WRITE THIS SECTION OF THE BOOK, I KNEW it was fraught with issues, especially who was not included and recognized in this chapter. A wonderful school such as Williston, as you may expect, has many dedicated alumni and friends. One such special person comes immediately to my mind is Dan Cain ('64), a dedicated alumnus, Trustee, and a thoughtful and generous person. In the early days when we were seemingly always dealing with survival issues, he not only was a friend but always there to lend an encouraging word and give financial support. Dan Prigmore ('64) would also be another alumnus who was very generous when it was most needed.

Because it would be practically impossible to write about all the Williston people who were dedicated and generous, I chose only seven people. These individuals were selected primarily because their significant generosity, treasure, and time came at a time when the school was facing a terrible financial disaster. Thus, their gifts and service to the school also helped me keep the school operating and gave me hope when there was very little.

Margaret Eastman French, Williston Trustee, Parent, and Grandparent

MARGARET EASTMAN FRENCH, BORN ON MARCH 30, 1907, WAS, IN many ways, a very special lady. Mrs. French had a strong relationship to The Northampton School for Girls, where her daughter Robin graduated in 1957. Mrs. F., as she was sometimes known, had been a Trustee at NSFG and then continued at the combined Williston – Northampton School (WNS). Her grandson, Scott, graduated from WNS in 1975 and her granddaughter, Laura, graduated in 1980. Thus, these schools were especially meaningful to her.

What began as a close working relationship between Mrs. French, the Chair of the Board's Buildings and Grounds Committee, and me, the Business Manager, eventually ended with my caring for her as she struggled with old age and medical issues. This story about Margret is a very personal story. She enthusiastically helped Williston and me for several years. And, when her health began to decline, I was pleased to be able to be of personal help for this special lady.

My very first encounter with Mrs. French was at one of my early Board of Trustees meetings in the Homestead. When the meeting was over, she said, "I want to show you some of the Williston buildings so you can see for yourself how desperately they need major physical work." We went out the rear door of the Homestead and over to the adjacent Memorial Dormitory, down the seemingly endless cinderblock corridor where everything just looked depressingly bleak.

The floor tiles were falling apart, the old acoustic ceiling tiles were water stained with many missing, the walls were marked up with graffiti. In some places, the paint was rubbed off to the bare cinderblocks, where the maintenance people had tried, over and over, to remove graffiti. We then went downstairs to the basement, which was essentially one big room with a single lonely, forlorn ping-pong table—a dark dungeon with almost no windows and few operating lights. The floor was covered with trash and the paint was absolutely awful. It was clear that little or no maintenance had been done to this building in years (see chapter on Buildings).

We went through three or four other buildings and the deferred maintenance was just as dreadful. The main classroom building, The Schoolhouse, was so run down it was embarrassing to me. The heating units in each classroom were covered with graffiti and the abused metal covers did not fit correctly on the units. They, too, needed paint. The lighting was terrible with old fluorescent fixtures, and the walls were painted with that awful institutional green color so many times that the paint had chipped off in large pieces, exposing the very attractive old bare brick of the once mill factory. This scenario was the same in almost every building, very depressing. The challenge of making the campus more

Memorial Dormitory 1967
(Memorial Dormitory Williston 1967 Log Yearbook)

livable and beautiful was fully accepted with amazing enthusiasm by Mrs. French. She clearly understood that prospective students and their parents expected much more, as this was to be their home away from home where they would live and learn.

In the beginning, Mrs. French and I met once or twice a month for lunch at the Lord Jeffery Inn, located in the center of nearby Amherst, the Inn where Robert Frost once resided. Eating there was quite special for me; it had a wonderful feeling of class and good food. The Inn was formally owned by Amherst College, so it was not unfamiliar to me. At the Lord Jeff, I got a very nice lunch and at the same time updated Mrs. French on the school's finances and the many physical plant projects, both in progress and waiting to begin. Maggie, as I affectionately called her, continued to personally keep a sharp eye on the campus, checking out the big projects, and when she saw something in need of repair, she would say to me, "What can we do about that mess? It is not good for our Admission Office people to have to show prospective students and their parents, this horrible unkept structure when they are on a campus tour." She also liked to talk with our Director of Admission, Tom Evans, and asked him about what he thought needed attention. Tom's great personality would truly encourage Mrs. French to do more.

Working so closely with Maggie, a Trustee, was exciting and challenging. When she visited the school to see me, she parked her big, bright emerald green Chrysler New Yorker just outside my office at the Schoolhouse. It was an impressive car with lots of chrome. The spare tire was mounted on the back inside a shiny circular case, in the grand, classic style. The vanity license plates proclaimed the car's owner: "Mrs. F." I never thought so much about that until one day a student, Roger Maroni ('77), said, "Wow you must be meeting with a big celebrity." She did show up often and we had very interesting and constructive conversations.

You have to remember that I was constantly dealing with the fact we had very little cash in the bank.

As you are about to read, Maggie was a Godsend. I think we have clearly established that there was almost no end to projects that needed our immediate attention. And, I think we have also established we had very little money to spend. Maggie knew this, and understood the importance of this, so she said to me, "George let's put some carpets in the corridors of Memorial Dormitory, and I will pay for them." That is the kind of Trustee every school wants on their board. It was also very uplifting to me because I knew seeing any beautification work being done meant a great deal to the students and the faculty.

Here are a few numbers that illustrate our financial challenges. For the fiscal year ending June 30, 1973 we had an operating deficit of $465,045.[90] That number was indeed very concerning.

We also borrowed funds from the school's Plant Funds (money restricted for plant projects) in the amount of $326,263.[91] And, we transferred funds from the Funds Function as Endowment to the Current Operating Fund in the amount of $938,063.[92] We did this while knowing we had funds coming from the sale of the NSFG campus that would partially offset this borrowing, also knowing this sale would reduce operating expenditures.

Being aware of how expensive it was to hire independent contractors to do a project, I began thinking how we could do jobs inside, that is, with our own workforce. Also, I personally had the knowledge to understand and even design major projects. As a matter of fact, I enjoyed running a project, especially when I had caring workers and an appreciative headmaster and faculty. Insisting on quality work added some to the project cost. For example, it meant replacing dormitory doors when they were very beat up, instead of trying to put more crack filler and paint on them.

Mrs. French was truly excited about seeing the projects underway and completed. It was equally exciting for me to share the visits with her while the projects were in progress. She was always appreciative of the workers and enjoyed telling them how much she valued them when on our walking tours. This really boosted the workers' spirits. A Trustee was a "big wheel" and the craftsmen knew she was knowledgeable of their work. They did not often get to meet or especially talk with a prominent Trustee.

To illustrate her enthusiasm and commitment for her role as Trustee, I clearly remember one day when I did not have the necessary cash in the bank to meet the school payroll. I was quite creative when it came to finding operating cash, but this time, I was really struggling to figure out how we could meet this challenge that was looming heavily upon us. I considered going to our local bank and securing a short-term loan, but I felt this would send a message of desperation, which I knew the bankers were possibly already thinking. So, I gathered up my courage and called Maggie, told her my dilemma and she generously said, "How much do you need? If you can come over and pick me up and take me to my bank, I'll give you a bank check." Bingo! The check was for $10,000, and it was a gift! While I felt like I had dodged another bullet, I also really enjoyed watching Mrs. French's pleasure in helping Williston.

Her biggest and perhaps the most significant addition to the campus was the construction of the Whitaker – Bement Center, which was designed by the Trustees and staff of the NSFG to be a "retreat" for the girls coming to the Williston campus for the first time. It was an architecturally well-designed structure, not like many other buildings on campus. NSFG, before merging with Williston, had planned to build a new facility on their campus and Mrs. French had already contributed $200,000 toward that project. The balance needed for construction came from NSFG gifts. When I arrived, the building foundation had been started and I immediately became the clerk of the works. Not only did I meet almost daily with the contractor and architect, but I met at least weekly with Maggie. I remember on one of my regular visits with Maggie, the contractor was doing the final grading around the building.

We were standing by the side of the building looking down the steep slope to Park Street and I said, "Maggie I am worried about trying to start a new lawn around this structure, as these steep slopes will make it difficult to get the grass seed to take hold, especially if we get a heavy rain. The topsoil will surely wash out. I would like to use sod because it eliminates the possibility of a wash-out, and it looks great immediately."

Without a minute's hesitation she said, "Yes, let's use sod," followed by the magic words, "I will pay for it!"

One day, as I was talking with one of our biology teachers, John Gow, affectionately called "Doc", he mentioned how much a greenhouse would add to his class curriculum. He always seemed to have some rather straggly plant thing growing in his classroom. I knew immediately Maggie would be interested in helping to acquire a greenhouse. She was always

Whitaker—Bement Center 2017

moved to action if a project directly benefited a faculty member and the students. So, I talked with her and showed her how it could be attached to Doc Gow's classroom. I did some research and found that we could get a well-equipped greenhouse, with automatic vents and plenty of room for plants for approximately $12,000. Our maintenance crew could build the brick foundation and hook up the water.

I called Maggie and told her what information I had found, and she said, "George, I would like to take on this project, so can you order it now?"

Williston was blessed with two outstanding theatre faculty members, Ellis Baker and Richard Gregory. These men were extremely skilled in the theater arts and were, in my opinion, perfectionists. Our theater, unfortunately, was rather run-down and shabby and Ellis, a very persuasive person, would chat with me, pleading for some help to improve his theater facilities. His list was long—sound system, lighting, chairs reconditioned and set-up so they could be moved easily, adding to the flexibility of a production, interior painting, and a new stage floor. Once again, I reached out to Maggie, who was already quite fond of both Ellis Baker and Richard Gregory, and asked her if she would like to become involved.

She responded, "The theatre certainly needs lots of fixing up, and the performances are always so wonderful. The theater program is an important asset to the school. Yes, I think that would be a project that I would enjoy seeing you undertake, and I will make a gift to get it done."

Her enthusiasm was powerful, and it made me feel very energized and excited. I knew she was not making gifts just because she was wealthy; I knew she was giving from her heart, and she participated with such joy.

On one of my many visits to her Pelham, Massachusetts home, I observed that her house exterior had been neglected for too many years. My memory says the house was sided in natural redwood, which was starting to deteriorate. So, I offered to get a contractor to restore this once-beautiful wood.

Then I mentioned the fact that we had discussed the need to build a garage-like structure to protect her car. Also, it would make it easier for her in the winter, when previously the car would have been covered with ice and snow. She was excited about this idea, and I contacted a local contractor who built the carport. I had always wondered why she never built a garage when she built the house.

Maggie's husband, Paul, had some health issues, which often made her life very difficult. For many years, Paul ran and owned the only bookstore in downtown Amherst. And, again, Margaret set him up and made it possible for him to own the store. As it happened, this store was used by Amherst College as their only bookstore. Hence, he sold textbooks to the Amherst College students. This fact had to be a major reason for the store being successful. The college eventually decided to operate their own bookstore, which led ultimately to the closing of Paul French's "village" bookstore. The closing of the store, in my opinion, exacerbated Paul's depression, which often outwardly appeared as ugliness around the home.

It is also of interest, as I have noted elsewhere in this book, that the connections between Amherst College and Williston ran deep, even up to modern times. Stanley King, a past President of Amherst College, in his book wrote, "The year 1895 is remembered today (1951) by our alumni because in that year, the College graduated two of its most distinguished sons, Calvin Coolidge and Dwight W. Morrow. Both later became trustees, as did two of their classmates, Herbert L. Pratt and Lucius R. Eastman." Lucius R. Eastman was Maggie's father.[93] Mr. King went on to say,

"In 1943 we received $10,000 from the estate of Lucius Root Eastman, '95. And in 1947 his widow added $40,000 to the Fund. Lucius Eastman was one of seven brothers who graduated from Amherst. His father was a member of the class of 1857, his grandfather, a member of the class of 1833; his great-grandfather was a contributor to the Charity Fund of the College in 1818-1819. His two sons graduated from the College, and his daughter (Margaret French) married a graduate (Paul French—Maggie's husband)... In 1905, her father became president of Hills Brothers Company, distributors of Dromedary Dates, and later of other food products, a concern in which his wife's family were the principal owners."[94] Nabisco eventually bought out this company and Maggie subsequentially traded her Hills Brother stock for Nabisco: a major source of her wealth.

She came to me on one of our visits and asked, "I want to move out of this house. Could you find me an apartment to move to?"

This was a rather shocking request, as I had no idea things were at that level of unpleasantness at the house. Immediately I said, "Maggie do you really want to do this and leave your beautiful home in the Pelham hills?"

She was emphatic and said, "Yes, all I want to bring to the new place is my bed and a couple of pieces of furniture."

As it so happened, they had just completed building an attractive apartment complex right in downtown Amherst. She could walk to her bank, Amherst's First National Bank, or the grocery store, Louis's Market; everything was convenient. She visited the empty, new apartment and immediately wanted to completely refurbish the interior. We had an interior designer come from a large Springfield department store. She designed all the window coverings and the wall paint. Maggie also wanted a new dryer and washer, which I got for her. She seemed to be anxious to move in and enjoyed watching the apartment become her "home." I clearly remember the day she finally told me she wanted to stay there. I could see she was uneasy, and she forced herself to do it because she had to. I offered to stay with her the first night, but she conjured up the courage to do it on her own.

If my memory is correct, I got a call from her the very next day, or shortly thereafter, and she told me, "I think I want to go back to my house."

Again, I went through the same drill, only in reverse, trying to make sure she did not want to give it a little more time before she made the move back. Maggie had a mind of her own, and when she made a decision, that was it!

All Maggie did for Williston, as well as the fact she became a real personal friend, made me become personally concerned for her deteriorating health. She lived in the home she built that was located on a hillside looking down over the Town of Amherst, but there were no close neighbors. To the best of my knowledge, she had no friends and her two children lived rather far away. So, when she stopped coming regularly to Williston, I increased my visits to her house.

On one of my visits, I remember her telling me about when she got married the first time, and it was not working out for her. Back in those days she said, "Divorce was not that acceptable." She did it anyway, and moved to Las Vegas, Nevada, where she bought a ranch and lived for a while enjoying her horses.

Back to the story—when she left the apartment, I offered to have the school's grounds crew come over and move her belongings out. Very little went to her Pelham home, and she said, "Would you take all of the other furniture, washer, and dryer back to the school and give it to the faculty who could really use it?"

By this time, her husband, Paul, had passed, and Maggie's health continued to slip. She was alone now and did not have anyone nearby to take care of her. I called on her several times during the week and brought food to her and we chatted. On one of my visits, she came to the door in a very flimsy nightgown. This was upsetting to me, as this certainly was not the Margaret French I knew. I immediately tried to get her to eat some food. She recently had befriended a cat and it was her close companion—her only companion. So, for the next few visits, my wife Ann was kind enough to come with me as I was not sure what might happen next. Things got worse and very upsetting to me; she absolutely did not want to go to the hospital or a care center.

Our next visit was the final one, as Maggie came to the door to meet us, with hardly anything on, and said, "I want you to come to my bedroom and see my babies." Not understanding what was going on, I followed her down the corridor to her bedroom. On the bed was her cat and three newborn kittens—her babies—born on the bed! I immediately called her doctor, as I could clearly see she was in need of fulltime medical help. It was a very sad time for me, and I never knew what happened after that. I assumed her family took over the situation.

Williston was Maggie's whole life, and she lived it fully. She thoroughly enjoyed working with members of the Williston family, especially Headmaster Robert A. Ward, Administrative Assistant Charlotte Turgeon, and me.

In 1977, Margaret E. French was honored, "In recognition of your outstanding devotion to Williston Northampton, you have been awarded the school's highest honor, the Distinguished Service Award. In acceptance of it, you do honor to the award and to your school."

I never worked with a Trustee so sincerely involved in the well-being of the school, and I truly believe she was one of a very few who played a major role in saving the school. Thank you, Maggie!

Roger P. Clapp, A Wonderful and Generous Human Being

ONE OF THE GREAT THINGS ABOUT BEING A BUSINESS MANAGER AT a private school is you have the opportunity to meet so many wonderful, and even extraordinary people.

One such story begins when I was busily working on a rather warm summer day in 1973, in my office in the Schoolhouse building. It was very quiet; few people worked a regular schedule in the summer time. There was a very gentle knock on my door and in a rather soft voice I heard, "Would you have a minute to talk with me?"

"Sure, come right in."

In walked a rather timid, older gentleman dressed in a not-so-special suit and a soft hat. He said in a quiet voice, "I am Roger Clapp, I hope I am not interrupting you."

Immediately I replied, "No, not at all, please come on in. Have a seat, and what can I do for you?"

"My dad was a graduate of Williston Academy in 1875, and a very active Trustee for many years. My father used to tell me all about the school and how it struggled, but had wonderful teachers. Being deeply involved in the school meant a lot to him and he talked about his experiences there all the time. Especially about working on the blueprints for Ford Hall." And then he said, "I am interested in what is happening now. I went to Exeter (Class of 1915) and to Harvard College (Class of 1919) and to the Harvard Business School, and all of these schools are in very good financial shape. [Never a truer word was spoken] So, I would like to see if I can be of help to Williston."

I sensed immediately he knew what he was doing and how a "business" should be run. He was, many years ago, a fund manager of Boston's Stone and Webster and a real entrepreneur. I told him, "The school has recently made some very good decisions, including hiring a new Headmaster, Robert A. Ward, and Williston has just merged with the Northampton School for Girls."

And, what a great school it was, with a strong faculty and fine students. I also told him about some of our difficulties.

We talked for about 45 minutes, then he said, "I have named Williston in a unitrust agreement, and it will be a substantial amount of money [$263,500]. I would like to meet with you often, if you have time. It is important to me to follow the school's academic programs, but also I would like to see monthly financial reports."

I thought to myself, *You bet I will have time—all the time you want!*

This began a long-term, wonderful, congenial relationship. I have always found that I enjoyed helping and talking with elderly people, and always felt they enjoyed sharing time with me. Our deepening relationship began by Roger inviting me to Boston, where we had lunch, usually at the Harvard Club or sometimes at State Street Bank. He might have been elderly, but I found myself breathing noticeably harder trying to follow him through the streets of Boston. On more than one occasion, he crossed the street without the crossing light. It concerned me very much, but it did not worry him in the slightest. Boston was his Town!

He really enjoyed telling me stories about his life, and each story was extremely fascinating. Roger was a detail man, so when he invited me to the Harvard Club, located near the corner of Massachusetts Avenue and Boylston Street, he would say to me, in great detail, "You should drive around to the back of the Club and tell the parking lot attendant that you were here to have lunch with Mr. Clapp. I have arranged for free parking."

This he worried about, as he did not want me to have to pay $10.00. Also, remember we were dining in the historic Harvard Club dining room with its very dark and rich-looking woodwork, high ceilings, and marble floors—very impressive, very old, stodgy, classy Harvard. About this same dining room, he told me that in the past, they would set-up a full-size boxing ring, and have serious boxing matches.

Dodge Brother's 1919 Touring Car[95]

I will try to recall a few more of his stories, as they both intrigued me and told me a great deal about this great man.

When he graduated from Harvard College in 1919, he told me he and his roommate had written letters to Mr. Dodge of the Dodge Motor Company, trying get him to lend them a new Dodge car to drive across the country.

Roger's sales pitch was that if they successfully drove across the country, it would be a great testimonial to the quality of the Dodge car. At this time, he reminded me, there was no transcontinental highway, therefore there were lots of dirt roads and mountainous roads in not very good condition. Hence, they had issues with the car along the way, but they did make it to California. Upon arriving, Roger declared the car not really useable.

Roger's career was absolutely fascinating, and he very much enjoyed telling me about it in great detail, as he was very proud of how he made his money from hard work. During World War II, he started a company that made steam valves for many of our war ships and for many steam boilers.

They were labeled Clapp Valves, and I believe we had one or two in the old gym boiler room at Williston that measured the steam pressure for the boilers that heated the gymnasium, Ford Hall, Memorial Dormitory, Schoolhouse, and the Language Building. Recently, Charles McCullagh, Chief Financial Officer, took me down to the old boiler room where we found the boilers completely dismantled, but I did not find the Clapp valve that I was hoping to find.

At each of our visits he would say to me, "I want to make another gift by a certain date, but remember, this is not a promise." Again, he would say, "You understand I will try, but it is not a promise." It puzzled me why he emphasized "it is not a promise." Was it because he knew how important his gifts were to the school and did not want us to count on receiving the gift in the event, for some reason, he could not give the gift when he said?

Ggauge by Clapp of Webster Mass. Appx 7 ½ O.D.
(Nautical Antiques & Tropical Décor 2202 Ship Mechanic Row, Galveston TX 77550)

One of his dates was, "I'll try to do something by Easter." Easter Sunday arrived, and I had totally forgotten his "promise." My wife, Ann, and our three children were walking out of the back door of Pitcher House, our campus home, to go to Steven's Chapel for Easter Services, when I heard the kitchen phone ring. For some reason, I ran back to answer the phone, and it was Roger Clapp.

He said, "George, I feel bad because, you remember, I said I would try to make another gift by Easter. Is it all right if I drive up to Williston now?"

Rather excitedly, I responded, "Sure, but I will be glad to drive to Cambridge and meet you."

He replied, "No, no."

Remember, he was elderly and drove a not-so-new Nash Rambler with New Hampshire plates. I noted his car had the New Hampshire plates, so I asked about it, and he said, "It is cheaper if I register my car there instead of Cambridge." He said he had a beautiful home in Meredith N. H. on Lake Winnipesauke. His head, when sitting behind the wheel of his car, was hardly above the wheel, very concerning to me.

I said, "Why don't we meet halfway?"

He replied, "OK, how about Howard Johnson's on the Massachusetts Turnpike in Sturbridge?"

This made me a little nervous, because in those days we did not have a GPS or even cell phones, thus we could not communicate if something went wrong. Our meeting place, Howard Johnson's, was on the Eastbound side of the turnpike. So, I left my family and hopped into the school car that was the gift from the McCormick estate, the Chrysler sedan, and traveled to Howard Johnson's on the turnpike. I drove into the parking lot and saw his rather old American Motors Nash Rambler with the New Hampshire license plates. What a relief! These meetings were very exciting for me, as I was always wondering what he would be doing for the school this time. I walked over to his car and got in the passenger seat and noticed two things: a full #10 envelope on the seat between us, and a toll ticket. I anxiously wanted to see what was in the envelope, but as I glanced at the ticket, I saw that it was a ticket for someone heading West. He was now heading East, the way we were going to have to travel

SCHOOL DAYS

when we left the parking lot! I thought to myself, how could that happen? No, please don't tell me he cut across the median! Yes, he certainly did!

I curiously said, "By the way, Roger, do you have a toll ticket for going to Boston?"

He replied, without a thought, that like this was no big deal, "No, I took a shortcut here, and cut across the median. I'll just tell them I lost the ticket."

That guy is amazing!

Then he proceeded to tell more of his amazing and interesting stories.

He said, "I do most of my own investing, so I always make sure I know everything about the companies I invested in. This was my business for several years." He went on to say, "Now George, I would like to recommend you hold this stock until I tell you to sell it. I know one of the cardinal rules for institutions is you never hold a stock gift."

I responded, "Sure Roger, I will do that. You just call me when you feel it is the best time to sell the stock."

It was a stock in a firm related to Colt Industries in Hartford. He said it should be worth somewhere around $100,000. The Finance Committee of the school was a little concerned when I told them of Roger's request, but they went along with the request. Time went by and the stock did not do much, and at one time it even started down.

I nervously called Roger and he said, "Do not worry, continue to hold the stock."

As I remember when he finally called me to tell me to sell the stock, it had gone up from its original value, just as he had predicted it would. Have faith, George!

Another similar story: I went to Boston to have lunch with him and he said, "I have some bonds, which I will give you, but hold on to them until I tell you to sell."

Curiously I said, "Sure I will hold the bonds. Roger, just call me when it is time for us to sell."

Listening intently, he told me, "The bonds are the Boston & Maine Railroad."

"Oh, oh," I said, rather sheepishly, "I thought they went out of business years ago."

He confidently said. "That is true, but I studied this company and bought the bonds after they went bankrupt. From my research, I saw how much property they owned all along their tracks and figured these bonds would be worth a fair amount someday."

He was right! Another amazing, or at least to me, amazing, example of how well he knew his business.

On another of my Boston visits, Roger took me over to his apartment in Cambridge, on the edge of the M.I.T. campus, to meet Winifred, his wife. It was a very modest place in Cambridge, no frills in or out, but it did have a nice view looking over the Charles River.

Winifred told me how much Roger enjoyed his involvement with Williston and she said, "You know, we each have our own projects." She went on to tell me about her interest in helping American Indians to attend private schools. She explained, "It is very hard to get the Native Americans to leave their reservation."

Winifred did have some success with this project, and she planned to continue her efforts. She also helped women prisoners, who wished to learn to write poetry.

Roger said of her, "She is a woman who does not like to drive on the red lines on a map." That was so true, and when he said it, it made me feel great tenderness towards him. It was such a wonderful and caring comment.

One of his first ventures happened as he and his out-of-work, former college roommate, S. Roberts (Bob) Dunham, sent out letters indicating their desire to purchase an ongoing manufacturing firm. They were introduced to a company going into receivership. One of its employees, L. Osbourne Waterhouse, had agreed to stay on to run the factory; Bob Dunham was going to handle the business end of the firm. Clapp and Dunham retained the majority of the stock. They pleaded with the president of the bank that was involved with the company to loan them money. The bank did. Roger decided to keep the name of the firm The Waterhouse Company, in tribute to the Waterhouse family's long association with coach building. In time, Roger became president and branched into several businesses. During the War, they converted the factory over to producing tents for the army.

SCHOOL DAYS

Roger said to me, "Tents were a natural fit, as the firm had made custom convertible tops for fancy cars."

He later started making custom cars for the very wealthy, here and in Europe. His car design won a first prize at the NY Auto Show. The NY Auto Show was the premiere show for anyone wishing to sell cars, and therefore a big deal in those days. He used the Lincoln chassis on which to build his custom cars. This launched his exclusive custom car business, some of which were sold to foreign leaders, princes, and kings. He told me a funny story about building a car for a Rockefeller where Rockefeller's wife wanted a speedometer built into the rear of the car so she could clearly see the speed. She wanted to control the speed, as she believed Mr. Rockefeller drove much too fast. Mr. Rockefeller had Roger design an odometer that was, unbeknownst to Mrs. Rockefeller, 10 miles slower than the actual speed.

His stories went on and on and all were extremely entertaining.

Roger Clapp felt very strongly that Bob Ward was right about the school needing a library and Mr. Clapp wanted to help Bob Ward achieve this dream. So, Roger Clapp seized this opportunity to memorialize his father on the campus of the school where his dad was an alumnus and had worked so hard as a Trustee. We had to deal with a few other challenges, one being that test borings found water on the site that was chosen for the building. There was an underground river, higher than the foundation would need to be deep. After discovering this problem, we did test borings on the upper campus in front of the gym. There were also some problems there. The contractor felt he could deal with the water problem, so we went ahead.

I enjoyed being the clerk of the works and carefully met, almost daily, with the contractor and the architect and, of course, Bob Ward. It was a great team and we had very few problems.

Roger was the person who truly made the library happen and he was very proud to build this in memory of his dad, Robert P. Clapp ('85). Roger Clapp went on to become one of Williston Northampton School's most generous donors. My surprised meeting with Roger on that warm summer day in my office sure did develop into an amazing friendship.

When Winfred passed, Roger was a lost soul. He also became very frail and eventually moved to an assisted living complex in Needham. This

The top photo is of the site where there were tennis courts. The lower photo shows the excavation of the library basement with George Dunnington, Business Manager, and Robert A. Ward, Head of School.

facility was built on a piece of property that belonged to Babson College. I visited Roger there and sadly, he was not doing well. When the love of his life died, I believe he also figured he was ready to go, and he was comfortable with his generous accomplishments and his full life.

My memories of my time spent with Roger Clapp are very precious to me, for he truly was a wonderful person in every sense of that word.

Robert P. Clapp '85 Library Cornerstone Laying June 1979

An Unusual But Special Gift— Paul V. McCormick ('24), Greenwich, New York

Early on in my time at WNS, I received a call from a lawyer who told me the school was the sole beneficiary of the estate of Paul V. McCormick ('24), a small-town lawyer, gentleman farmer, and alum from Greenwich, NY. As I recall, at the time I could find almost nothing in our alumni records, certainly nothing that would indicate he was a potential major donor. Mr. McCormick attended Williston for only one year. He then went on to graduate from Colgate University in 1929. He was a decorated World War II veteran.

As you have read, this was a difficult time financially at the school, so when the attorney told me it could be a sizable gift, I was very excited. I immediately drove up to Greenwich, a very small town in upstate NY, the acclaimed home of "Apple Pie and Ice Cream." Also, in the past, the town was known for mining slate for roof shingles. Although slate was very beautiful and long lasting, the cost of slate shingles was very high. Their use dwindled with the ever-increasing cost, and were primarily used only in high quality institutional and commercial construction.

The estate included a Gulf gas station (the only gas station in town), an office building (for Mr. McCormick's Law Office) which was also the Town Hall, a large working farm with 900 head of Hereford cattle, farm tractors and implements, a pair of prize draft horses, a Chrysler sedan, and a Willy's Jeep with a plow.

You can only imagine what I was thinking, not being at all familiar with running a farm, a large one, at that. When the size of the estate became known, the estate attorney wisely suggested that he search for any living relatives of Mr. McCormick's to be sure that there would not be any questioning of the estate There were two distant aunts in NYC. He offered them $500.00 each to sign off, and they accepted.

Now began the fun. On my first visit to the farm, I asked Homer Perkins, President of the WNS Board of Trustees, to travel with me so he might observe what we were going to be dealing with.

Strange as this may seem, when we got out of the car, Homer said, rather softly, "Hi Frank." The farmhand, with a real country drawl, said back, "Hi Homer."

When I got a moment, I asked Homer, "How in the heck do you know this guy?"

He replied, "We went to second grade together in Easthampton."

They hardly spoke after that first meeting, even though it had been many, many years since seeing each other.

Walking through the main house I saw lots of ammunition but no guns. Pictures on the wall showed oriental rugs on the floor, but there were no rugs in the house. I confronted the farmhand/caretaker and he denied there were rugs or guns. I debated confronting Frank as to where these things might be found, but, decided not to do so, because if he left me, I would not know what to do with a large active farm. We got an inventory of the giant tractors, huge, prize draft horses, Hereford cattle, and vehicles. The people in the Town Hall pleaded with me not to sell the building, which appeared to me to be an old 1920s bank, with its giant safe and teller stations still there.

The gas station had a five-year net lease, fortunately making the renter company completely responsible for all financial obligations, taxes, repairs, electric costs, etc. After the lease expired, it was sold back to the gas company at a preset price.

I immediately drove Mr. McCormick's Chrysler sedan to Easthampton, as our WNS vehicles were all in disrepair. On our next visit, my assistant, Rick Stafford, drove the Jeep Wrangler with the snowplow back to the school. Thanks to Rick's strong back, we were able to take back to Easthampton, from the second-floor office, the copiers, typewriters, and other office equipment, using our school van to transport the items.

I never could figure how anyone could count 900 cows. I remember sitting on the fence surrounding the cattle and looking across a sea of cattle. They just would not stand still for me! The farmhand said it was possible, but I never could figure out how to do that.

It was summer, and I enjoyed spending weekends with my family on our 26' sailboat in Mystic, CT. We always thought our boat was comfortable, even for the five of us. In those days (the 1970s), to make a telephone call from the boat to someone on shore, you had to contact the marine operator in New London using a ship-to-shore radio. A unique thing about ship-to-shore radios was any boat in the area could listen in on the conversation. Often this was an evening's entertainment.

I had a simply wonderful, very competent, and very prim and proper secretary, Terry Favire (since passed and sadly missed). She called me on the boat through the New London Marine Operator and said, "There is a problem on the farm."

I detected uneasiness in her voice and said, "Well Terry, tell me what is going on."

She promptly replied, "No! You need to talk with the farmhand directly."

I immediately called the New London marine operator and got in the queue (only one person could talk at a time) for my call. Also, on our boat, at this time was my wife, Ann, and our best friends, Fred and Ann Larson. So, we were all listening to the various conversations between other boats and the shore. It was a fun and entertaining thing to eavesdrop on all the ship to shore radio traffic.

Soon came our turn on the radio, and the marine operator said, "Suannamy (my boat's name), your party is on the line."

I asked, "What is going on Frank?"

He said, "One of the cow's uteruses fell out!"

Pause. I was caught completely off guard. Meanwhile, my buddy Fred started uncontrollably rolling on the floor laughing. I am sure other boaters must also have been taken aback, as this was not an everyday boating conversation.

I said, "Frank, what do you usually do with this problem?"

He replied, in his farm drawl, "You can take her to market and you get so much a hundred weight. Or, you can call the vet and he can push the uterus back."

Being somewhat sympathetic for old Betsy, I elected the latter. Believe it or not, it happened again, and I could not help but wonder what other boaters were thinking when they heard this conversation repeated. This time. I elected to send her to market. All in a day's work for a business manager! And unforgettable entertainment for the Long Island Sound boaters.

Sometime later, I got another call from the farm and was told, "One of the prize pulling horses died." This seemed strange to me, but what did I know about horses? It was sold to the "glue factory," his words. I learned that these animals once were appraised at $1,200.00 each. Since the horses were trained over many years as a pair of pulling horses, their value was as a pair. However, only one horse was worth $400. The farm and cattle were sold to an Albany, NY slaughterhouse.

In the Autumn of 1973, we received one very generous payment: $402,285, from the Estate of Paul V. McCormick ('24).[96]

So ended my days as a farmer on a cattle ranch. Yippy Yi Oh.

This gift was very timely, for we continued to desperately need funds to use in making the campus more presentable, as we knew our admission problems often hinged on the looks of the campus.

The Board of Trustees of The Williston Northampton School, in 1992, posthumously recognized Mr. McCormick's generosity and love for his school with the Board of Trustees Citation, and on this special occasion they launched the Elm Tree Associates.

Charles H. Peter Derby ('28) Estate

In May 1983, I received a call from Attorney Jessie D. Deely of Lee, Massachusetts, informing me of Mr. Derby's recent death. He told me that, "Mr. Derby essentially left his whole estate to Williston, and it will likely be a sizeable amount."

This was truly exciting news for the school. I was most anxious to go to Becket, Massachusetts and see the property that was included in the estate.

I had not previously known of Mr. Derby, even though I had tried earlier to discover who in our alumni body might have the potential to be a major donor. What I finally found out was that Charles Derby entered Williston as a freshman in the fall of 1924, a member of the Class of 1928, but left the school after only one year. His brother William ('25) attended Williston for two years, his senior year coinciding with Charles's only year at Williston. During World War II, Mr. Charles Derby was part of the Signal Corps stationed in Burma. His mother, Ruth Derby, was very fond of Williston and on her own visited several times without talking with anyone in the school administration. She died in 1980, leaving one-quarter of her estate in a trust of which Williston was the ultimate beneficiary.

Soon after being notified of the estate, I met with a real estate agent who had a key to the home. On arriving, I found a modest, 1790, Cape Cod-style home in need of some repair. The Derbys referred to it as the farmhouse. When we opened the door to go in, I was shocked because I could hardly get past the door. "Stuff," for want of a better word, was piled from the floor to the ceiling, leaving only a small pathway through the various rooms of the house. The house was very old and still had no electricity on the second floor. The kitchen sink had a working hand pump as the only source of water.

As I slowly walked through the house, I observed numerous antiques, some of which I thought might be very valuable. Fortunately, I acted on this belief and contacted Robert W. Skinner Incorporated, Auctioneers and Appraisers in Boston, Massachusetts. As I was leaving to return to campus, I noticed a large carved decoy of a preening Canada goose. It appealed to me, so I took it back to my house on campus. This is not the end of this tale. Stand by for further details.

The Skinner representative and I made arrangements to meet and view the myriad of exquisite furniture, jewelry, and other bric-à-brac. After a very short time, the Skinner representative said, "George, there is a small fortune here and I will have to send up three of our trucks to pack it correctly for travel and take it all back to Boston to be appraised."

As we were parting I pointed to the mantel where there was a carving of a standing goose and asked, "What is something like that carving worth?"

She replied, "Could be as much as $20,000, but if you had its mate it might be worth twice that amount!"

I gulped and said stutteringly, "I believe we do have its mate, and I will see that you get it."

Immediately I began to worry about the mate sitting on the Pitcher House fireplace hearth, right in a place where one of my children or one of the students might choose to play with it. I remember being very concerned about how all these valuable items would arrive safely in Boston. My initial instinct was to try and inventory the items, but I soon realized that would be impossible.

The Skinners had multiple, specialized auctions and for each, an elaborate catalog was composed detailing the highlights of each item. A memo from Skinner, dated February 9, 1984, highlighted a few things from the auction. Referring to the Derby auctions it said, "over one half million dollars realized from the Robert W. Skinner Incorporated auctions...The collections represent two lifetimes of great vitality: those of Charles Peter Derby, who died recently, and his mother Ruth I. Derby (1886-1970)[97]...A two-day auction of most of the Derby house contents offered more than 700 lots of remarkable quality and diversity." The above information gives one some appreciation of the size, the number of items, and the value of this estate. I will share with you a few specific items and their sale price. Again, from the Skinner memo dated February 9, 1984, "Of nine lots placed in Skinner's annual October Americana, one set a new auction record: $44,000 for an A. Elmer Crowell preening Canada goose decoy (remember the one at Pitcher House? That was it—Wow!) Its mate, a mantel carving of a standing goose, went for $28,000." I had no idea of the value of the decoy of that goose sitting on my fireplace hearth.

The chair pictured below is from the cover of the Skinner catalog announcing the auction: "The Estate of Charles H. Peter Derby of Becket,

The needlepoint seat cover is worked in a bold, irregular, dark blue and green wave patterns.

SCHOOL DAYS

Massachusetts, in two sessions, Session 1: Sale 936, Friday, October 14, 1983 at 1 p.m. in Copley Sq. It is item 565. Chippendale Mahogany Corner Chair, Massachusetts, ca. 1780, shaped and curved crest above curved back continuing two shaped hand holds above three block and turned supports and shape solid splats, serpentine seat frame with slip seat, on cabriole front leg, ending in claw and ball foot and block and turned rear legs, joined by block and turned X stretcher, (slip seat reupholstered), ht. 32 ½ in." According to the *Berkshire Eagle*, dated October 21, 1983, "this item was estimated at $3,000 to $5,000."

This treasured item was sold for the grand sum of $35,000.00, and was the top sale item of the auction. So much for an educated estimate!

Believe it or not, there were several other auctions, some in his house at Becket, Massachusetts.

In addition to Charles Peter Derby's many antiques that he collected and were sold for a substantial amount of money, he also had several pieces of property in the Town of Becket, Massachusetts. Mr. Derby claimed to be a gemologist. A small structure behind his home looked as though it could have been his workshop. Otherwise, I saw no evidence of his work or collection.

I personally worked hard at trying to sell 55 acres of land located near the rather famous Jacob's Pillow Dance Festival, Inc. As the organization was a non-profit, many people had to be involved in the decision to buy the property. The age-old not-for-profit question was, where are we going to get the money? They were hoping I might reduce the selling price, but I was convinced it was a fair price. I talked to members of their Board in NYC and to local members who were most anxious to have the land. On April 30, 1986, the "CLOSING STATEMENT" showed the land was finally sold to Jacob's Pillow for $40,000.00. Another "CLOSING STATEMENT" dated November 22, 1985 stated we sold 5.633 acres on George Carter Road, Becket, Massachusetts for $45,000.00. And lastly, a "CLOSING STATEMENT" dated April 30, 1986, showed we sold "Easterly and Westerly sides of George Carter Road, Becket, Massachusetts" for $135,000.00. Just the sale of the land and buildings added $205,727.50 to the scholarship fund.

All the proceeds from the sale of antiques and the property went to fund the endowment for the Ruth I. Derby Memorial Scholarship at Williston. As of June 30, 2017, the market value of the funds was $783,675.00 and provided $42,643 in scholarships that year. In the beginning of this endeavor I must say, I never in my wildest dreams expected all the house "clutter" to approach a gift of this size. This example clearly shows how beneficial an endowed fund can be to a wonderful school such as Williston-Northampton.

Yes, the estate was one of the most complicated, multifaceted estates I ever had to deal with, but as you can clearly see, it was worth the effort.

George E. Clapp ('20) Estate

THE GEORGE E. CLAPP STORY IS YET ANOTHER INTERESTING STORY I have selected to share. Mr. Clapp was an honor student at Williston and after a long career in the newspaper business he ended up working at *The New London Day* in New London, Connecticut. After 37 years in various positions, he finally became editor for nine years, retiring in 1967.

It is a little comical as to how I learned of the fact that he had left his entire, but modest, estate to WNS. Just before moving to the Williston Campus, my family and I were living in Old Saybrook, Connecticut and I was working at Wesleyan University in Middletown, Connecticut.

Our nextdoor neighbor and a very good friend was also the Senior Trust Officer of the Hartford National Bank in their New London office. He, Fred Larson, his wife Ann, myself and my wife Ann often played cards together. We joked and played pranks on each other. From my familiarity with not-for-profit institutions, I was aware that a bank Trust Officer often managed estates when trusts were left to their organizations. As I was transitioning to Williston I joked with Fred, saying, "We really need some big gifts at Williston. Please start working on getting Williston a large estate from one of your trust clients." Why not?

This story is hard to believe, but while I was actually in the process of moving to Williston in Easthampton, Fred called me at my office and said, "I have a very nice estate for Williston, from a graduate by the name of George E. Clapp."

I replied to Fred saying, "Please do not bother me with any small gifts, I am very busy."

Naturally I was thinking this was just another one of Fred's practical jokes. After all, my wish for a bequest of an estate could not possibly happen this quickly! Soon thereafter, his Administrative Assistant, Millie

Devine called and said, "George you need to start immediately to sell Mr. Clapp's house in Quaker Hill, CT, and his car has to be moved from the New London parking garage."

I replied and said, "Millie (whom I knew), I told Fred that if the car was not a Mercedes, please do not to bother me." I was quite naturally sure this surprising gift could not be true, not in such a short time after starting to work at Williston.

Finally, I realized this bequest was indeed real, so I drove down to New London, and picked up the keys to Mr. Clapp's house and to his car and made plans to empty the contents of the house. I also contacted a realtor and authorized the house to be sold on the real estate market.

It was a modest home, but I felt it would be very marketable. After my inspection of the contents of the home I knew we could use much of the items for faculty apartments back at the school. I did distribute the furniture to the various, mostly single teachers, who usually had sparsely furnished campus apartments. The furniture was greatly appreciated as it was both functional and made these stark apartments a little homier.

Mr. Clapp was an ardent hunter and sports fisherman as was evident from the significant amount of L.L.Bean fishing rods, hiking boots and fishing gear. Some of this gear got sold at our Parents Association annual fundraiser and the rest was given away. As it turned out, the car was real—not the Mercedes I asked for, but a brand new (1976) American Motors Rambler. At this large fundraiser auction, planned and organized by one of the parents and Janet Evans, wife of Admission Director Tom, a feature of the auction was an art dealer who came to campus with many valuable art pieces to be auctioned off in Steven's Chapel. In conjunction with that, we had the tag sale in the gym and sold all kinds of generously donated stuff, including the brand-new Nash Rambler.

This was but another completely unexpected, generous gift that came at a very opportune time in 1976, as our finances continued to be stretched to the limit.

One great thing about schools is that many of their alumni have deep and meaningful feelings for their Alma Mater. Unfortunately, the school does not always discover this fact in the routine process of raising money for their annual fund. Likewise, the alums do not always act on their feelings nor advise the school of their gift intentions while they are living. It is but another reason a school needs a Development and Annual Fund Office that is continually researching its alumni.

Mr. Clapp, thank you again—you are truly among the school's "Great People" for remembering your school in your will; it made an important difference. Again, this gift was a complete surprise to us, and his name was not on the active list of alumni. As had often happened during the prior administration, when an alum did not make a gift for several years, the potential alumni donor was removed from the files. The effect of this action was it made the giving statistics look better, a goal of the headmaster. It was, however, a big mistake!

Dr. Antonio J. Giacomini ('31)

Again, in the schoolhouse, on one of my many lonely summer days in 1976, working quietly in my office, an older gentleman came to my office door. He looked as though he had just run a marathon; his shirt was wet with perspiration, and he said to me, "Do you have a few minutes to talk with me?"

I said, "Of course, come in and sit down. (Reminiscent of Roger Clapp's visit.) Let me get you something to drink."

He introduced himself as Dr. Antonio J. Giacomini, Class of 1931. He went on to say, in a very passionate voice, how much he enjoyed Williston and how it helped him all through his life. He was a dentist.

Then he said, "I have always wanted to establish an endowed scholarship fund so I might help some other student attend Williston. I could not have attended Williston without financial aid, so I kind of want to pay it back."

Anxiously, I had been waiting to ask him how he got to Williston that day, seeing him all sweaty and out of breath. I finally got my chance.

"Doctor, how did you get to Williston? You look like you might have walked?"

"No," said he. "My car broke down just before the Easthampton exit on Route 91."

I replied, "Did you walk all the way from there, up over Mount Tom and down to the Schoolhouse?"

He casually said, "Yes."

I said, "Wow, I do not think I could do that."

Fortunately, the school had a gas station nearby that serviced all the school's vehicles, and the owner was a friend. So, I said, "Why don't I drive you to the gas station so I can make sure someone goes immediately to your car and makes the necessary repairs to get the car running again?"

Now for the real shocker—remember that he was very excited and emotional when he told me about his gift intentions. He said, "George, that would be good, because I left $5,000.00 in cash under the front seat in a paper bag. I would feel better if we could go and get it as soon as possible."

I cannot possibly tell you how I felt on hearing this story; my heart went into my throat, while my mind kept thinking of all the possible bad things that could happen while we were sitting at the Schoolhouse. I drove rather quickly over Mt. Tom and down to Interstate 91, all the while the doctor kept telling me his many Williston stories. There, on the side of the highway, was his car—not so new, but looking whole, i.e. no broken windows. Dr. Giacomini unlocked the car and reached under the seat and then raised his hand up to show me a well-used paper bag. What a relief!

One of those stories he told me on our ride was about his wife. It seemed she was not of the same persuasion as the Doc when it came to making gifts to Williston, so this meant he had to hide the gift money where she could not find it. Hence, all the cash in an old brown paper bag—lots of cavities!

And, he said, "Can you make sure this gift does not become public for a while?"

"No problem, I will personally make sure it is anonymous until you tell me otherwise."

Dr. Giacomini was given the "The Samuel and Emily Williston Award," which is presented to a male graduate of the school who has demonstrated outstanding loyalty and devotion to the school. In an article he wrote in the *Summer 1977 - The Bulletin* he said, "I am most happy to have received the Samuel and Emily Williston Award. The fact the school deemed me worthy of this great honor fills me with great pride." He went on to say, "I feel that I owe much to Williston and I am proud to be one of her alumni—'Long may we cherish Williston!'"[98]

I am pleased to say this gift has been providing Williston students with scholarship money ever since 1976, and the principal market value as of June 30, 2019 is $77,043.

In the early 70s, the school continued to struggle, especially as we had many physical plant projects happening, so a gift like this one made me very grateful and joyous. Again, I believe Dr. Giacomini's name had been stricken from the alumni list by the prior administration as he was not a giver. A lesson to be learned, and fortunately, Williston now does an excellent job at staying in touch with its alumni and friends no matter what they give.

Theodore (Ted) Adams, the School's Independent Plummer

It may seem to the reader a little strange that I chose to include Ted Adams in this section of my book where I discuss people who gave gifts at a time when the school was in great need. After reading this story, I think you will agree with my decision.

Ted Adams, the school plumber, was a very special person in many ways. He cared deeply for the school. His father, Ted Sr., before him, was also the school plumber for decades. I had the pleasure of meeting him on the job just before he retired when he was in his 80s. In the basement of the Schoolhouse, he and Ted were mixing powdered asbestos to put on the steam pipe using their bare hands. How dangerous was that!

Ted and his wife, Vera, had two daughters who attended NSFG. Sandra was in the Class of 1964 and Karen was a member of the Class of 1968. Bob Adams, Ted's brother, often accompanied Ted as he worked on school projects. So, you could say it was a family thing for them.

Let me try to explain why I think Ted was also a hero to the school.

Ted Adams was legally an "independent contractor," not an employee of Williston, but I would estimate he worked 98 percent of his time for the school and its faculty. Many times, I asked him to come on the staff and be an employee. He refused and said, "The school would have nothing to gain by making me an employee, and I always put the school first in my business."

There was little doubt about that. I could call him any time of the day or night when there was a plumbing or heating issue, and he would either come immediately to the school or talk me through the problem so I could attempt to fix it. His dad was the plumber for 50 or more years and I was told he was just as caring about the school. My predecessor, Mr. Babcock, also relied on Ted and/or his father throughout most of his time as Business Manager at the school. Plumbing issues by nature were often ones that needed immediate attention. Ted was always available and lived only a few miles from the school, hence, he responded in minutes, prepared to tackle the issue of the moment.

Ted stories could fill a book, so I will just mention a few specific ones at this time to illustrate my point about his importance to the success of the school. There will be more stories in other parts of my book.

When the cost of energy became a real concern in the 1970s, Ted worked with me on numerous energy-saving projects. One, in particular, was his solution to a problem that had concerned me a great deal. The steam kettles, used for cooking in the school's kitchen, required live steam and that steam was generated by a large boiler, a football field away in the gym basement. A great many energy-wasting steam-pipe feet away from the dining hall kitchen. I did not understand why live steam was continually going to these kettles that were not being used.

Ted, with his own problem-solving ingenuity, came up with the idea to install an electric eye in the attic of Ford Hall, the building that housed the dining hall. A sensor installed in the kitchen was triggered by the real need for steam, and this, in turn, triggered an electric eye, several hundred feet away in the attic of the gym, which then turned on the large oil-burning boiler to generate the required steam. For many years, the cost of number six fuel oil (a commercial large boiler fuel oil) was not significant, so the business manager did not worry about saving energy/money. But times and the price of oil changed. We needed an inexpensive solution. I doubt very much if you could find another plumbing firm that would be able to accomplish this task at a minimal cost, or, as a matter of fact, even dream up this solution. More than likely, if a plumbing firm was given this issue to solve, they would have hired a very expensive engineering firm to design a solution to this problem! Ted was both a very intelligent person and a very clever guy.

To offer another example of Ted's creative genius is what he did in the Lossone Hockey Rink, another building that was a very expensive, high-energy user. Much of the wastefulness of energy in the rink was because, like most buildings on campus at this time, it had been completely neglected of maintenance, both routine and major: false economy for sure. Electricity was becoming more and more expensive and the rink used a lot of it, for the high intensity lighting, for the very large cooling and dehumidifying equipment, for making locker room and Zamboni hot water, and for making ice for the skating rink. Ted's part in this was trying to reduce the cost of the electricity required for heating water. He devised a unique system to capture the "wasted heat" from the two large electric compressors that made ice for the rink. With this system, the captured heat was used to heat water for the rink locker room showers and also the hot water used by the ice-grooming machine, known by its brand name, the Zamboni.

David Adamski was my newly appointed rink manager, the first full-time manager, and he commented, "The quality of the ice itself, the most important feature of a good rink, is also much better and can be adjusted in thickness to the size of the crowd that is using the ice at a given time. The compressors that make the ice and the engines that drive them have had a complete overhaul, and the tank-like vehicle, the Zamboni, now floods the ice with hot water, which is much more effective than cold water in ice-making."[99]

Previously, the cold water was either the only available water because the hot water provider did not work—because of poor maintenance and/or it was too expensive to operate.

Again, a huge cost-saving design that, most likely, would not have been a solution conceived by most plumbers.

Remember, the school continued to be in dire financial straits, so any opportunity I could save a few dollars by doing something myself instead of paying overtime to a maintenance person or calling in Ted Adams, I did. Hence, when I got a call after normal school working hours about a failed heater in a dormitory, a faculty house, or other building, I tried to respond first, so we did not have to call Ted Adams to campus. For example, the simple Dunnington-level problem might be the heater was just out of oil, or the circuit breaker was tripped. However, with Ted's help and willingness, he taught me things that I could do to solve some problems before it was necessary to call him to come to campus. I also learned a lot about how to fix a failed oil-heating boiler from Ted, by assisting him (or rather, mostly watching him in the middle of the night). Also, we would talk on the phone (not a cell phone), when he would instruct me what to do.

He also always responded to our faculties' plumbing and heating needs in their own homes. And, I know, some never received a bill for his services.

In spite of our very tight cash situation, I did try to pay Ted something every month, but never close to the amount he was really owed. He knew we did not have the funds to pay him in full for all his services over the years. Mr. Babcock told me about Ted's bookkeeping and, because the school simply did not always have the money to pay him in full, he did not pay him anywhere near what he was owed.

When I asked Ted how much we owed him, Ted would respond by asking me, "How much is the school able to pay?"

I shared this information with our auditors, Coopers and Lybrand, and they insisted we needed to recognize this significant liability on the schools' balance sheet. I agreed with that accounting principle, and also wanted Ted to see that the school recognized this liability. So, on numerous occasions, I also tried to find out how much the school really owed Ted, but to no avail. Ted met with the auditors once, but that did not help either. Ted kept meticulous notes about every job, from every $.10 pipe nipple to a major piece of the often-failing steam line. This detail was shown on his bills. The materials were not just lumped all together on his invoices labeled "materials," which is the custom of most pluming firms, showing only a total dollar amount for labor and material.

However, when we needed a major piece of equipment for a job, such as when the hot water tank in the gymnasium failed, we would pay for it directly to the vendor. Sometimes I was able to save money by reaching out to alumni and student families who may have been in the business where the part was manufactured or sold. The gymnasium water tank was such an example.

I enjoyed talking to parents whenever they were on campus and often asked, "What is your business?"

Fortunately, I recalled a parent saying that his company made large water tanks. We got a nice deal. That parent was the father of a student,

John Hazen White Jr. ('76). John now runs that company and also became a Trustee and Chair of the Board of Trustees of Williston. What a wonderful example of caring and support.

My recollection was I put on the balance sheet, $50,000. as the amount of the liability owed to Ted. I asked him about the amount again and he inferred it was not enough.

Then he said, "George, what good does it do for me to even bother to figure all this out? Because I doubt if you could pay it now. But, maybe someday."

So, it was clear he expected to be paid sometime in the future.

A few other Ted (our Ted, not the TV Ted) stories might help to appreciate why I feel Ted played such an important role in saving the school. I must emphasize, for over many, many years in the 1950s, 1960s and 1970s, the school did only minimal repairs to its buildings and equipment. Mostly, the maintenance amounted to just putting on more and more paint, and at that, only on the fronts of the buildings. Hence, most of the heating plants, items not visible, were very old and never got meaningful routine maintenance (often that would have saved money in the long run). It was only crisis maintenance, i.e., when the boiler stopped, usually on a very cold day or night.

The old factory building, purchased from United Elastic in 1950, later the Language Building, was situated behind the Schoolhouse and the Plimpton Student Center and served many purposes over the years, but little or nothing was ever done to maintain its structural integrity. As I previously said, the wind blew through the frames of the many huge single-pane windows so that it was very uncomfortable in the classrooms where the faculty and students were trying to learn. The unit-heaters, at one time located in each classroom, were in disrepair and therefore were never functioning correctly or often did not work at all, thus exaggerating the discomfort.

We did not have the many thousands of dollars to make the needed major repairs, such as the heating system, replacing the roof, or the windows. So, I worked with Ted to see what we could do to fix the heating problems. Ted again devised a whole new system that would let each classroom have its own thermostat and the whole system was on a timer that automatically lowered the heat when it was unoccupied. Did I pay for this at the time? Probably not.

Early on in my Williston experience, I went into the small Plimpton Library to the far left of the Schoolhouse (later it was the Student Center and then the History Department). One evening I noticed water dripping from the ceiling. So, I found a ladder, climbed up, and removed a ceiling tile—and saw the water was coming from the sprinkler system's old iron pipes. When I shined my flashlight around, I saw that there was black plastic tape wrapped around the pipes in many, many places! Remembering now that I was very new at the school, the first thing that went through my mind was, Mr. Babcock was being cheated by our plumber, Ted Adams. Really? I immediately called Ted Adams and he met me at the Plimpton Library.

I said, "What the hell is this tape doing on the sprinkler piping?"

Ted, in his calm and gentle voice said, "George this system is what is known as a 'dry' sprinkler system, which means there is very little water, under no pressure, in the pipes, unless a fire triggers the water valve to fill the holey pipes with water. The pipes are old, rusted iron pipes and have needed replacing for many years. Mr. Babcock said, "We do not have the money to do the job. Hence tape was used, and yes, it worked for our annual, required sprinkler test." That encounter was a real eye-opener for me. It was one of my first face-to-face meetings with our "miracle worker" plumber. The laugh was on me.

Ted Adams was truly a generous, faithful craftsman extraordinaire whose time holding the Williston plumbing systems together was only a part of this hero's life.

During World War II, Ted was a radioman on a fighter plane that was based on the aircraft carrier, Wasp in the Pacific. He flew many combat missions and was shot down and crashed into the Pacific Ocean *two* times. As if that was not enough, the *third* time, he crashed again into the ocean when the plane he was in, on its return trip to the aircraft carrier, ran out of fuel. This time, he ended up on a raft for three days before being rescued. He was awarded the Distinguished Flying Cross for "heroism and extraordinary achievement." The medal was for saving his pilot's life. Truly a hero.

His daughter, Sandra Adams, Northampton School for Girls Class of 1964, told me in correspondence, "He was offered a position in naval intelligence in Washington DC, but his father, Ted Sr., asked him to return to Easthampton to work in the business." [100]

As mentioned earlier, many of the calls to Ted for help were in the middle of the night, and were answered by his wife, Vera—what delicious chocolate chip cookies she made and shared. She always was very pleasant and gracious sounding, like she was just waiting for my call.

Sandra went on to say, "As for my mother, her years as a telephone operator served her well as my father's 'answering service.'" [101]

I am told Ted's many years of devoted service to Williston ended in a very unpleasant way. After I left the school in 1986, I was replaced by Jim Reagan. Ted's billing system was very unique, for sure, as he did not submit all his bills for his services until many months after he did the work. This practice was known by me and our auditors, Coopers and Lybrand.

I explained this practice to Jim Reagan and told him, "I only recognized $50,000 of our debt on the balance sheet." I also said the real amount was not known.

As mentioned earlier in the book, my predecessor, Business Manager Wilmot Babcock, often told Ted he simply did not have the money to pay him in full. Ted accommodated his request out of concern for the school's well-being. Can you imagine what would have happened if Ted had required the school to pay what was owed each time he did a job? In those early years, this more than likely would have forced the school into some form of financial crisis, or at the very least forced the school to cut budgets so severely the programs would not have been successful. Remember, in my opinion, Philips Stevens and Wilmont Babcock had cut all operating budgets to a barely subsistence level.

As noted earlier, I attempted to pay Ted something each year, hopefully more than the expense we incurred in the year. I clearly knew the school owed him much more, an amount Ted never revealed. But when Ted retired from his business, I was no longer at the school. I am told he finally presented the school all his unpaid invoices, planning on this hard-earned money for his hard-earned retirement. The school challenged the amount, and I believe they did not pay all that he was legitimately owed.

Unfortunately, Ted Adams never contacted me to ask for help or even to inform me of what was happening. If that had happened, I would have, without hesitation, gone to the Board of Trustees and pled his case. It was a very sad way to treat a man who probably did as much as anybody to keep the school alive through those many financially difficult years. This is such a sad story and a blemish on Williston's character.

I ask, "How did this terrible issue get to this level of not paying Ted what Williston owed to its faithful plumber for so many years?" I would like to offer a few thoughts. First, I am guessing Business Manager Jim Reagan did not fully appreciate Ted's many years of service, nor did he appreciate what a deplorable condition the school was in when I became the new business manager in 1972. Jim may not have fully appreciated the dire conditions of the physical plant and how it was negatively affecting the critical admission process. The school's enrollment was down in my early years at Williston, contributing to the significant deficits. Jim may not have understood that Ted's delayed billing was completely legitimate and done to help the school survive. Still, why, after I had alerted him in 1986, of this issue with Ted, did he not call me, consult with the Buildings & Grounds Committee of the Board of Trustees and, of course, Head of School Dennis Grubbs? It saddens me greatly. The school should have developed a plan to pay Ted Adams, in full, for his decades of dedicated services to Williston. In hindsight, I guess I need to take my share of the blame for not dealing with the amount of money the school owed Ted. Perhaps, if I had entered on the balance sheet, a liability much greater and more realistic than the $50,000 I did, it would have helped the school to realize what was truly owed Ted Adams.

I can only say, "I appreciate what you did to help the school survive." Thanks so much Ted!

Miscellaneous Attempts to Raise Funds For Survival

1961 Capital Campaign—"Progress Fund"

IN DECEMBER 1961, WILLISTON ACADEMY ANNOUNCED "THE WILLISton Progress Fund." The President of the Trustees, John P. Wright ('24), wrote the cover note, stating the campaign goal was $775,000 to be raised by June 1962. He went on to say, "The Trustees have been impressed by the wise and thoughtful recommendations of the management team which, last winter, studied exhaustively the school's resources and potential. Only after lengthy debate and profound thought has your Board decided to appeal generally for funds to help Williston progress."[102] The brochure went on to say, "Currently, however, enrollment cannot be increased unless the capacity of certain facilities is enlarged…The long-range plan is gradually, without changing the traditional character of the school, to expand to 470 boarding students."

The Chart Enrollment Boarding and Day casts many aspersions on the school achieving a boarding enrollment of 470 students. The Chart depicts both Day and Boarding enrollment (Day student enrollment was not significant).

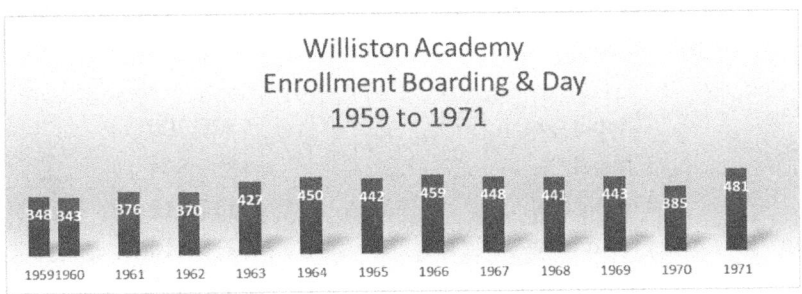

The enrollment numbers shown above include both boarding and day students. For example, in 1969, there were 393 boarding and 50 day students. Part of the campaign included building out the campus so the facilities could accommodate 470 boarding students. In 1961, this enrollment goal seemed to me to have been a real stretch. Increasing the boarding enrollment, as a boys' school, would be extremely challenging given the existing physical plant needs.

Looking back at the Audited Financial Statements, the only campaign facts that could be found that showed the projects that were selected to be included in the campaign included:

1. Chapel Organ
2. Chapel
3. Dormitory
4. Dining Hall Extension
5. Skating Rink

The Williston archivist was not able to locate any fundraising materials that would show what projects were actually selected and/or what was the budgeted goal for each project. This kind of information is basic to any promotional material in a campaign. It appears to me that it did not exist. Perhaps all the brochures were thrown away so there was no trace of what the campaign was to include.

Again, looking at the audited financial statements, the total contributions to the campaign were $523,069, and the expenses were $66,422, providing the school a net gift amount of $456,647 to supposedly spend on the projects.

The projects delineated in the financial statements as of June, 1965, indicate the following expenditures:

Chapel Organ	$20,300
Chapel	$359,824
Dining Hall Ext.	$117,315
Dormitory	$279,146
Skating Rink	$368,887
Total	**$1,145,472**

Assuming the above projects were the only ones undertaken in that time period, totaling $1,145.472, this meant there was, at that time, a cash shortfall of $688,825. Unfortunately, it would take too much time to discern exactly what other projects may have been built in the time period 1960 to 1972, and how they were paid for, i.e. from gifts, from operations, from bank borrowing, etc. Were these facts known to the Board?

It was often the custom for educational institutions to hire fundraising consultants, pay them significant amounts of money, and then find that the rendered, often voluminous reports just sat on someone's desk.

In the mid 1960s, I was asked to speak at a conference of college and university business managers on the subject of using consultants. I often believed the consultant was used as a protection blanket for whomever hired the consultant. One big question, I believe, that should be asked before hiring a consultant is, "Are you, the school, prepared to spend the money that will likely be recommended?" It is not hard for the school to make a few educated guesses as to what would be recommended for projects and their costs. If, after doing this exercise you then conclude the amounts you have estimated are not feasible, then do not continue the plan until you can get comfortable with a realistic plan.

The academy made that mistake. They hired two consultants, Booz-Allen-Hamilton, to do a survey. In fiscal 1961, they paid the firm $5,468.24. They also hired the fundraising consulting firm, Marts and Lundy, to do a capital fund survey.

The campaign was announced on December 24, 1961, and immediately the school made an attempt to raise money. Did they follow a professional consultant's plan? It seems to me that they did not. My experience would clearly say there was not nearly enough time to do all the traditional planning that was usually recommended and required for a successful campaign.

Approximately six months later, June 25, 1962, Marts and Lundy presented a detailed report on the status of the Progress Fund. They also included a "Cost of Campaign" statement. Their "Total Operating Expenses" were $17,846 and their "Fee" was $31,500. A total of $49,346. Their project "Budget" was $64,000."[103] This difference of $14,654 makes me suspicious that the service was ended before it was completed. I wonder, was it the academy or was it Marts and Lundy who ended the consultant project/campaign plans?

It is the author's opinion that the progress fund was another failed attempt by the academy to raise capital funds. My opinion was based on the simple facts that the stated goal of the progress fund was $775,000, and at best, they raised $456,577. In the school's history, I have never discovered any truly successful capital campaigns, going all the way back to the 1800s. The Head of School, Philips Stevens, left no clear signs that he was willing to do the "asking" from alumni who had the ability to donate meaningful gifts. He had a similar problem when approaching the people he asked to be on the Board. Thus, the leadership did not help raise gifts and some did not give gifts at all! Quite predictably, with a Board not being major donors, failure is almost a certainty. There also was no evidence of an administrative office with the qualified staff necessary to support a campaign.

Fortunately, in the 1970s and 1980s, the administration began the process of establishing a fundraising office with a professional staff that had the knowledge as to what had to be done to conduct a campaign. Reconnecting with alumni, parents, and friends was a large initial undertaking. Both Headmaster Ward and Headmaster Corkery guided this process, and there was evidence of success in the annual giving results. It was when Headmaster Denny Grubbs took office that the school started raising significant capital gifts. From these struggling times to June 1986, it is great to see how successful the school has become at raising capital gifts and building out a truly beautiful campus.

With this brief overview of the school's finances, it is easy to conclude that budgets could not be balanced by reducing expenses, as the prior administration had tried. The only immediate alternative was to increase the sources of income. A potential major source of income was for us to work very hard at recruiting new students, a subject we addressed in the section on admission. We then looked carefully at all the potential income-producing functions, however small. To mention a few: the Skating Rink, Bookstore, Snack Bar, use of campus assets, etc. A rather unexpected and seemingly innocuous income generator came from diligently investing our free cash.

Short-Term Money Market Income

This unexpected new source of income deserves mentioning as it illustrates how I would search for and try anything that had the potential of adding income to our finances. It came to my attention from a friend who worked for the investment firm, Kidder Peabody. He explained that I could invest our "free" cash for just overnight and for the weekends. At first, I wondered what we would have that would qualify as "free cash." Cash was something we did not have much of, most of the time. In the early 70s, the bank "float," the time period between when a check was written/mailed and when it was finally deducted from the school's bank account, could be as many as five days, especially on checks mailed far away. Free Cash!

Williston employed a part-time women's basketball coach and dorm parent, Leslie Harrison. Because she was a coach, she had mornings free and could work for me heading up the task of maximizing the income from the money market. Leslie got to be a real pro at identifying the float-time when our cash was not being used.

In the chart below, "Short Term Money Market Investment Income," in fiscal year 1982, we earned $84,756 with very little expense to the school.

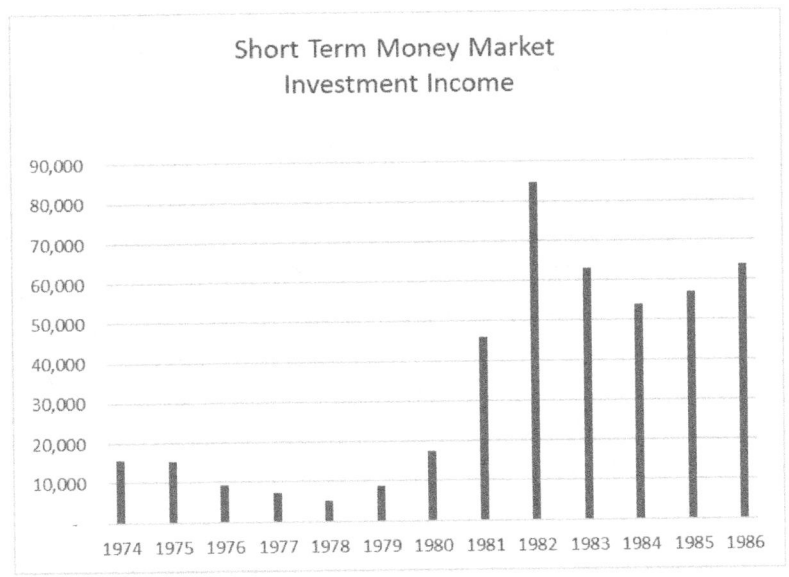

We plugged along, trying to enhance our potential sources of income, often using our existing human resources. Productivity?

The most successful schools and colleges, such as Andover Academy and Harvard University, have endowment funds sufficient to produce income that enables them to add considerably to their programs. This would include scholarships that would strengthen the enrollment and the quality of the student body, as well as professorships and many other quality-enhancing programs. The struggles to add to our endowment investments was discussed elsewhere in the book. For most of the years for both Williston Seminary and Williston Academy, it was a liturgy of failures. The charts below, "Endowment Assets" and "Endowment Income," remained relatively flat from 1960 to 1972.

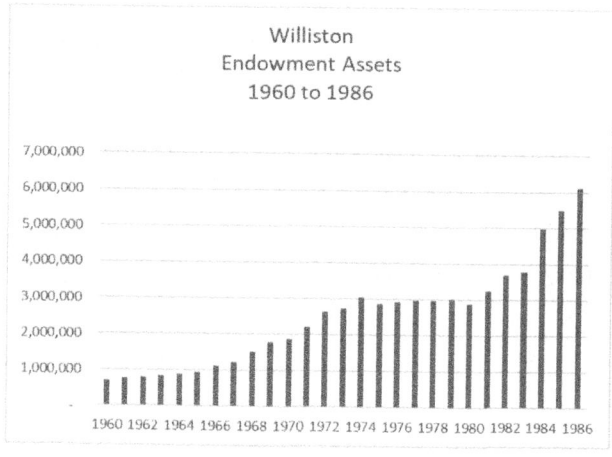

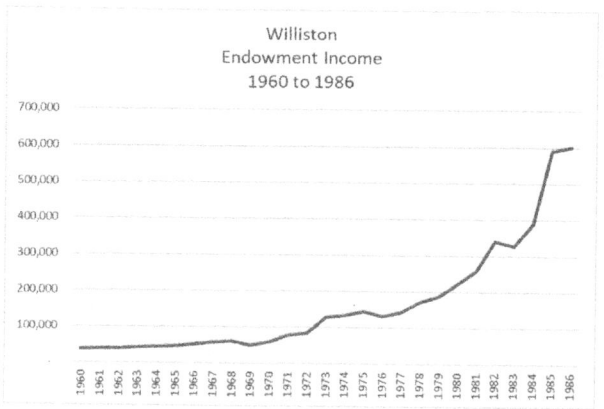

In the Stevens years, 1960 to 1971, the endowment more than tripled, going from $722,473 to $2,228,527. From my limited research and knowing what I have learned in researching this book, I would feel comfortable saying this growth was from both market appreciation and alums who left gifts to the school in their wills, but not gifts resulting from direct solicitations.

The income from the endowment investments more than doubled in this timeframe, going from $37,599 to $78,741, a very important happening during these times of need. For example, in my last year, 1986, Endowment Income was 9.6 percent of total income. If we compare this to 2017-18, Endowment Income is 15 percent, a much more impressive amount.

Looking at my time at Williston, 1972 to 1986, and that of Headmasters Ward, Corkery, and Grubbs (one year), the principal increased from $2,648,418 to $6,111,976, or 130.8 percent. Again, we were fortunate to have received many gifts that were previously in the donor's plans, i.e. planned giving. Discovering these donors made us wonder why they were not on our potential donor screen to explore and develop. For those donors who were still living, we enjoyed developing the relationship and encouraged the donors to increase the initial amount of their gift. What did happen in this time period was that a plan was made and implemented to solicit both capital gifts as well as annual fund gifts and to develop a plan to become more involved with the alumni and parents.

In the years after 1986, Williston has, in my opinion, done a spectacular job building the school in so many ways, including the physical plant, endowment, and the quality of the faculty.

The School's Major Asset— The Physical Plant

As you have read, the Ward-Dunnington administration was facing many demanding physical plant issues, some because the structures were so deficient that something had to be done immediately to preserve their integrity and make them useable, i.e., roofs leaking. The admission office's recruitment of new students was being affected negatively because the disrepair was unsightly in many of these buildings—a real turn-off. These situations, very limited money, and physical plant needs were the preverbal "rock and hard place."

As previously stated, with very limited resources we chose to borrow physical plant improvements money from our Unrestricted Endowment Funds, whereas the previous administration chose to borrow primarily from the bank. Mainly because of this decision, the Stevens-Babcock administration left the school with an outstanding bank note of $1,100,000.

We were very fortunate to have received two unexpected, sizeable, unrestricted gifts in the early 70s, just when we most needed the money for plant improvements.

When the academy moved from downtown Easthampton to the present campus location, there was a need for new buildings: dormitories, science/theatre building, and chapel. In my readings I did not find any indication that there was money raised to support this significant and costly move.

As was told over and over, Williston had, for far too many years, a very poor experience trying to raise money to build new buildings. That failure did not stop Phillips Stevens from building new buildings. That lack of capital gifts unfortunately meant a good portion of the cost of construction was robbed from the school's scarce operating/program funds. As was said by a person who shall remain nameless about Phil Stevens, "Everything was in the window and very little was on the shelves."

He enjoyed flaunting his accomplishments, as he wrote so flatteringly in his book, *The Plus Decade*[104]. This, I believe, was true when he built a new building—he loved the glory of a groundbreaking or dedication. Then again, most school heads would also enjoy this.

When your author retired as the business manager at the end of fiscal 1986, he left the school with the plant fund owing the endowment fund $413,987. There was no longer any external debt, i.e., bank notes.

In the approximate fourteen years of the Dunnington administration, we invested into the plant assets $2,841,764. The four largest projects were: Memorial Dormitory, $858,551; Lossone Hockey Rink, $558,596; The Schoolhouse, $315,555; The Whitaker – Bement Center, $300,016. What is interesting to note is that these projects, except for Whitaker – Bement Center, were newly purchased or built early in the beginning of the Stevens-Babcock Administration. Sadly, these expenditures were largely in response to deferred maintenance issues.

I did not find any indication that there was money raised to support this significant move. Several years later in 1960, they did attempt to raise money for these projects in a fundraising campaign called the progress fund.

Unfortunately, the net proceeds of this fundraising from the parents and alumni were not adequate for their plans. Thus, a good portion of the cost of construction was robbed from the school's scarce operating funds, and the school borrowed considerable money from the bank. I could also observe some of the construction costs were reduced not by scaling down the size of a building, but by reducing the quality of the construction materials and using a cheaper design, i.e., flat ugly roofs and lots of cinder blocks. Thus, these buildings certainly were not of the same quality as Ford Hall and the gym.

Unfortunately, during my time as Business Manager, the school was not able to raise significant capital gifts. We were not prepared to do so, as our focus had to be on setting up and staffing an alumni/development

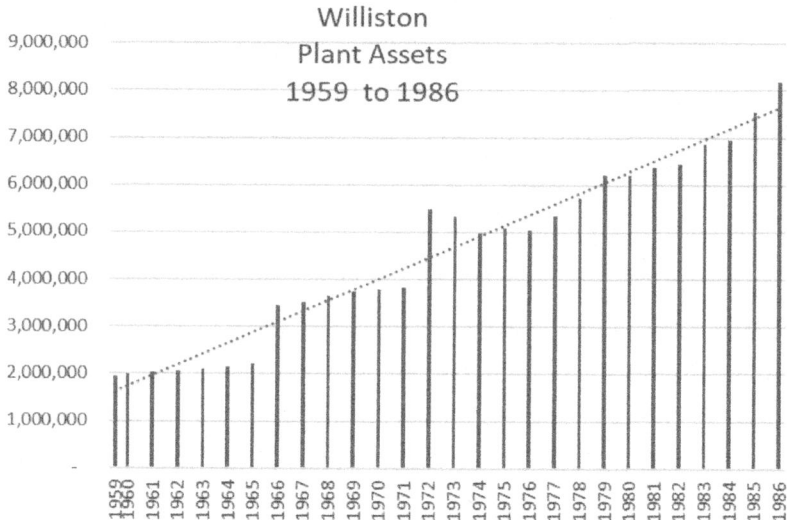

The information is from the Williston Annual Financial Reports

office, the required backbone for fundraising. This also necessitated updating all alumni biographical information and attempting to draw the alumni back into a more active status. In my last year, 1985-86, Denny Grubbs did begin to raise some capital gifts.

A Few Special Stories

An entire book could be written telling terrible stories about the condition of Williston's buildings in 1972. Their physical condition was one of neglect, yes—serious neglect for many years. At first, I thought the terrible condition of the school's physical assets were simply because of the lack of the required money to do regular maintenance. Then I believed it was because of the choices that were made to spend money on building new structures, instead of on the overall required maintenance on existing structures. But, on further analysis, I questioned those reasons. For the years 1960 through the first two years of the 1970s, Williston Academy showed on its financial statements a decent "profit" from operations – how was that possible? Most likely, it probably was not possible.

What was left for the new merged schools to work with and use in their programs were buildings in very poor shape, which needed urgent repairs.

When I look back to 1972, on becoming Assistant Treasurer and Business Manager, my first concern was, is it possible for the school to continue as a "going enterprise?" Could the School actually survive these issues?

I will share with the reader a few words about some of the plant assets that challenged me.

The Gym

This gym was, in its day, an eloquent, well-designed, and well-built structure, but it was designed for a much smaller school. The gym was completely rebuilt recently, however the very attractive, wood-paneled Dodge room stayed as it was when the gym was constructed in 1931. An amusing story that happened in the Dodge Room—Headmaster Archibald V. Galbraith was well-connected to the poet Robert Frost, who was then a teacher at Amherst College. At his request, Frost came every year to the campus to read his poetry. In 1938, when Frost was at the campus reading his poetry in the Dodge Room, all the boys were sitting on the hardwood floor of this handsomely paneled room in what was referred to as the "New Gymnasium," listening carefully to the "Bard." A typical boys' stunt happened after Frost had been reading for an hour and half. Suddenly, a loud "fart" resounded!

This occasioned embarrassed laughter among the students, to which the poet responded, "Would you like me to go on?" Hearing no answer, he said, "Very well, I will continue." [105]

The gym swimming pool housed one of the many private school's most successful swim teams. Interestingly, in 1974, Director of Athletics Rick Francis said, "Our four-lane pool no longer conforms to recent rule changes, and the ceiling is too low to meet the minimum specifications for diving."[106]

The wooden basketball court, sitting on numerous small metal springs, had not had the playing surface properly refinished for years. There were spots where the wood had rotted from water leaks in the roof.

The huge, beautiful, multi-pane windows surrounding the basketball court were neglected for so long that the glazing was virtually missing from each pane of glass, with the wind blowing through all the cracks—to say nothing of the costly energy drain.

Now, with the merger, Williston became coed. One of the sports added to the gyms schedule was women's basketball, making the already too-small floor space issue much more critical. You have to say, Rick Frances, the athletic director, and Sue Curry, girls' basketball coach, tried very hard to make things work, but it was nearly an impossible scheduling task. The NSFG Campus remained unsold, so the girls went to the gym on that campus to practice. This was very unfair for the girls. It meant traveling between campuses, which made it difficult for the students to attend and cheer on our own team at the games.

Out of necessity, they undertook many small gym construction projects preparing for the merger, such as adding a girls' shower room and locker room, etc. Sadly, the real issues, like lack of playing space, could only be addressed by a major capital expenditure—something we simply could not even contemplate at that time. The windows demanded immediate attention, so I put together a group of students to work all summer, re-glazing the glass and painting the windows and frames. Bob Couch, a faculty member and Class of 1950, headed up the various student paint crews. There was also a crew headed up by Roger Maroni ('77), and he and Chris McCarty ('76) worked with several others. They worked very hard, did a real professional job, and finished all the windows. An amazing accomplishment!

I have to mention a very funny paint crew crises. There were so many coats of paint on the gym's very attractive, Georgian-style front doorways that, to restore them and make the entrances look beautiful again, it was necessary to have the student painters take a blowtorch and burn off the many, many layers of peeling paint.

Soon after they got started, I got a panic call in my office from Roger Maroni saying, "With our blow torches we started a fire, back inside the beautiful and elaborate door frame. It's hard to extinguish." When I arrived it was still smoking, but they had succeeded in putting out the fire.

While many deferred maintenance issues could be seen when you looked around the campus, there was one that could not be seen—the 5,000-gallon oil tank that supplied the main campus heating boilers in the basement of the gym. I always attempted to make the most cost-effective oil purchases as possible. Oil, when purchased by the truckload, usually resulted in saving a few pennies per gallon. When I inquired from the oil company why they were not making larger "drops," (full truck loads) they replied, "That is all your tank will hold."

I conferred with our plumbing and heating person, Ted Adams and immediately he said, "The tank has never been cleaned out from many, many years of accumulated sludge. And Mr. Babcock told me not to bother, as it did not affect the oil burners operation."

That may be true, but it prevented me from buying the very pricey oil at the best price possible, because I could not buy the maximum gallons of oil at one delivery. And, by the way, the sludge would have eventually caused serious problems with the oil burner. I was simply amazed when I visited the tank site to find that Ted Adams had crawled down a small round hatch door on top of the huge tank and was filling up buckets of oily sludge. His brother Bob was up top, hauling the buckets up and out. The smell in the tank had to be toxic, but the tank was finally cleaned and it could again hold 5,000 gallons of oil. I had to swear to absolute secrecy as to where all the sludge went!

The Language Building

This structure served many purposes while being used by the academy. For a while it was the chapel, the all-school study hall, and classrooms. It was, at first, an 1800s factory building, now with its same flat, leaky roof and a rotted, ground-level, wood-plank, floor. The floor was sitting close to the dirt and hence, there were many holes rotted in the floor. Strangely, these holes were patched with many layers of electrical tape. Huge, multi-pane windows, again with most of the glazing missing, were also leaking air, allowing frigid air to blow through the rooms at will. The heating was from the central steam boilers in the gym, but the individual room heatalators were not always repositioned, as the use and layout of the floors were changed numerous times over the years. Hence,

Language Building
(Rick Teller Williston Archivist)

thermostats and the heaters were not always located in the same physical area. We had also converted two classrooms into a popular dance studio.

Since this was a major classroom building, we had to address some of these issues using our meager funds. To do something soon was almost a demand from Tom Evans and Deborah Hayward, the Admission Office leadership team. Cosmetic-type decorations were done throughout the building, helping us present ourselves in a more appealing way. Our plumber, Ted Adams, had no choice but to completely re-plumb, with many feet of new copper pipe feeding the rooms' heating units, and each room was equipped with its own energy-saving thermostat. This work bought us a few more years of use before we determined it would be much too expensive to make the building functional and attractive. This decision made it necessary for Director of Studies Karin O'Neil to find new homes for all the classrooms we would lose. This was a huge task for her to accomplish. I bravely decided to recommend we demolish the entire building that had served the school for so many years. Not every Business Manager gets to make a decision such as this.

The Language Building Being Demolished 1981
(Williston Northampton School Archives)

The Schoolhouse

The Schoolhouse, another large, restored, 1895 factory building acquired by the academy on December 1, 1949, also suffered from years of neglect. This building was one of our most-used structures as it housed many administrative offices, including those of the Headmaster and the Business Manager, the Business Office, the Director of Studies, the Dean and more. It had classrooms and faculty offices on the second and third floors, and the lower level housed the Business Office, Post Office, Faculty Lounge, and copier room.

In days of old, the cost of number six fuel oil was not a real concern, so the fact that the numerous windows were falling apart, as in other buildings, and the heat was pouring out and the cold was pouring in, mattered very little. Soon, all this changed in the mid-seventies, when the prices of fossil fuel went to record prices. Our faculty teaching in this building seldom complained of being uncomfortable. The comfort of the students was not a seemingly big concern—"Tuff it out, boys and girls!" The faculty and students were hardy! I might add, while some occupants froze, others had to open the windows to let the heat out, even on the coldest days. Students of those days are likely to remember this experience.

Again, it was another case where there was virtually no maintenance performed on all the individual room heaters. Early on, it was essential that a new rubber-membrane roof had to be installed, as the old roof was leaking in numerous places.

As could be expected, this major building also challenged our admission team when taking students and parents on a campus tour. They knew competitors had much better facilities, which frustrated them.

There was only one way to refurbish this building to make it look like it was a "classy," institutional structure. It was very large, three floors and a full basement. The town records showed that it was 56,344 square feet. To make this happen, I determined we had to completely gut the entire interior of this building. A scary thought, but necessary. Fortunately, the Board of Trustees, led by Margaret French, Chair of the B & G Committee, allowed me to do this project using our own augmented staff, something that never could have been done in the past.

First, nothing really had changed significantly with our limited finances. As previously mentioned, we did have a couple large gifts that gave us a little breathing room. However, the cost of hiring an architect was out of the question, as was hiring a contractor, both of which I deemed to be unnecessary. I felt comfortable and able to assume these roles. I do not believe this was in my job description—really.

I began the renovation task by sketching out a floor plan from the basement to all the above three floors. This was only a sketch, not a scale drawing.

Next, the most important part of the plan was to assemble a skilled, in-house construction team.

First to be signed up was Ted Adams, our plumber who had to redesign the entire heating system from the point where the steam entered the building in the basement to every floor and every room. Energy efficient controls needed to be installed in each room, along with new modern heating units. Also, he installed a totally new sprinkler system.

Second was the addition of a carpenter to the team who had the experience and training to do high-quality finish work. I hired Larry Lepien, who, conveniently, lived just up the street. He was a very quiet, very skilled carpenter who could translate my very sketchy plans into classrooms and offices.

Thirdly, we added an (outside contractor) electrician, Ralph Miller, a parent of a Williston student ('77). He was most dedicated and clever at finding ways to properly wire and light this enormous project.

And lastly, we completed our team when we added Fran Perrier for our painter, a very diligent worker.

This team worked together amazingly well. They respected each other as a person as well as they respected their individual skills. We had a real team—if the plumber needed help the painter was right there to lend a hand, etc.

A brief word about the size of this undertaking. We began by totally gutting the 1950s, second- and third-floor walls and ceilings of this old factory building. This meant removing all the walls and ceilings back to the bare, red-brick outer walls and to the roof rafters. The flooring was stripped down to the original. I think it was four-inch-thick, oiled walnut plank. It reminded me how it must have looked when it was a factory, but without the huge machines roaring away.

This may be hard to imagine, but each floor area was so huge, in order to set the ceilings level, I used a beautiful, antique brass transit, which had an equally beautiful case. This had been recently donated by an alum for the school archives. When I received this gift, I had no idea we would ever use it, but it did the job. With this brass transit I was able to set the ceiling lines level all the way around this giant space.

I should also mention that our team included many students. As might be expected, they lugged supplies up to the second floor and up to the third floor, the heavy pieces of sheetrock, wood, and other supplies. The unwritten rule was, no one, including faculty and guests, could go up the stairs without taking some piece of wood or construction material with them.

It is here that I must again give considerable credit to Director of Studies Karin O'Neil for being very understanding of the project and for working many hours on finding everyone a substitute classroom while the construction was happening. She was a great part of our team.

I decided to do the interior wood trim in red oak. This was in fashion at the time, and it went extremely well with the restored brick walls.

I need to say a word about the restored brick walls, as that took a herculean effort. Remember the Williston green walls we had previously talked about? These walls were painted so many times from the day the school bought this structure in the 1950s that you would think it was green cement. We wanted the beautiful red bricks to be the visual feature. We had only one way to accomplish this, and that was by sand blasting the paint off the wall until the nice old red bricks appeared! Also, since the paint was so thick, it took hundreds of pounds of "Black Beauty," a blasting sand, to remove the many hundreds of pounds of paint. It was a huge mess, and as hard as we tried to stop the blasted-off, very fine sand and paint from going down through the numerous cracks in the floor, the sand found its way all the way down to the offices on the first floor. It just kept coming down, even months after we were done.

Lastly, and I am sure of no surprise to the reader, is that all of the windows were in need of being replaced. While I cannot say for certain, these many windows, sashes, and frames were likely the original factory windows. We ordered all new windows for the entire building, albeit not of the quality I would have like to have purchased—i.e., double-sash

Schoolhouse Classroom, 2018
(Photo by George Dunnington)

Schoolhouse with Portico from Downtown Middle Hall
(Photo by George Dunnington, 2018)

insulated glass. Our carpenter, Larry Lapine, built all the sills and the window frames out of the beautiful red oak, and, our painter, Fran Perrier, stained and varnished the wood trim.

This project was very involved and huge in scope. Our own in-house task force of four craftsmen did a spectacular job saving the school many thousands of dollars. Or, looking at the project from another way, it simply could not have happened if we had had to contract with an outside architect, contractors, etc.

This enormous job I am very proud of making happen. The quality of the workmanship was outstanding.

Memorial Dormitory Improvements— Faculty Housing

One thing that seems to be somewhat universal in private secondary schools is, if a school has a good reputation, it is usually because it has a dedicated, well-trained faculty. Williston had a dedicated faculty, and they worked extremely hard with little physical accoutrements and with below average salaries. Also, as a residential school, the Williston faculty had less than great housing. Good, comfortable, private housing connected to a dormitory is necessary in order attract new faculty. Faculty living in a residence hall is hugely important to a residential school's success. It is often where the faculty observe a student's personal needs, provide the students with a personal camaraderie, and provide academic counseling. Our residence halls were in need of significant upgrading. For example, on one of my walks through buildings, I was in Memorial Dorm, built in the 1950s, when I observed the ceilings on the top floor were green with mold where water had seeped through the concrete ceiling/roof.

The faculty apartments were very inadequate, especially on the south end, where the new, single faculty lived. These units were extremely small and the only entrance was through the dormitory hallway. No privacy!

I was discussing this with a Trustee, architect and alum John Seiler, Class of 1945. He was a Harvard College graduate and taught architecture there. After hearing my tale of woe, he offered to help redesign this building with full-size, new apartments at the south end, and completely remodel the north end apartments. Also, to try to make the structure look like a "prep" school building, not just a big square box, as it was. This was a most generous offer, for again, money continued to be a limiting

Original Memorial Dormitory, with flat roof and box-like appearance, 1950s
(Williston Yearbook)

Memorial Dormitory (2020) Showing Peaked Roof Installed 1983 and The Spacious New Faculty Apartments on the South End

factor. A friend of mine, Raymond Vincuas, owned a large, prefabricated building company in nearby Westfield, and he also offered to help. He explained to me the principle of saving construction costs is to not let architects draw up rooms and corridors with odd, wasteful measurements, etc. With his advice and John Seiler's help, we turned the leaky, ugly, flat roof (I was told it leaked the first year it was built) to one with a peak and, most importantly, added two beautiful, spacious faculty residences on the south end of the dorm. We were fortunate to have hired Philip E. Shumway, Williston Class of 1942, from Amherst, Massachusetts, who built the new, peaked-roof structure.

We also addressed the basement level, a disgusting, dark space, by opening it up with a bright, open stairway to an outside patio, where the students could gather to socialize in an open common area. We designed a new, enlarged snack bar on that level. The horrible Mem Dorm, an admission office nightmare, was now a positive location for campus tours.[107]

I am particularly proud of the decision-making process that happened regarding the changes to this facility. "The idea behind the Campus Center, explains Business Manager George Dunnington, is to provide a social setting for all of Williston's population—faculty, staff, and students—to mix informally." Before the decision was made, the administration discussed the project with the faculty and the students. All supported the original Campus Center construction plans and voted to break ground for the Campus Center.

Headmaster Corkery agreed, and added that the "facility would enhance the quality of life of all those living in the Williston Northampton community." George Dunnington is still excited about the whole decision-making process. "I feel the students and faculty showed great leadership throughout the discussions. The kids played a key role with excellent, sound reasoning. Everybody thought of the common good. Ground was broken August 5, 1982, and from then on, the project went as planned…This feeling from the constituents is very rewarding as many projects always have their dissenters and many decisions have to be made by the Business Manager."[108]

Ford Fire

The opening of school is an intense time period, especially for our maintenance and housekeeping staffs. All the student rooms need a thorough cleaning, and all the beds need to be made with fresh linens. Our senior boys' dorm, Ford Hall, was all cleaned and ready to welcome back our senior boys in September. At one end of Ford Hall, on the lower level, was a very old, attractive, wood-paneled lounge area. This area was an entranceway into the dining room. On Labor Day weekend, after regular working hours, a fire started in one of the couches in the lounge. The old, beautiful wood paneling served as fuel to get the fire roaring. The heat was so intense that it ripped through and up the stairwell into the halls, scorching the paint off the walls all the way up to the third floor and filling each room with soot. This was a devastating happening. Because of the fact the students were not yet in the building, all the fire doors were propped open to allow our workers easy access, as were the individual room doors. All the rooms were smoke damaged and the building was not useable. Under Headmaster Ward's leadership, the whole school pulled together and the 34 senior boys were placed in other rooms around campus. This meant a sacrifice for many students, as some rooms had to now accommodate three students when there should only be two. Mr. Ward personally decided to take all of the students on a tour through the burned-out and soot-filled Ford Hall. He was trying to help them to understand why we were having to double up our rooms, and also to show how devasting and dangerous a fire can be.

The William J. Lossone Hockey Rink

The "Progress Fund" capital campaign contributed to the construction of the rink, built in 1965-66, when it first appeared on the financial statements at $368,887. Evidently, there was still work being done on the building because in 1967, its value was $427,785. While we have previously talked about buildings suffering from severe deferred maintenance, the rink, in 1972, if not the worst building on campus, was one of the worst. The rink was an income-generating building and yet it was not managed well, not cared for, and it carelessly used enormous amounts of energy. Unfortunately, I did not give this my attention upon starting my job in March at Williston. It was at the outer most edge of campus and not in use at that time. I am not sure who was responsible for the annual rink close-downs for school vacations, but it appeared no one seemed to have assumed that responsibility. Since it wasn't shut down correctly, the two huge, very expensive electric motors that drove the compressors burned up, because these two compressors that made ice simple ran out of oil and blew up. Now the electric motors and compressors were nothing but junk. This I did not discover until we began thinking about starting up the rink for a new season. Again, I called on Ted Adams to fix the problem. This time, we discussed what had happened and how we could prevent such an accident in the future. Ted installed an automatic shut-off on the compressors that would trigger a shut down if they overheated or ran out of oil. It would also shut down the huge electric motors that powered the compressors.

As I studied the electric bills I saw on the bill something called a "demand charge." The power coming to the rink was from three 220-volt cables requiring their own transformer and a demand charge meter. Obviously, no one in the management chain knew about this, or, I think, they would have taken action long before now. I was not familiar with a "demand charge." Briefly, what happens is, once a month when the rink electric power comes on, based on the demand at that brief period in time, the demand charge (electric rate) is established for the month. The rink skating operations usually start in the afternoon, when the hockey teams come to practice. When they enter a dark rink and go to the circuit breakers and throw all breakers on at once, the large, inefficient rink light bulbs use a huge amount of energy. Also, the compressors would likely come on, as would the hot water heaters. BANG! That electrical surge sets our demand rate, which is very high for the month. Our electrician, Ralph Miller, made changes so the required power could only happen in a set sequence. Ted Adams designed a system where we could get the residual heat for our hot water system directly from the rink compressors. This was a huge savings, as the ice-making Zamboni used a lot of hot water and the locker room showers also used their share of hot water. At this time, there was no summer skating program, hence we did not have condensers to remove the moisture from the air, and that would also be an added energy user.

The Zamboni, the ice-making machine, was very old. I believe it was an original piece of equipment with a gas, carbon-dioxide-spewing engine. It had been operating poorly for many years. This had to be returned to the factory to be reconditioned for about $13,000!

We had to replace all the plexiglass and the surrounding fencing boards around the ice.

Making visits to the rink in the time periods after 10:00 p.m., I discovered that pick-up rentals, of which there were many, were not being recorded and sizeable amounts of cash were being stolen. This was a difficult issue to resolve, because these rentals were paid for in cash, but we eventually did stop most of it.

When I hired Mr. Adamski as a professional rink manager, he hired a staff to properly clean and care for the equipment, making our rink one that Williston could be proud of.

The rink served not just the Williston hockey team's requirements; it was also open to the public. David Adamski said, "The ice is in use a minimum of 10 hours a day during the week and 17-18 hours on both

Saturdays and Sundays...Evening ice is used by younger boys' teams from Easthampton and neighboring towns."[109]

The school continued to invest in this property, so by the end of the 1985-1986 school year the value on the financial statements was $558,596. It now was equipped to operate throughout the year, not just winters. One big addition was a large condenser to remove the warm summer moisture in the air.

The Williston Pond

In the early 1970s, I became concerned about how low the water in the pond was. You could easily see, on the bottom, all the dining hall "sleds"—i.e., trays—and also the many discarded porcelain coffee cups. The water was barely, flowing over the spillway and down-stream. *The Willistonian* said, "Dunnington Acts to Clean Pond." They quoted me, "The pond is a very important asset that is rapidly deteriorating. For the past five years the Buildings and Grounds Committee of the Board has discussed this problem and unfortunately, financial priorities, i.e., roof on John Wright and Arts and Science Building, necessitated postponing any action."[110]

Finally, after getting the various permits and an engineer to do a topographical survey of the pond's bottom, we were ready to remove tons of sludge. I was told by several people that we would have to be prepared to clean up the roads after the large dump trucks, full of wet mud, dripped out on the roads. This would have to be cleaned up every night by the school. Then, where would we find a place to dump the many hundreds of yards of muck? We were most fortunate that the town still had an active dump—or, as it became called, a landfill. It was required that every so often they had to cover the rubbish/garbage with clean fill. That was a wonderful discovery, because the town gladly used their trucks to haul pond muck to their landfill at no cost to the school or the town. It was an interesting project to watch, as they cut a gully from the water source to the spillway, thus letting the water run a narrow stream through the pond, out of the pond area, thereby not interfering with the digging. The job was finished in late summer 1980, thus preserving this very attractive feature of the campus.

The Beautiful Campus Pond
(Williston Northampton School Annual Report 2016-17 Page 19)

Campus Beauty Trees and Lampposts

To add to yet another campus eye-sore was the fact that the academy symbol, the giant elm trees, were all dying from the Dutch elm tree disease. Anyone familiar with the school knows the song "Sammy" written by Paul H. Johnson, Class of 1905: "Sammy my, my Sammy, my heart yearns for thee, Yearns for your campus and Your Old Elm Tree…" [111]

There was no cure for Dutch elm disease, not because of lack of trying, as many institutions across the country were experiencing the same issues. Our grounds crew worked very hard to care for the trees, but eventually they had to be sawn down.

We replaced the old elms with new maple saplings, perhaps 15 feet high. So, it was many years before we had full-grown trees to admire, as in the picture above.

Early Elm Trees 1916
(Williston Archive Blogs)

Williston Entrance with Maple Trees

We also undertook a big job which involved lighting all the main campus walks. We chose a very classic lamp with a bulb in the top and the bottom of the lamp, making the lamp appear to be a gas lamp.

It was a classic-looking, very heavy, well-built lamppost. The grounds crew dug holes and made a frame into which they poured concrete and inserted the bolts to hold the many lampposts. Ralph Miller did all the underground wiring. They added real class to the campus and provided greatly improved lighting for better safety.

In this chapter, I chose just a few examples of the work that was completed, mostly by our own craftsmen, so the reader could get an appreciation of what was done all over the campus. If I included all the projects we undertook, it would take several pages.

The Progress Fund ran from 1961 to 1966, and the Plant Fund,

Campus Lamp post

as shown on the financials assets, increased in that period of time by $1,410,114.

The major projects included were: Rink $368,887, Dormitory $279,146, Chapel $359,824, Dining Hall $117,315. In total, the Stevens tenure, 1959 to 1972, expended $3,535,867 on construction projects.

In the Dunnington time period as Business Manager, we expended $2,841,764. Even with the limitation of scarce resources, we were able to buy some time, making the campus more attractive, thereby helping the recruitment of new students. We also avoided borrowing money from external sources by using our own restricted funds. Our projects also made the campus more functional and enhanced the quality of campus life.

Dennis H. Grubbs, Headmaster 1984–1999

THINGS AT THE SCHOOL WERE BECOMING MORE NORMAL, ESPEcially the finances. Dennis Grubb's arrival was the fourth head of school I had the privilege to work with.

Denny landed on campus running and was the first Head of School since its founding, that I can recall, to go out and successfully solicit major gifts. This represented a new and important characteristic of the head of school. The previous heads that I worked for, including Phillips Stevens, the retiring head in 1972-73, Robert A. Ward and Cristopher Corkery, were mainly concerned with the rebuilding of the basic components for a successful school.

In the Williston 1986 Annual Report, Denny writes, "Annual Fund gifts to the school set a record in 1985-86."

This was a good omen for what was to come.

In talking with Denny about his tenure at the school (I will paraphrase what he said), he said, "we all worked very hard." He emphasized this fact over and over as they were trying to do everything better. He had to make some important upper management appointments, as well as work closely with Karin O'Neil on faculty and curriculum matters.

He also said, "I am pleased with the work I was able to continue in improving the relationship we had with the Northampton School for Girls alumna."

During my time at the school, this relationship was very precarious, even including what the name of the merged school should be. Headmaster Ward was the master at healing relationships and was continually confronted by NSFG issues, so this important issue was one that needed a lot of attention and time for healing. Denny, in my opinion, by his caring ways, brought this issue to near normality.

He also said, "I felt the school had a great alumni body and I had the pleasure of working with many of them."

It is absolutely essential, for a school to be strong and successful, to raise significant gifts, both for supporting the current operations of the school as well as for guaranteeing its future by building the endowment.

Denny was well settled into the school by the end of the 1985 – 1986 School year. And I felt I had been a part of an era to right a sinking ship and that was mostly completed. Now, it was time for others to do great things. So, it was time for me to move from Williston and try a new venture.

Endnotes

1. Amherst College 1969 Olio
2. Wesleyan Argus February 5, 2071, source of numbers
3. The Wesleyan Argus October 27, 1970, Page 6 an article by D.B. Thompson, Staff Writer
4. A History of Williston Seminary, by Joseph Henry Sawyer 1917, Page 329
5. A History of Williston Seminary by Joseph Henry Sawyer, Cover Page
6. A History of Williston Seminary by Joseph Henry Sawyer, Page 15
7. A History of Williston Seminary by Joseph Henry Sawyer Page 41
8. Page 41
9. Page 41
10. Page 42
11. A History of Williston Seminary by Joseph Henry Sawyer Page 64
12. God's Stewards, Samuel & Emily Williston, by Frank P. Conant Page 84
13. Massachusetts Legislature
14. A History of Williston Seminary by Joseph Henry Sawyer, Page 8
15. Mt Holyoke Archives
16. Mt Holyoke Archives "Remarks by Anna C. Edwards" a Seminary teacher.
17. Remarks by Anna C. Edwards Mount Holyoke College Archives
18. Same
19. A History of Williston Seminary by Joseph Henry Sawyer Page 119
20. A History of the Endowment of Amherst College, by Stanley King 1951, Page 40
21. A History of Williston Seminary by Joseph Henry Sawyer Page 119
22. A History of Williston Seminary by Joseph Henry Sawyer Page 144
23. A History of Williston Seminary by Joseph Henry Sawyer Page 182
24. A History of Williston Seminary by Joseph Henry Sawyer Page 185
25. A History of Williston Seminary by Joseph Henry Sawyer Page 197
26. Boston Globe July 1, 1874
27. A History of Williston Seminary by Joseph Henry Sawyer Page 198
28. A History of Williston Seminary by Joseph Henry Sawyer Page 198
29. History of Amherst Endowment, Stanley King 1951 Pages 101 and 102
30. Amherst Graduates Quarterly May 1941, "Mr. Samuel and Mrs. Williston" by Annette Esty

31 The Williston Northampton School Annual Report 2017-18 Endowed Funds Page 51-54
32 Amherst Graduates' Quarterly May 1941
33 A History of Williston Seminary by Joseph Henry Sawyer, Page 199
34 A History of Williston Seminary by Joseph Henry Sawyer Page 203 paraphrased
35 A History of Williston Seminary by Joseph Henry Sawyer Page 215
36 A History of Williston Seminary by Joseph Henry Sawyer Page 215
37 A History of Williston Seminary by Joseph Henry Sawyer Page 219
38 A History of Williston Seminary by Joseph Henry Sawyer Page 228
39 A History of Williston Seminary by Joseph Henry Sawyer Page 244
40 A History of Williston Seminary by Joseph Henry Sawyer Page 257
41 A History of Williston Seminary by Joseph Henry Sawyer Page 273
42 The original book values and the 2018 Market Values were provided by the Amherst College Treasure's Office.
43 A History of Williston Seminary by Joseph Henry Sawyer Page 307
44 A History of Williston Seminary by Joseph Henry Sawyer Page 313
45 A History of Williston Seminary by Joseph Henry Sawyer Page 322
46 A History of Williston Seminary by Joseph Henry Sawyer Page 322
47 A History of Williston Seminary by Joseph Henry Sawyer Page 325
48 A History of Williston Seminary by Joseph Henry Sawyer Page 328
49 1971 Williston Yearbook interview with Williston Head Philip Stevens and Northampton School Head Nathan Fuller
50 Williston Academy Comparative Operating Accounts, Year Ended June 30, 1971 and June 30 1970.
51 The Bulletin Summer 1978, Page 2
52 Same A Message from the Headmaster Page 3
53 Williston Northampton Bulletin winter, 1973 Page 3 A Message from the Headmaster
54 The News Press January 21, 2018 'Greatest Showman' film stirs new interest in PT Barnum Page 20A
55 Williston Northampton Bulletin, Autumn 1971 Page 23
56 Same as before.
57 Modern American Poetry Page 1 from "Hawthorne and Frost: The Making of a Poem." Frost: Centennial Essays. Copyright 1973 by University Press of Mississippi.
58 Spring Log 1979 [no page numbers]

59 Williston – Northampton Bulletin Vol. 64 No 4 Summer 1978 Headmaster Bis Farewell to Class of 1978 Page 1
60 Memo to Richard Teller, Archivist from Karin O'Neil former Director of Studies and teacher, dated July 18, 2005
61 Memo from Coach Rick Francis to Rick Teller, Archivist, dated July 17, 2005.
62 Williston Northampton School Willistonian, September 10, 1979
63 Williston The Bulletin Spring 1982 Corkery's Corner page 2
64 The Bulletin Summer 1983 Williston Northampton School Page 3
65 Memo dated July 14, 2005 to Rick Teller, Williston Archivist from Cathleen Robinson Brown printed in the Williston Bulletin the Pages 52- 53. I quoted liberally from that article.
66 The Bulletin Summer 1983, The Williston Northampton School, Page 3
67 Letter to the author dated August 6, 2005 from former teacher Richard Gregory
68 From the Archives Sharing Williston Northampton and Local History, October 11, 2011 Richard Teller Archivist
69 NSFG Property Committee Meeting Minutes of September 25, 1970
70 Mr. Zabriskie's letter to The Honorable Edward M. Kennedy dated November 9, 1972
71 On Amherst College letterhead Dated October 4, 1972, Robert A. Ward wrote to Senator Kennedy urging him to help with the sale of the campus.
72 Springfield Republican newspaper January 20, 1974
73 This statement was sent by George Dunnington to Trustees, Ted Daggett, John Reed, & Homer Perkins, April 11, 1974
74 The History of Williston Seminary. Page 144
75 The History of Williston Seminary, by Joseph Henry Sawyer, 1917 Page 243
76 History of Williston Seminary Page 245
77 Page 244
78 Letter to George Dunnington from Anne Ritchie, May 2020
79 Williston Northampton Bulletin Autumn 1971 page 32
80 Williston Northampton Bulletin Autumn 1974, page 4
81 From an undated memo written by Ann Dunnington, RN and Pat Davy, RN Co-Directors of Health Center.
82 Same letter
83 Much of this chapter's contents were from Gloria Granfield, Administrative Computing Director July 1982 to January 2010.

84 Williston Northampton Bulletin winter, 1973 Page 12 Jack Cody
85 Penney Mitchell letter to George Dunnington, not dated
86 A letter from Dick Gregory to me dated March 21, 2017
87 Letter to me from Dick Gregory dated August 6, 2005
88 Penny Mitchell responded to my request for information on the Summer Programs. It was not dated.
89 Williston Northampton Bulletin winter, 1973 Page 15
90 WNS Statement of Income and Expenditures July 1, 1972 – June 30, 1973 Page 2
91 WNS Balance Sheet June 30, 1973 Plant Funds Page 4
92 WNS Endowment Fund Changes Year Ended June 30, 1973 Page 8
93 The History of the Endowment of Amherst College, 1951 Stanley King page 106
94 King Page 184, 185
95 Not the actual car used by Mr. Clapp.
96 Williston Northampton Bulletin, Autumn 1973, page 12
97 Skinner memo dated February 9, 1984. Release: HALF-MILLION DOLLAR DERBY ESTATE SETS TWO AUCTION RECORDS
98 The Bulletin Spring 1977 Page 5
99 Williston Northampton Bulletin Winter 1974 page 15
100 Sandra R. Adams NSFG '64, December 5, 2018 Letter to George Dunnington
101 Same
102 The Williston Progress Fund brochure December 1961
103 Marts and Lundy Survey Report, Crawford L. Gilligan, Director
104 The Plus decade Copyright 1961 by Williston Academy Easthampton, Massachusetts
105 This rather comical story was written by Lewis W. Miller he and his bride, Jean Miller '36 sent five of their children to the NSFG and to WNS. Thanks again to the Williston Archivist, Richard Teller for his faithful help.
106 Williston Northampton Bulletin, Winter 1974 Page 4
107 Courtesy of Helen Stauder, Director of Research, Williston Advancement Office
108 Williston Bulletin Fall 1985
109 The Williston Northampton Bulletin, Winter 1974, Page 16
110 The Willistonian Letter to the editor, December 14, 1979
111 The Plus Decade by Philips Stevens, copywrite 1961 by Williston Academy

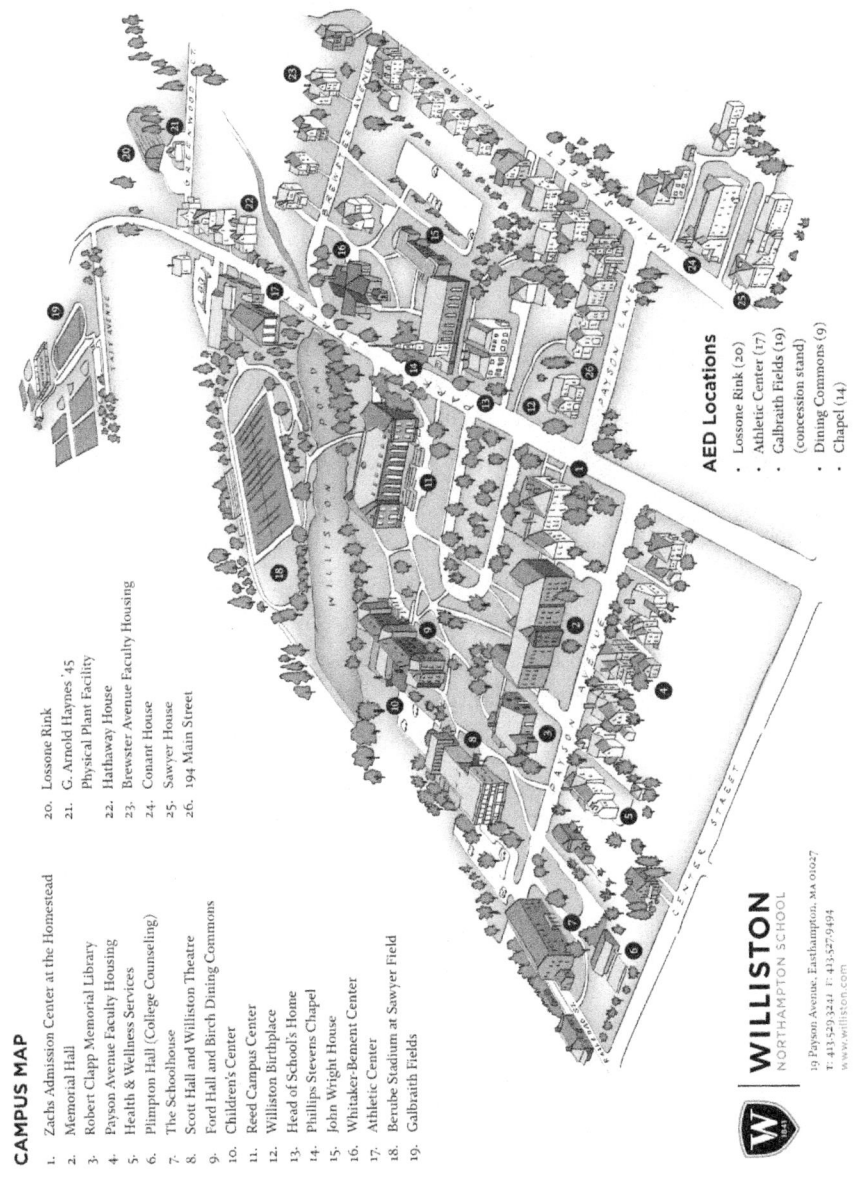

CAMPUS MAP

1. Zachs Admission Center at the Homestead
2. Memorial Hall
3. Robert Clapp Memorial Library
4. Payson Avenue Faculty Housing
5. Health & Wellness Services
6. Plimpton Hall (College Counseling)
7. The Schoolhouse
8. Scott Hall and Williston Theatre
9. Ford Hall and Birch Dining Commons
10. Children's Center
11. Reed Campus Center
12. Williston Birthplace
13. Head of School's Home
14. Phillips Stevens Chapel
15. John Wright House
16. Whitaker-Bement Center
17. Athletic Center
18. Berube Stadium at Sawyer Field
19. Galbraith Fields
20. Lossone Rink
21. G. Arnold Haynes '45 Physical Plant Facility
22. Hathaway House
23. Brewster Avenue Faculty Housing
24. Conant House
25. Sawyer House
26. 194 Main Street

AED Locations

- Lossone Rink (20)
- Athletic Center (17)
- Galbraith Fields (19) (concession stand)
- Dining Commons (9)
- Chapel (14)

WILLISTON NORTHAMPTON SCHOOL

19 Payson Avenue, Easthampton, MA 01027
T: 413.529.3241 F: 413.527.9494
www.williston.com

About the Author

Your author has spent almost his entire working career in the field of higher education and in private secondary schools. I was fortunate to have been given the opportunity to delve into college finances, starting with all handmade accounting entries to developing computer centers for both the academic and administrative functions at a time when computers were virtually non-existent in small institutions. Perhaps my biggest challenge was trying to save Williston from financial disaster. Huge bank debt and all programs cut to barely substistence levels required my immediate action. During this time, I found time to have fun which I will share with the reader. What made my career especially rewarding was my meaningful interactions with the faculties and the students.

Made in the USA
Columbia, SC
12 June 2022